THE COMMAND OF THE HOWE BROTHERS
DURING THE AMERICAN REVOLUTION

SIR WILLIAM HOWE

LORD RICHARD HOWE

THE COMMAND OF
THE HOWE BROTHERS
DURING THE
AMERICAN REVOLUTION

BY

TROYER STEELE ANDERSON

OXFORD UNIVERSITY PRESS
NEW YORK · LONDON
1936

PREFACE

THIS book has grown out of an interest in the border-land that lies between military and political history. The trend toward specialization in history has often left the connexion between political and military events on the fringe of one specialty or the other. The historian has usually focused his attention upon the heart of his specialty and skimped the fringes. The fact that specialties happen to have been delimited in the prevailing fashion has therefore tended to divert attention away from the critical problems that have to do with the co-ordination of political and military effort.

That shortcoming has been particularly apparent in the accounts of the command of the Howe brothers during the American Revolution. Both political and military historians have criticized the Howes without adequate allowance for the fact that the British commanders had to be politicians and military men at the same time. In view of this temptation to judge them by either a purely political or military standard, it is not surprising that the failure of the Howes has become a sort of mystery, something that has led many to suppose it can be explained only by very curious and secret reasons. It is my belief that the failure of the Howes is a mystery only because the conventional division between military and political history has diverted attention away from the points that serve best to explain the conduct of British operations in America. In this study I have tried to concentrate attention upon the junction between military and political policy in the hope that by doing so a rational understanding of the work of the Howes can be reached.

In view of the direction I plan to give it, this will not be a military history in the conventional sense. I have left out, for the most part, the usual detailed accounts of battles and marches. I have gone minutely into these details only at points at which it has been claimed that the Howes made serious mistakes. Much of my time has been devoted to the broad concepts of policy that were at work in the minds of the two men and to an examination of the measure of co-ordination achieved between the policy of the Howes and that of the government in England. If I have had to devote an apparently inordinate amount of time to Sir William Howe, it is both because he was the more controversial figure of the two and because the obstacles facing the commander of the army, and hence his responsibilities, were greater than those facing the leader of the naval forces.

It will be noticed that I have given very little attention to the picture of events as seen from the American side. This has been deliberate, for it is not so much the events but the reflection of events in the minds of the British commanders that is our problem. We shall probably appreciate more accurately what they were trying to do if we see only what they saw and deny ourselves the historian's privilege of knowing what was seen and felt on the other side of the battle line. As this is a study, not of military operations in full detail, but of the British command, we cannot appreciate the problems of command unless we can see things through the eyes and with a sense of the limitations of those who had to make decisions at the time.

I want to take this opportunity to express my gratitude to those who have helped me in the preparation of this book.   I owe my greatest debt to my father, Professor Frank Maloy Anderson, of Dartmouth, who first called my attention to the problem of the Howes as one particularly suited to my interests.   He has, throughout the preparation of the manuscript, given me most valuable and painstaking advice and has helped to sustain my enthusiasm as well as to correct my faults.

The late Mr. William L. Clements very kindly gave me access to the Clinton papers.   The hospitality of his home, which he and Mrs. Clements extended to me while I was at work on the papers, remains a very pleasant recollection.   I am also indebted to Mr. Randolph G. Adams, the librarian of the William L. Clements Library, and to Professor Verner W. Crane, of the University of Michigan, for helping me to secure access to material which otherwise I would not have been able to use.

I owe a very special debt to Miss Jane Clark, who was Mr. Clements's secretary and archivist.   Without her assistance it would have been impossible for me to make intelligent use of the Clinton papers; and, it must be added, without her ability to decipher Clinton's handwriting, I probably could not even have read them.   The present usefulness of this collection to historians depends in large measure upon her work.

Professor Henry S. Commager of New York University has also been of great help to me by going carefully over the manuscript and suggesting many improvements which I have endeavoured to incorporate in the final draft.

ACKNOWLEDGEMENTS

I AM very much indebted to The Macmillan Company for permission to quote from Sir John Fortescue's *Correspondence of George III*; to Goodspeed's Book Shop for permission to quote from C. K. Bolton's *Letters of Hugh Earl Percy*; to Houghton Mifflin Company for permission to quote from Harold Murdock's *Bunker Hill*; to The Dial Press for permission to quote from *The Journal of Nicholas Cresswell*; to Sampson Low, Marston and Company, Ltd. for permission to quote from *The Diary of Thomas Hutchinson*; and to John Lane, The Boadley Head, Ltd. for permission to quote from *Walpole's Last Journals*. Their courtesy has been of great help to me.

T.S.A.

CONTENTS

MAPS

THE COMMAND OF THE HOWE BROTHERS
DURING THE AMERICAN REVOLUTION

CHAPTER I

FEW periods in history have been more thoroughly studied than the American Revolution, but there remains a fundamental problem. Why did Great Britain fail to defeat the colonists? Many explanations have been advanced, some specific, some general, and all have received a measure of recognition from historians. But it cannot be said that any consensus of opinion has been reached. So far as any general agreement can be found, it lies in the view that Great Britain could not hope to hold permanently so vast a population and area at such a distance from Europe.

This conclusion, however, seems too theoretical. Mere distance and size do not automatically make continued allegiance impossible. It must be shown that they provoked some definite form of hostility and prevented any reconciliation before we can say that a geographical situation prevented continued political connexion between Great Britain and her colonies.

Historians have dealt at great length with the economic and political causes of the conflict between Great Britain and her American colonies and also with the complicated story of alternate provocation and concession that preceded the outbreak of war. Less has been written, however, about the reasons for Great Britain's failure to subdue the revolution once the point of open hostility had been reached.

There has been a tendency to assume that, once the contestants had come to blows, ultimate reconciliation was impossible. From that assumption has followed a lack of curiosity about the reasons for the immediate failure of the British efforts to subdue the revolt. But recent British imperial history throws doubt upon the validity of that assumption. South Africa was subdued by force of arms and brought once more within the Empire. Why could not the same have been done for those colonies that became the United States? The assumption that it was fundamentally impossible seems rather dubious in the light of later events and we are compelled to turn our attention towards more immediate and specific reasons for British failure. It is the purpose of this study to discover to what extent the conduct of the British command, as exercised by Lord Richard and Sir William Howe, contributed to the final defeat of Great Britain.

It is safe to say that the war of the American Revolution was won and lost during the first three years. There never would have been a Yorktown had the expectations of the British government in 1776 been realized, and the events of the early years of the war were decisive in making that government ready to accept Yorktown as a final verdict.

Except for the first few months of the fighting round Boston, the commander of the British army in America during the first period of the war was Sir William Howe. With the beginning of the summer of 1776 his older brother, Lord Richard Howe, held the naval command. Any explanation of British failure during these years thus becomes a verdict upon the conduct of the two brothers.

Both of these men had most creditable records in their respective services and it was generally believed at the time that better appointments could scarcely have been made. The armament with which they were supplied was, by standards of the day, exceptionally large and powerful. In betting parlance the two brothers should have been 'odds on favourites' to accomplish their purpose.

But failure met their efforts, and the sanguine hopes which their reputations had prompted made more bitter the disappointment the British nation had to endure. It seemed to contemporaries almost incredible that such extensive efforts could have missed their mark without egregious mismanagement or worse. Partisan spirit contributed to the dissatisfaction with the conduct of affairs, but a large part of the criticism and disappointment was genuine. After the recall of the Howes in 1778 this dispute waxed yet more furious and became hopelessly enmeshed in factional politics. The ministry, smarting under its inability to bring the war to a successful conclusion, wished to make it appear that the failure had been due to the mismanagement of the Howes and sought to convince the country that competent officers, with the forces available, could have brought the revolution to a speedy end. In this campaign the ministers had the support of a number of disgruntled Loyalist refugees from America, notably Joseph Galloway, who contributed their personal knowledge of American conditions to building up a case against the Howes.

The two brothers had earnest defenders among the Opposition. That group had opposed the war from the first. Did not the failure of such armaments under such reputable commanders but signify the accuracy of their predictions? Although not members of the Opposition, the Howes had been recognized before the war as well disposed towards the colonists and hence served as symbols of generous and forbearing treatment. The case of Burgoyne was also brought into the discussion.   That general, torn between the temptation to blame the Howes or the ministry for his humiliation, finally decided to blame the ministry.

This dispute over the responsibility for the American disaster led to a bitter pamphlet war.   Some of these publications were genuine statements of opinion or fact; others were mere paid pamphleteering such as was generally employed by political factions of the day.   We have traces also of the discussions of the case which took place in countless London drawing rooms and of the flood of innuendo and conjecture that followed.

The upshot of it all was a parliamentary investigation in 1779, held at the demand of the Howe brothers, who had come to feel they could not permit the campaign of detraction to continue without taking some public steps to call their critics to account.   This inquiry, like so many parliamentary investigations of military failures, led to the gathering of voluminous evidence, but the affair died a natural death from the adjournment of Parliament without any conclusion.

The problem which Parliament thus dropped historians have touched upon ever and anon since that time.   No critical work on the American Revolution can be written without some allusion to it.   Most writers offer no conclusion of their own but mention the chief lines of criticism of the Howes and leave the reader to take his choice.   Only a few have come out with very definite points of view.[1]

The most severe modern criticism of the Howes is found in a long article contributed by Charles Francis Adams to the *Proceedings of the Massachusetts His-*

[1] Probably the most accurate analysis of the motives of the Howes is that of Charlemagne Tower in his *Essays Political and Historical.*

torical Society for 1910.[2]   Adams condemned the conduct of the British campaign as incompetent beyond words, as of such sort that, had Washington designed it for his own ends, it would not have been very different.   One cannot but feel, however, that Mr. Adams was thinking all the time of the campaigns in the American Civil War, in which he participated. In his recollection of the manner in which the soldiers on both sides developed a knack of adjusting their military technique to the peculiar conditions of the country over which they fought, he tends to forget that it is not altogether reasonable to expect British soldiers of the eighteenth century, who received their military education under much more formalized conditions, to show the same adaptability.

At the opposite extreme stands Sir John Fortescue in his *History of the British Army*.   He thinks the command in America was exercised, on the whole, wisely and efficiently and lays the blame for failure on blundering by the civil heads of the government at home.   It must be remembered, however, that Fortescue is almost always exceedingly critical of the civil authorities wherever they come into contact with the military and especially where there has been a miscarriage that might be attributed to either.

One other opinion requires particular mention.   It has been asserted the Howes did not really wish to win.   Such a charge was levelled against them at the time and has frequently been repeated since.[3]   It rests primarily on two ideas: first, that the brothers were politically friendly with the Opposition and had opposed the use of severe measures against the colonists;

[2] *Massachusetts Historical Society, Proceedings* XLIV, pp. 13-65.   Reprinted in C. F. Adams, *Studies Military and Diplomatic*, pp. 114-173.
   [3] The late Professor Egerton, in discussing this topic with me, expressed it as his opinion that the Howes did not want to win.

and, secondly, that their conduct of the operations in America was such as to make a show of victory, while allowing its substance to escape them.

Of those who, in the course of general histories of the American Revolution, go at some length into the conduct of the Howes, probably the most balanced and understanding analysis is to be found in S. G. Fisher's *The Struggle for American Independence*. But we still lack a thorough study of the problem.[4] Even Charles Francis Adams was careful to say that his views were to be regarded only as suggestions and that he would not wish to set up his conclusions as in any sense definitive.

This book is undertaken in the hope that an intensive study of the problem will do something towards removing the American command of the Howes from the list of historical enigmas. There is no need for retelling the details of the American war, nor the ins and outs of the dispute that precipitated the conflict. The emphasis will be placed upon the problem of the British command, what those in authority had to do, the means at their disposal, and the process of selection of means and opportunities that led them to the course they took.

The problem of the conduct of the Howe brothers presents one very special difficulty. When we endeavour to explore the motives of two such men, motives that were more than usually mysterious to their contemporaries, we should welcome the discovery of hitherto unknown documents, especially private correspondence, which would reveal the innermost

---

[4] Since this chapter was written Bellamy Partridge has published a volume on "Sir Billy Howe." As the emphasis is on Howe's personality and the intricate interplay of political and military factors is not thoroughly worked out, it sheds little new light upon the problem under consideration.

thoughts of the chief actors.   Unfortunately we shall
never see the private papers of the Howe family, for
they were destroyed in a fire.[5]   It is, however, my opinion that the loss to this study is not as great as might
at first sight be supposed.   Both the brothers were
extremely taciturn.   It was the universal testimony of
those in the official family of the Howes that never
did two men keep their own counsel more carefully.
There seems little reason to suppose that their private
letters would have shown a taste for confession which
neither man ever showed in the slightest degree elsewhere.

Those who suspect the Howes of definite collusion
with the Opposition for the purpose of losing the war
may feel that there would have been some trace of it
in the private correspondence.   It seems, however,
unlikely.   Such evidence would more probably be
found in the papers of some member of the Opposition
who lacked the necessity of personal honour to prompt
him to discretion.   One would be surprised to discover it in the letters of the two men whose reputations would have been blasted by the discovery of
such an arrangement.

The only material useful to this study that has not
been long known to historians is that comprised in
the papers of Sir Henry Clinton, now in the library
accumulated by the late Mr. William L. Clements.
This collection, although the greater part of it naturally concerns the later years of the Revolution, is,
nevertheless, extremely valuable for the period of the
Howes' command.   It sheds new light upon many
details of the British campaign and particularly upon
the relationship of Sir William Howe to the Burgoyne
expedition.

[5] Barrow, *Life of Howe*, Introduction, viii.

The solution of the problem is not, however, to be found in the discovery of something new and startling, in some sensational revelation, but in the mobilization of all existing material. Much of it, especially the official despatches of the Howes, is very familiar, although still in manuscript form. The present-day emphasis upon the new and startling, although proof of a laudable eagerness to uncover the last shred of evidence, must not tempt us to believe that the latest bit, if it puts a slightly different interpretation upon a few points, completely replaces the obvious sources from which the bulk of the information must be drawn.

It is frequently assumed that official despatches, being prepared for the perusal of the public or official critics, cannot divulge real motives. This might be true if a military commander could sit down at the end of a campaign and compose the whole volume of his official correspondence, having in mind the failures to be explained, the successes to be exploited. But despatches are not prepared in that way. No commander knows what awaits him. He cannot write with an eye solely to self-defence before a commission of inquiry. He must from time to time ask for reinforcements and supplies, and to justify his requests he must divulge what he hopes to do with them. By comparison of his description of conditions, needs, and expectations in one despatch after another, it is usually possible to discover the real intentions and opinions of a commander of an army. Not infrequently the restraint of an official despatch is more conducive to exact truth than is the irresponsibility of a private letter.

It is my intention in this study to sketch the problem facing the British army and navy as it appeared to Sir William and Lord Richard Howe, to picture what they knew and what they necessarily could not have known, to point out their estimate of the situation, and to discover how far that estimate was in accord with their knowledge of the facts and with contemporary military doctrine.   Only when we see the situation as they saw it can we presume to decide whether the two brothers acted wisely on the basis of what they knew or whether they acted in a fashion that betrayed incompetence or some ulterior purpose.

The conclusion ought to do something either to vindicate the Howes or to reinforce the accusations levelled at them by their critics.   But this verdict upon two individuals is not the sole interest of this study.   I hope it may shed further light upon the degree to which individual judgement and discretion, as contrasted with the inescapable press of events, shaped the course of the American Revolution.   I shall endeavour to paint the difficulties faced by the British commanders, the gaps in their knowledge, the conflicting considerations that determined their actions ; in a word, to show the complexity and uncertainty of those actions which have been so readily praised or condemned.

CHAPTER II

THE task facing the Howe brothers when they undertook the command of the British forces in the American Revolution cannot be understood without examining the special features of the situation in America. A failure to make allowance for the peculiarities of the struggle has been the most frequent cause of mistaken judgements about the conduct of the war.

The American Revolution was not a war in the usual sense of a contest between two well established nations : it was a revolt. That statement, apparently so obvious, contains implications that have sometimes been ignored. When a nation goes to war with another nation its purpose is usually to compel its opponent to desist from some particular policy or to surrender some privilege or possession. The government of the enemy usually remains intact and the bitter taste left by defeat need not worry the victor if the vanquished is unable to seek revenge.

With a revolution, such as that in America, the problem was very different. The British government could not content itself with imposing certain pains and penalties upon the American government : it had to destroy that government. Furthermore, and this was the more difficult task, it had to destroy the revolutionary organization in such fashion that a majority of the people in the colonies would, after the first disappointment of defeat, be reasonably content under the restored British rule. A British triumph that left discontent ready to break out again at the first opportunity would be of little use.

This necessity ruled out immediately the use of mere force. Force there must be, but it had to be mixed with persuasion and designed to strike at the vulnerable points of revolutionary morale. The more subtle the unhinging of the American will to resist, the smaller would be the aftermath of discontent.

The order set up by the American Revolution had certain weaknesses which gave the British an opportunity. Like all newly constituted governments, it lacked traditional support. People did not remain loyal to it from force of habit. Probably the majority of Americans were uncertain enough in their attitude toward the struggle to make it possible for them to turn either way in response to the fortunes of war. Consequently the American cause was in its early stages very susceptible to the influence of defeat. The defeat might be, from a military point of view, unimportant, but if it persuaded the lay mind that things were going badly for the revolutionary arms it might prove disastrous to the morale of the cause. One or two spectacular British victories in the early stages of the war might have unhinged the American resistance.

At the same time the rather embryonic character of the American organization gave it some strength. Most wars are not fought to a finish but to the point at which the ultimate result becomes obvious. When the victor reaches that point he expects the vanquished to surrender. Occasionally, however, that does not happen. Because of heroism or stupidity the adherents of a hopeless cause may fight on. And by doing so they sometimes are able to snatch victory out of defeat because their opponents, confident that the contest is practically over, have relaxed their efforts.

Such a course of events was especially probable in the American Revolution if the Americans survived the first shock.   The Americans had no traditions which, in such a war as they were fighting, would indicate to them the point at which defeat ought to be confessed.   In one case they might be too easily discouraged by misfortune, but in another refuse to abandon hope when, by European standards, they ought to have done so.   As events were to show, the British were in constant danger of assuming that the American resistance had been defeated beyond recovery, only to have it burst forth again in most unreasonable fashion when they were off their guard.

The American resistance was further strengthened by the fact that the revolution had either to triumph or to collapse completely.   Individuals might compromise with the British government: the revolutionary organization could not, once independence had been declared.   That vigorous minority that was irretrievably committed to the cause of independence would, therefore, fight on even after reverses sufficient to destroy the support of the lukewarm majority.   That remaining kernel of resistance was likely to be just the thing for which the British had not made allowance.

We can see, therefore, that the subduing of the American Revolution presented a problem different from that involved when one independent state attempts to coerce another by war.   The revolution was likely to be brittle in its early stages; but, if it did not fall apart in the first few months of the war, it might show a capacity to resist in the face of misfortunes that would have persuaded most governments to sue for peace.

When the Howes began to plan their operations against the colonies several obvious alternatives were open to them. Force without stint or limit, the making of life as unbearable as possible for the Americans, might have been attempted. This, however, would have defeated the real purpose of the British government, which was to make the colonies once more useful parts of the empire.

There was some suggestion that the most rebellious areas, such as New England, might be quarantined by a blockade by land and sea. This, it was argued, would prevent the disaffection spreading into the more loyal sections and would, in course of time and by the pressure of the blockade, impose such inconvenience and loss upon the blockaded region that the public would eventually clamour for reconciliation.

This scheme, however, faced certain difficulties. It was a question whether the resistance was sufficiently localized to be subject to successful quarantine. Even if it were, and if the blockade were as effective as could be hoped, a long period would have to elapse before surrender could be expected. During that time, when a large British force was locked up in America, dangerous foreign complications might arise that would render the whole plan impracticable. It would certainly need time for success and time could not be guaranteed.

Going to the other extreme, the British commanders might have attempted a headlong military advance, striking with the utmost rapidity and frequency, in an effort to rush the American army off its feet. If such a policy could have destroyed the American armed forces, it would have been the best possible choice for it would have avoided the hazards of a protracted conflict and it would probably have caused

AREA OF THE HOWES'
OPERATIONS

Areas reported
to contain
many Loyalists

The reader should notice how the relatively narrow district between the sea and the mountains is divided by the lines of the Hudson, the Delaware, and the Chesapeake.

less annoyance to the civil population than would have any other. Furthermore, it would have impressed the Americans more than could have anything else with the hopelessness of resistance.

But a policy of impetuous advance faced dangers as well. If the drive fell short of annihilating the American army it might leave the British so exhausted as to imperil the results already won. An offensive at all costs is likely to be very expensive. If the British closed a headlong campaign without complete success and with their forces badly worn and diminished by the strain of constant action, the following campaign might find the Americans with their ranks replenished and the British without reinforcement from home sufficient to compensate for the loss of the previous year. The prospects for complete victory had to be very bright to justify such a risk.

A fourth plan of operations was piecemeal reconquest, the re-establishment of British authority upon a firm basis in one district before moving on to the next. This plan had some merits; the British army was strong enough to control at least one region at a time without taking serious risks. The scheme did not depend upon a subtle calculation of American psychology.

But it had faults as well. It would be slow and expensive. Most serious of all, the work of pacification had to be done in such fashion as to endure after the army had passed on to the next stage of its advance. So long as the American army remained in the field, the adherents of the Revolution could not be expected to resign themselves to inaction, unless some strong organization were provided for keeping them in order.

This is the point at which the Loyalists entered the

British plans.[1] There has been considerable misunderstanding of their rôle.   It has sometimes been supposed that the Loyalists, if adequately used, might have supplied most of the personnel for the British force in America, supplemented by only a small nucleus of regulars.   This view has been supported by the claim that the Loyalists actually enlisted were at times more numerous than the army that Washington had in the field.   The argument, however, neglects the fact that these troops would have had to be equipped from England and put through a long period of training before they could have attained an excellence sufficient to warrant their being treated as the mainstay of the army.   All in all, it was probably quicker and no more expensive for the British to send regular troops to America than it would have been to build up an equally powerful force through the enlistment of Loyalists.

The real use to which the Loyalists could be put was rather different.   Many of the British believed that the Revolution was the work of a belligerent minority that had intimidated the friendly or indifferent majority.[2]   They thought that this minority had succeeded because, as is the wont with dissatisfied groups, it had been organized effectively before any countermeasures could be taken by the friends of the government.   If this revolutionary faction could once be put to flight, it would then be possible for the Loyalists to organize themselves strongly enough to hold the situation in hand after the regular army had moved on to other fields of action.   The Loyalists were not supposed to defeat the American army, but to retain

---

[1] Sympathizers with the Revolution usually called them Tories, but historians have generally preferred the term by which these supporters of the Crown called themselves.

[2] See the pamphlet by Joseph Galloway entitled, *Plain Truth.*

control of the recaptured districts against further local efforts to stir up revolution.[3]

This scheme, plausible enough at first sight, was in reality not easy to put into effect. The Loyalists have sometimes been estimated at as much as half the population of the colonies. Although this figure seems too high, we need not quarrel with it here. Certainly those willing to lend active assistance to the British government were far less numerous. Furthermore, the scheme for the use of the Loyalists, as outlined above, would have required a fairly even distribution of Loyalist strength.[4] The opposite was the case: they were strong in some districts and weak in others. In many sections they would have been unable to set up an organization strong enough to keep the upper hand after the regular troops were removed. The mob, always an effective instrument in such cases, would usually have sided with the revolutionary party. It may be doubted whether a sufficient proportion of the country could have been held this way to place the revolution at a decisive disadvantage.

Thus every promising method of military operation had shortcomings. Those that offered a possibility of rapid victory were attended by heavy risk. Those that would proceed more cautiously were expensive and faced the danger of interruption from outside events. Any plan adopted was likely to be a combination of two or more methods but it would be exceedingly difficult to determine the best proportions.

In addition to these perplexities, the British commander in America, in forming his plans, had to know

[3] Evidence of General Robertson before the Inquiry. Dom. State Papers, Geo. III, 18.

[4] Galloway admitted as much in his evidence before the Parliamentary Inquiry and also in his pamphlet entitled, *A View of the Evidence.* Hereafter cited as *A View, etc.*

how much support the British government was prepared to give him.   If he could count on generous
support over a long period, the expensive but safer
plan was best.   If his support was limited in amount
or in time, he needed to take risks for the sake of
rapid victory.   It was difficult, at a distance of three
thousand miles, bridged only by sailing ships, to know
for long what support the home government would
provide.   Even the government, in the difficult political situation in which the American war placed it,
could not be sure of its own intentions far in advance.
There was infinite opportunity for confusion and misunderstanding.

In all this the military commander was in a most
uncomfortable position.   His task called for real statesmanship, a nice blending of military pressure and persuasion, a policy that might prompt him at times to
desist from the full use of one means in order to assist
the operation of the other.   Yet, since he held a military title and commanded an army, he would almost
certainly be judged by purely military standards,
should any mischance overtake him.   Nor would
hostile critics be likely to make allowance for the
confusion for which time and distance were responsible.

Critics of the Howes, of Sir William in particular,
have often committed a further injustice ; they have
made insufficient allowance for the qualities of the
instrument available.   The size of the forces put at
the disposal of the Howes was determined, of course,
by the British government's estimate of the seriousness
of the opposition.   What that estimate was, however,
is the subject of a separate chapter.   Attention will
be devoted here to the quality of the principal instrument, the army.   Although the navy played a vitally

important part, the British were so overwhelmingly superior upon the water, except for the annoyance caused by privateers, that the exact quality of the fleet does not require detailed examination.

The layman usually expects unreasonable things of an army. He reads in his morning paper that the enemy has been defeated, and then feels it to be outrageous if the army does not rush ahead after the retreating enemy or into some new attack. He often fails to realize that an army is an intricate mechanism, that it is subject to fatigue, to confusion, to shortage of supply, and to the thousand and one other things that can never be entirely avoided by even the best of planning and organization. He forgets that before condemning a military commander for lack of vigour he ought to know very accurately the character and capacity of the organization he commands.

By any modern standard of good management the British army of the 18th century was an inefficient organization.[5] It was badly recruited, inadequately commanded, imperfectly supplied and maintained. Its ability to fight was its redeeming quality, but between battles its imperfections were apparent.[6] The most eloquent authority for these deficiencies is Wellington. Times without number, in his despatches, he complained of the quality of the army. Yet he was no mediocre commander seeking to excuse his own failures. He may have been a little too severe at times, but the faults of which he complained were

[5] E. E. Curtis, *The Organization of the British Army in the American Revolution.*

[6] Fonblanque, in his *Life of Burgoyne,* quotes on p. 33 the opinion of the Duke of Braunschweig-Luneburg about British troops. 'Braver troops cannot be found in the world when in the battlefield and under arms before the enemy ; but here ends their military merit. . . Their home customs incline them to the indulgences of life, and nearly without exception, they all expect to have comfortable means of sleep.'

real and embarrassed Sir William Howe just as much as they did the Iron Duke.

The British army could fight. Seldom was there any complaint about the bravery or steadiness of British troops. But their excellence in battle was secured by a tactical system designed primarily for use in open country and for getting the most out of troops who, individually, came from the poorest elements in the population. The maintenance of order and alignment, rather than speed, was the criterion of good tactical management. Flexibility and independent initiative were thought likely to produce confusion and disaster.

All action on the field of battle was, therefore, slow and according to rule. The system sufficed in Europe against a foe who employed similar methods. In America, although it would win battles, it would seldom annihilate a defeated enemy whose retreat was not embarrassed by a similar routine. If the British attempted a drastic pursuit it was likely to end in serious confusion for the pursuing troops. Wellington said that the British troops could stand anything but victory. The effectiveness of rapid pursuit was further diminished by the fact that the Americans, for all their unsteadiness on the field of battle, often showed a surprising tenacity in keeping together some sort of organization after defeat. Their inadequacy in routine discipline that was so often disastrous in pitched battle probably preserved in some measure the individual initiative that hastened recovery after defeat.

The British authorities were aware of the rigidity of the traditional tactics and endeavoured in the years before the Revolution to remedy the deficiency.[7] Sir William Howe had contributed personally to the de-

[7] See J. F. C. Fuller, *British Light Infantry in the 18th Century.*

velopment of the light troops that were designed to give greater flexibility to British tactics. But the difficulty remained, although perhaps less marked than it had been earlier in the century.

The cumbersomeness of the British tactics was made more serious in America by the rough and broken character of much of the countryside. Cornwallis and others testified to the importance of this factor.[8] Under such conditions it was not easy to manage the regular formations required by orthodox tactics and effective pursuit was very difficult without radical departure from the usual discipline.[9] Against an enemy adept in escape, and possessing an organization so loose that it could be broken and reformed a few days later without disastrous results, it was very hard to strike a decisive blow.

A reading of his despatches leaves one with the impression that Sir William Howe was not a man likely to break with orthodox methods when confronted by unusual conditions. Rather he was inclined to take refuge from the unusual and perplexing in a more rigid orthodoxy. But we must not be too ready to condemn him for this. In his situation the penalties of an unsuccessful experiment would have been unusually severe. If any of Howe's ventures turned out disastrously and led to the loss of a large part of his army, nothing could be done to repair the damage for months to come. Thanks to his distance from

[8] Evidence of Cornwallis and General Grey before the Parliamentary Inquiry. Dom. State Papers, Geo. III, 18.

[9] Another factor that militated against effective pursuit was the dependence of the British army upon its baggage trains. For some curious reason British troops never developed much of a knack of living off the country. Where a French army would manage to support itself comfortably, the British would be in distress if anything delayed their supply trains. Both Generals Grey and Robertson testified to the influence of this dependence upon British operations in America. See Dom. State Papers, Geo. III, 18.

England, in any given campaign he had to seek victory with the means then at his disposal. There was no time to send home for reinforcements to make good the losses of a promising but unlucky experiment.

The wastage of war is not confined to losses in battle. Desertion and sickness take a heavy toll that is greatly increased if the army is subjected to unusual strain. Losses from these causes have usually exceeded by a wide margin the losses in battle. An army as accustomed to rigid discipline as was the British was particularly likely to suffer from these causes if the troops were allowed to get out of hand through operations too hastily planned or too impetuously pushed.[10] No commander can treat his army as if it were a piece of machinery, able to keep going indefinitely if supplied with fuel and oil. An army must be rested and, in addition to physical recuperation, must have time every so often to put things in order, to repair the confusion that inevitably creeps in during the pressure of an active campaign.

These limitations have too frequently been ignored by the critics of Sir William Howe. They have tended to assume that he could have pushed on without pause and have failed to realize that the speed of the British pursuit could have equalled that of the American retreat only at the risk of confusion that might have nullified the British superiority and brought losses which would have been irreplaceable. They have sometimes forgotten the susceptibility of the British army of the eighteenth century to loss and confusion unless kept well in hand. Although an impetuous campaign might have secured victory for the British in the early stages of the war, any result short of a

---

[10] Evidence of General Grey before the Inquiry. Dom. State Papers, Geo. III, 18.

decision might have exhausted the army and left it helpless in the ensuing campaign.

It is not my intention to suggest that Sir William Howe was justified in all the caution that he observed : that question must be decided later. I only wish to make it clear that both the nature of the army under his command and the general character of the struggle provided arguments for caution. It is an old military adage that the general wins who has the last reserves. In the American Revolution that side would win which could summon the greatest strength at the moment of final decision. If Sir William Howe shot his bolt in the first campaign and missed a decision there would be small prospect of better luck next time. But if he proceeded more cautiously, if he always kept a little something in hand, then, if the moment of decision were postponed to a subsequent campaign, he might still hold the advantage.

On the other hand, the general who has the last reserves does not win unless he is able to use them. The mere conservation of the British forces would avail nothing unless it made possible a more effective pressure upon the Americans at the crucial moment. If the crucial moment were allowed to pass and the force were not utilized to the full, nothing would have been gained by conserving it. But it was a terribly difficult task to discover the crucial point. It could not be readily determined in advance and it might pass unrecognized at the time. The particular scheme of operations adopted by the Howes might hasten or postpone it, but it might come uncontrolled and unannounced, from the luck of war or from the intrusion of an outside influence.

It seems abundantly clear that military commanders have seldom been placed in more perplexing circumstances than were the Howes. The military forces they commanded were, for that day, exceedingly powerful. But victory in battle would not, of itself, guarantee the accomplishment of their real purpose, the restoration of British control over the colonies. They had to fight opponents that were in some ways unusually weak, but in others exceptionally strong. The British army was poorly adapted to the exploitation of victory against so elusive an adversary as the American in his home country. Beyond the battlefield lay the will of the American populace to resist. This had to be undermined before success was assured. Various forms of pressure, each with advantages and disadvantages, could be brought to bear upon the Americans to persuade them to give up the struggle, but the discovery of the proper proportions for the remedy was extremely puzzling.

To cap the climax of difficulty came the danger of confusion and misunderstanding occasioned by the great distance between Great Britain and America. With the best of sympathy and good will the Howes and the government would have been lucky to escape conflict of purpose. Such a misunderstanding, if it arose, might render worthless a plan which, if based upon accurate agreement between the Howes and the government, might have been excellent. In spite of the strength of the forces originally put at their disposal, few military commanders have had more difficult calculations to make, more subtle factors to weigh, more incalculable elements to allow for than did Lord Richard and Sir William Howe. This is not said to acquit them in advance of the responsibility for the British failure. But we shall not do them justice or really understand the struggle between Great Britain and her American colonies if we fail to keep the complexity of the situation constantly in mind.

CHAPTER III

WE MUST now inquire what view the British government took of the crisis. We need to know how serious a resistance was expected from the Americans, how effective the British government thought its forces would be in subduing the revolt, how many of the colonists were believed to be ready to come to terms with the government, and how much assistance it was supposed would be given to the British commanders by those friendly to the government. In a word, we wish to discover what information influenced ministers and generals when calculating the effort necessary to subdue the revolution.

A nation, like an individual, is limited in resource, whether of time, energy, or money. A variety of complex problems require a careful allotment of available resources. Those allotted to any particular purpose will be in proportion to the importance of the task and to the effort which it is believed will prove necessary for the accomplishment of the undertaking.

As national resources must usually be allotted well in advance, it is of great moment that estimates of the importance of a task and of the forces needed for its accomplishment should be accurate. If the apportionment for some vital undertaking proves too meagre, confusion and waste, perhaps serious defeat, will follow and the effort required for the completion of the job will be much greater than would have been needed had the original calculation been accurate. If the original estimate is exaggerated, then support is needlessly denied to other important tasks.

This careful apportionment cannot be made entirely upon the basis of expert advice. Public opinion must be consulted. Ministers and legislators cannot, as a matter of practical politics, devote government resources to a given purpose much beyond the point that public opinion believes necessary. It was therefore exceedingly important that Sir William Howe should estimate accurately how far public opinion would support the British efforts in America. If he thought the nation would support a vigorous effort, but only for a brief time, his plans ought to have been built accordingly. If a more meagre but steady support seemed likely, a different course was indicated. The assurance of generous support would have justified cautious measures that trusted to the weight of British resources to overwhelm the revolution. An expectation of slender support would have required a more risky course, one that might, if lucky, win rather cheaply.

If the appropriate measures were to be chosen, Sir William Howe had also to estimate accurately the magnitude of his task. If he underestimated it, he might have regarded slender resources as adequate and have pursued a methodical course when he ought to have taken risks. If he overestimated his adversary, he might have taken risks when steady pressure would have sufficed. Thus, from every point of view, the contemporary estimate of the resistance to be expected from the Americans was more important than any other single thing in determining the British plan of operations.

Amid the mass of information that came from Amer-

ica to England, or that was dished up for public con-
sumption by those already in England who professed
personal knowledge of the colonies, there was much
that would incline the British public to believe
that the reconquest of the colonies would not prove
difficult.   As was pointed out in the preceding chapter, the most sanguine British hopes rested on the
belief that there were enough enthusiastic Loyalists
so that, if properly led, they could bring a decisive
addition to British strength.   Even General Gage,
British commander in America, who was not given to
undue optimism, at times led the government to expect a good deal from the Loyalists.   He wrote to
Lord Dartmouth, the Colonial Secretary, on 5 July
1774:

> I have done all in my power to spirit up every friend to
> government, and the measures taken by administration
> encourage many to speak and act publicly in a manner
> they have not dared to do for a long time past.   Your
> lordship will observe that there is now an open opposi-
> tion to the faction, carried on with a warmth and spirit
> unknown before, which it is highly proper and necessary
> to cherish and support by every means; and I hope it will
> not be very long before it produces very salutary effects
> . . . the terror of mobs is over and the press is becoming
> free.[1]

He added encouraging words about similar prospects
at New York and Philadelphia.

From the southern colonies came even more promising assurances.   Governor Martin in North Carolina thought that with a little support he might win
back the colony.   Dartmouth, although inclined to
discount this optimism a little, thought there was

---

[1] *Parliamentary History,* vol. 18, p. 88.   From the papers on American
conditions submitted by the government to Parliament.

enough in it to justify support for the attempt.[2] Dunmore wrote in similar vein from Georgia, and Dartmouth wrote to Sir William Howe that his own earlier scepticism had been shaken by advices which confirmed the reports of the two governors. Consequently he proposed to assist Loyalist efforts by occupying successively the various districts with regular troops, halting long enough in each district to enable the Loyalists to organize for the maintenance of their position.[3] The King felt so sanguine about this scheme that he thought it quite possible the south might be reconquered in time for the troops to return north for the summer campaign.[4] Dartmouth thought well enough of the Loyalists to admit that expectation of assistance from them was the sole excuse for sending troops to the south.

Other reports came in, tending to show that the revolutionary zeal of the colonies was not so great as had at first sight appeared and might either be killed by a not very expensive kindness or die of its own lack of vitality. A Philadelphia merchant wrote to Sir Robert Herries that if any terms of reconciliation were offered that Congress ought to accept they would be embraced.[5] Lieutenant-Governor Colden fairly bombarded Dartmouth with letters assuring him that colonial opinion was not so disaffected as appeared on the surface. He wrote in August 1774:

From a view of the numerous resolves of the people in all the colonies, which appear in every newspaper, your

2 Dartmouth to Howe, 15 September, 1775, Colonial Office Records, Class 5, vol. 92, pp. 491-4. Hereafter these records will be cited so that the above would appear as C.O.5/92, pp. 491-4. Where the name Howe is used alone it will refer to Sir William.

3 C.O.5/92, pp. 539-52. Dartmouth to Howe, 22 October 1775.

4 Ibid.

5 Historical Manuscript Commission Reports, Mss. of Mrs. Stopford-Sackville, vol. 2, p. 21. Hereafter these will be mentioned as H.M.C., with the name of the particular report.

lordship might be led to think a stupid fatal hardiness intoxicated the whole. But there are everywhere many people who are seriously alarmed at the critical posture of the contention between Great Britain and her colonies; they look forward with the deepest anxiety, and would rejoice in any prudent plan for restoring harmony and security.[6]

A month later he still felt able to write:

I think I may continue to assure your lordship, that a great majority in this province are very far from approving of the extravagant and dangerous measures of the New England governments, that they abhor the thoughts of a civil war, and desire nothing so much as to have an end put to this unhappy dispute with the mother country.[7]

Word also came that the tendency of certain elements among the colonists to take steps in the direction of independence was producing a serious rift. The informant stated it to be the purpose of the New York delegates to leave the Congress if independence were declared, and passed on a rumour that another petition was to be sent in order to secure an accommodation of the dispute.[8] Tryon reported to Howe as late as December 1775 that the spirit of rebellion in New York was much abated and that he awaited only the arrival of five thousand regulars to restore the government.[9]

In addition to reports from America which painted the resistance to the Crown as lukewarm, certain elements in England made light of anything even the most determined sort of rebellion could accomplish. T. Townshend lamented before Parliament the sad

[6] *Parliamentary History*, vol. 18, p. 124, Colden-Dartmouth, New York, 5 October 1774.

[7] Ibid., p. 127, Colden-Dartmouth, New York, 2 November 1774.

[8] C.O.5/93, pp. 89-90. Secret intelligence enclosed in Howe's letter of 16 January 1776 to Dartmouth.

[9] C.O.5/93, pp. 79-80. Tryon to Gen. Howe from New York, 3 December 1775.

fate of the army and naval officer, 'who would have nothing to do but burn, sink and destroy.'[10]   Rigby confidently declared, 'He should disdain to treat with America.   It was romantic to think they would fight; it was an idea thrown out to frighten women and children.   There was more military prowess in a militia drummer.'[11]   Although such disdainful opinions must by no means be considered as general, there was a hope, which in many quarters amounted to a belief, that when it came to a crisis the prospect of a real war with the mother country would make the Americans recoil from extreme measures.   Those who felt inclined to believe that the Americans would yield to rigorous pressure could take heart from the opinion of General Haldimand, who felt that the Boston Port Bill had done something to make the temper of the colonists more tractable.[12]   Even more emphatic was the evidence of Colonel Grant, who assured the House of Commons that he 'knew the Americans well, was certain they would not fight.   They would never dare face an English army, and did not possess any of the qualifications necessary to make a good soldier.'[13] Little wonder that men like Townshend and Rigby could assert dogmatically that Americans were cowards, when a man with personal knowledge of them could be so sure of his opinion.   Even Gage felt that the forceful measure of the Boston Port Bill had a good deal staggered even the most presumptive, although, with characteristic caution, he wished his opinion to be taken as only tentative.[14]

[10] Walpole, *Last Journals*, vol. 1, p. 442.
[11] Ibid.
[12] Haldimand to Amherst, New York, 1 June 1774, British Museum Additional Manuscripts 21,661, ff. 348-9. Hereafter mentioned as B.M.Add.Mss., with the proper number.
[13] *Parliamentary History*, vol. 18, p. 226.
[14] Ibid., p. 84, Gage to Dartmouth, 19 and 31 May 1775.

Some who were not quite so optimistic as to suppose the colonists would be afraid to resist, believed, nevertheless, that their armed resistance could not be effective.   Lord North assured the House of Commons in March 1774 that 'the militia of Boston were no match for the force of this country.'[15]   Dartmouth, in directing the despatch of troops to the south late in 1775, assumed that the Americans would not risk an action.[16]   After Bunker Hill Dartmouth could scarcely have believed the Americans incapable of fighting, but he apparently considered them so far inferior to the British troops in the field that only unusual conditions, such as those found at Bunker Hill, could tempt them to a regular resistance.

There was thus a large amount of evidence to support those who claimed that the revolt in the colonies was an unsubstantial affair, the work of a bellicose minority brave only because hitherto unmolested.   It could also be argued plausibly that throughout most of the colonies would be found great numbers of people who disapproved the course taken by the extremists and only waited a convenient moment and a reasonably safe opportunity to rise against their local tyrants and restore the government of the Crown.   Optimists could also believe that the vast majority of the colonists, even if not disposed to such positive efforts to restore British government, were at least disgusted by the violence and radicalism of the revolutionaries and ready for almost any reasonable measure of conciliation that would save them from being pushed into a course of action they both disliked and feared.   Men agreeing with these estimates naturally expected an easy victory for the government and did not anticipate

[15] Walpole, *Last Journals*, vol. 1, p. 317.
[16] C.O.5/92, pp. 539-52.   Dartmouth-Howe, 22 October 1775.

the necessity of any phenomenal exertion to secure it nor any serious delay in its accomplishment.

But this view of the situation was not universal. From many sources came a much more pessimistic account. Warnings arrived against relying too much upon Loyalist support. The Earl of Dunmore wrote to Dartmouth in the summer of 1774 that there was 'too much cause to apprehend that the prudent views, and the regard to justice and equity, as well as loyalty and affection, which is publicly declared by many families of distinction here, will avail itself little against the turbulence and prejudice which prevails throughout the country.'[17] From New York, later in the same year, Lieutenant-Governor Colden testified to the weakness of the Loyalists by saying that many of these well disposed gentlemen felt obliged to support the measures of Congress lest their failure to do so would throw the game into more dangerous hands.[18]

Those who minimized the enthusiasm and determination of the revolutionary element could not complain that they had not been warned of their mistake. Governor Wright wrote from Georgia that the civil power in the colonies was far too weak to accomplish anything, that prosecutions would only be laughed at, and those who sought to carry them out subjected to insult and abuse.[19] At the end of 1774 he wrote again :

. . . the sanction given to the rebellion by the resolves and proceedings of that congress has greatly encouraged the spirit of political enthusiasm, which many were possessed of before, and raised it to such a height of phrenzy,

[17] *Parliamentary History,* vol. 18, p. 137, Dunmore-Dartmouth, Williamsburg, 6 June 1774.
[18] Ibid., p. 129, Colden-Dartmouth, 7 December 1774.
[19] Ibid., p. 142, Wright-Dartmouth, Savannah, 24 August 1774.

that God knows what the consequence may be, or what man, or whose property may escape their resentment.[20]

Lest some at home be inclined to label the popular enthusiasm a mere excitement of the moment, Gage took pains to express the contrary opinion. He wrote to Dartmouth in August 1775:

The designs of the leaders of the rebellion are plain, and every day confirms the truth of what was asserted years ago by many intelligent people, that a plan was laid in this province and adjusted with some of the same stamp in others for a total independence.[21]

From South Carolina came similar information, sent by Lieutenant Governor Bull in the summer of 1774:

I had expectation that the measures taken by the Parliament relative to Boston would have had some happy effect towards composing the disturbances in this province, which seemed to have subsided a little last winter, but it has taken a contrary turn. Their own apprehensions and thoughts, confirmed by the resolutions and correspondence from other colonies, have raised an universal spirit of jealousy against Great Britain and of unanimity toward each other.[22]

He went on to say that the more violent section even talked of resistance at any cost, and that others, more moderate, who thought such language too extreme, were often overborne by the extremists.

Very pessimistic reports also came in about the prospects for reconciliation by compromise. Haldimand wrote Amherst late in 1774 that, in his judgement, force was the only means of restoring order, although he apparently thought the display of force

[20] Ibid., p. 144, Wright-Dartmouth, Savannah, 13 December 1774.
[21] C.O.5/92, pp. 497-9.
[22] Parliamentary History, vol. 18, p. 138, Bull-Dartmouth, Charles Town, 31 July 1774.

could be confined to a general naval blockade and an army large enough to subdue the New England colonies.[23]   It is interesting to note that even so firm an advocate of force as Haldimand, although he was in New York at the time, did not foresee the future spread of the revolution.   Nine months later, after his return to England, he believed even more emphatically that it would be not only futile but dangerous to listen to any proposal from the colonies until they had suffered for their conduct, since they gave not the slightest indication of wishing to recede from the stand they had taken.[24]   Those who preached the futility of attempting to negotiate with the Americans made sufficient impression in England to lead Horace Walpole to sneer at the announced intention of the government to send commissioners to treat with the colonists as something worthy only of childish or utterly despairing minds.[25]

Those who warned the government that force would be needed for the reconquest of the colonies took pains to state that this force would have to be extensive and that effective measures could not be carried out cheaply.   Even Earl Percy, who had a youthful and aristocratic contempt for the Americans, expected no easy victory.   He wrote to General Harvey late in the summer of 1774:

> I am certain it will require a great length of time, much steadiness, and many troops to reestablish good order and government. . . I plainly foresee that there is not a new councillor or magistrate who will dare to act without at least a regiment at his heels.[26]

[23] B.M.Add.Mss. 21,661, ff. 364-5. Haldimand-Amherst, 15 December 1774.

[24] Donne, *Correspondence of Geo. III with Lord North*, vol. 1, p. 244. Hereafter mentioned simply as Donne, without the title.

[25] Walpole, *Last Journals*, vol. 1, p. 483.

[26] *Letters of Hugh, Earl Percy*, Letter of 21 August 1774 to General Harvey, from Boston. Pp. 35-7.

He hoped that the coming congress would cripple the colonists by its dissensions, but predicted that there will be more work cut out for Administration in America than perhaps they are aware of.'

Percy's belief that the government faced a hard task if the matter came to blows was confirmed by his experiences on the 19th of April, 1775. He wrote just afterward to Harvey, 'Whoever looks upon them [the colonists] as an irregular mob, will find himself much mistaken. They have men amongst them who know very well what they are about.'[27]

Shortly afterward Haldimand warned Amherst from Boston that if the Continental Congress voted money for an army the difficulties in the way of the British would be very great. Chatham had already told the House of Lords in January of that year that it took forty thousand men to conquer America from France when the task was not complicated by domestic strife with the English colonists.[28] From these and other opinions it is clear that the authorities in Great Britain did not lack warning that the work of reconquering the colonies by force would demand a great expenditure of effort.

Thus some advisers of the government ridiculed the idea that the colonists could or would offer any serious resistance to the Crown, while others prophesied that the uprising would prove formidable enough to require the most strenuous efforts of Great Britain before it could be subdued. No clearly defined middle opinion existed to relieve the perplexity of a statesman puzzling between the two extremes. The man who, of all the British representatives in America, was most likely to hold such a view was General Gage.

---

[27] Ibid., Percy-General Harvey, Boston, 20 April 1775, pp. 52-3.
[28] *Parliamentary History*, vol. 18, p. 209.

But a perusal of his correspondence shows no consistent estimate which would guide a puzzled minister between the Scylla of making too much of his task and the Charybdis of making too little.

Gage wrote in August of 1774 that it was agreed that the popular fury was never greater than at that moment, yet he assured the government that the demagogues who were spurring things on in Massachusetts did so from a confidence in the long forbearance of government and a feeling that they were safe from punishment. If their methods, which had hitherto been a sort of moral attrition, should take more positive and open shape, they could expect no assistance from any other colony but Connecticut.[29] In December of the same year Gage wrote that the hot headed party sought to raise troops and to have other colonies contribute toward their expense. He then went on to say:

> Their violence terrified many of their party who have given assistance to preserve peace and quiet, by which people have had time to cool and hearken more to reason, but I do not infer that they are more inclined to receive the new laws, or that a little matter would not raise them up again. But people who have been mal-treated for their attachments to government have recovered themselves during the calm and in several places have associated for their mutual defence.[30]

Then, to add to the ambiguity of his information, he expressed serious doubt about the value of these associations.

Yet, between the despatch of these two somewhat hopeful letters, Gage had sent home three epistles

[29] *Parliamentary History*, vol. 18, p. 93, Gage-Dartmouth, 27 August 1774.
[30] Ibid., p. 107, Gage-Dartmouth, 15 December 1774.

painting conditions in colours of the blackest hue. He wrote on September 2 :

> Civil government is near its end ; . . . your lordship will permit me to mention that as it is judged here, that it will be resolved to stem the torrent, and not yield to it, that a very respectable force should take the field, . . . nothing that is said at present can palliate ; conciliating, moderation, reason is over ; nothing can be done but by forceable means.[31]

Later Gage reported that the country people throughout New England were drilling and that even places esteemed loyal had caught the rebellious infection.[32] On September 25 he wrote further :

> We hear of nothing but extravagancies in some part or another, and of military preparations from this place to the province of New York, in which the whole seems to be united. . . Your lordship will know from the various accounts the extremities to which affairs are brought, and how this province is supported and abetted by others beyond the conception of most people and foreseen by none.[33]

During the rest of the autumn Gage had his ups and downs of hope and fear. At the end of October he felt that 'the people would cool was not some means taken to keep up their enthusiasm.' Three days later he was more pessimistic :

> This province is without courts of justice or a legislature — the whole country is in a ferment — many parts of it, I may say, actually in arms, and ready to unite. Letters from the other provinces tell us they are violent everywhere, and that no decency is observed in any place but New York.[34]

[31] Ibid., pp. 96-7, Gage-Dartmouth, 2 September 1774.
[32] Ibid., vol. 18, p. 99, Gage-Dartmouth, 20 September 1774.
[33] Ibid., p. 100, Gage-Dartmouth, 25 September 1774.
[34] Ibid., p. 105, Gage-Dartmouth, 30 October 1774.

But he felt encouraged when he wrote to Dartmouth three days later:

This provincial Congress has been encouraged by the general union and readiness shown by the rest of the New England provinces to appear in arms at their call to go the lengths they have. I transmit to your lordship a proclamation against the proceedings of their last meeting, and I hope it will have some effect, for I learn that people are cooler than they were and grow apprehensive of consequences. The congresses have gone greater lengths than was expected.[35]

Gage has been so much criticized that one is tempted at first not to attach great importance to his reports. But it must be remembered that his inadequacy was not known at the time and that the government certainly paid close attention to what he wrote.[36]   There were, in addition, other accounts of affairs in America which, if not quite so changeable from day to day, must have left those in Great Britain almost equally puzzled to know what to expect from the colonists. John Wentworth, governor of New Hampshire, who had the advantage of some measure of detachment without so much isolation as to vitiate his judgement, wrote to Dartmouth in September 1774:

Notwithstanding I can still have the pleasure to represent to your lordship that this province continues more moderate than any to the southward; yet, at the same time, truth requires me to suggest, that the union of the colonies in sentiment is not divided nor lost in New Hampshire, although they have hitherto been prevailed

---

[35] Ibid., p. 105, Gage-Dartmouth, 15 November 1774.
[36] The importance attached by the government to the letters from Gage is shown by the frequency with which they occur among the papers presented to Parliament concerning conditions in America. These papers, found in vol. 18 of the *Parliamentary History*, furnished the evidence which the government wished Parliament to use in drawing its conclusions about the situation in the colonies, and hence mirror, to a considerable degree, the ministerial mind.

upon to abstain from acts of violence and outrage, and the laws have their course. How long it will remain so is impossible to foresee. I confess much good may not reasonably be counted upon while the unhappy distractions in the Massachusetts Bay gain ground and spread with such violence as cannot but be extremely deplored in every considerate man.[37]

General Haldimand, staunch believer in force as the only specific for the disease of rebellion, was not always certain it would come to such an extreme. He wrote from New York on 1 June 1774:

I think it my duty to acquaint your lordship with the apparent effect, which the late vigourous measures adopted by the Parliament of Great Britain have made on the minds of the people of this country; the few who entertained more loyal and liberal ideas of government are now induced and encouraged to speak their minds with more freedom, and fear not to disapprove the rash proceedings of their countrymen, blindly led by a few hotheaded and designing men.[38]

Yet he also cautioned Dartmouth that too much trust ought not to be placed in such appearances.

Thus the British government was bombarded with news, opinions, and advice of exceedingly varied complexion. The majority of its informants admitted the existence of a serious situation in America, but some believed the remedy would not prove very costly. Others represented any but the most strenuous measures as so much wasted time. Amid this perplexity Lord North and his colleagues merit some sympathy. They were playing a difficult game, to keep in power and to forward the plans of the King. While they

---

[37] *Parliamentary History*, vol. 18, pp. 116-17, Wentworth-Dartmouth, 13 September 1774.
[38] Ibid., vol. 18, p. 120, Haldimand-Dartmouth, New York, 1 June 1774.

were engaged in that delicate operation, any prospect of unusual expense was extremely unpalatable, not to say dangerous. It was a tremendous temptation, in the face of an emergency like the American Revolution, to calculate the matter very closely in order to get out of it as cheaply as possible.

That there was considerable doubt and perplexity on the part of the ministry is sufficiently evident. Walpole records the general surprise at some of the twistings and turnings of governmental intention; the determination in February 1775 to offer terms of pacification; the determination in June to prosecute the war.[39] In his opinion they were 'aground.' Some allowance should be made for the prejudice of the diarist, but it is clear that the ministers did not feel at all sure what course they ought to follow. In view of the contradictory evidence presented to them this indecision offers no occasion for surprise.

The King, almost alone, seems to have been fairly consistent in his views, although only after some early uncertainty. By September 1774 he had fully decided that there must be no retreat on principle, although he hoped that the colonies would submit when they saw the firm attitude of the government.[40] By the middle of November, however, he felt certain that blows alone could decide the dispute.[41] Leniency now would only convince the colonies that the mother country was afraid.[42] He even felt reluctant to send commissioners to settle the dispute, for he thought it made Great Britain appear afraid of the struggle; and he dwelt on the importance of taking a firm stand, not

---

[39] Walpole, *Last Journals*, vol. 1, p. 467.
[40] Fortescue, *Correspondence of George III*, vol. 3, no. 1508. This collection will hereafter be referred to simply as Fortescue.
[41] Ibid., no. 1556.
[42] Ibid., no. 1557.

only for the sake of its effect upon the colonies, but also for its influence at home.[43]

In general, however, confusion dogged the footsteps of governmental thinking. It was a confusion of belief about the seriousness of the revolt in America and about the effectiveness of the means available for subduing it. Such confusion was fraught with danger. Even those who felt convinced that extensive measures must be taken to end the revolution were probably influenced, subconsciously, by the more optimistic reports from America to hope that Great Britain might, after all, get out of the contest more cheaply than they at first feared. That frame of mind probably made them less patient than they otherwise might have been in their support of the military commanders in America. It appears to have made them and the general public more ready to hunt a scapegoat when things did not go well. But most of all, this general confusion of mind about the magnitude of the task ahead meant that those in charge of affairs, and particularly those in America, could not know with any certainty to what degree opinion would permit the devotion of the resources of the nation to crushing the revolution. In such uncertainty, the adoption of a plan appropriate to the resources available was extremely difficult, for no one could tell, except for a brief period, what those resources would be.

[43] Fortescue, vol. 3, nos. 1563 and 1600.

CHAPTER IV

THE BRITISH PREPARATION FOR THE WAR

WE MUST now examine the preparations made by the British government for carrying on the war against the revolted colonies. This chapter will discuss, first, the steps that led to the appointment of the Howe brothers to the command in America; and, secondly, the general adequacy of the measures undertaken to support their efforts. To explore the latter problem we shall not need a highly detailed catalogue of troops recruited, transports fitted out, regiments embarked, and supplies purchased. Such statistics are likely to mislead a generation accustomed to operations on a very different scale from those of the 18th century. Our purpose will be better served by discovering whether the measures taken were adequate according to contemporary opinion. We shall also need to know whether they corresponded to the expectations of the commanders sent to America, for upon that point must hinge in no small measure our allocation of the responsibility for the failure of the British efforts. A perfectly good plan of operations might miscarry completely if the government failed to support it in the fashion the military commanders had a legitimate reason to expect. Or a plausible plan might be hopelessly bad because based upon an assumption of support which the commanders ought to have known could never be afforded them.

The sending of the Howe brothers to America was

not a sudden decision taken after the war had begun. As early as November 1774, George III discussed with Lord North the advisability of sending some additional major-general to America, the suggestion apparently having come from the minister.[1] By the middle of the next month the idea of sending commissioners to America to settle the dispute had been born, although the King was not at all enamoured of it. He feared it would but prolong the dispute by making the colonists think the mother country feared them.[2] The 18th of December the King wrote as if the sending of a major-general was fully decided and expressed his approval. By that time his only fear was that the immediate sending of the officer might prevent the proper forming of a general plan. He also mentioned the possibility of giving the chief command to Sir Jeffrey Amherst, in which case Sir Jeffrey would wish to be consulted about the appointment of his chief subordinate.[3]

It was natural that Sir William Howe should be a candidate for this post, for few officers in the British army were more highly regarded than he. Practically all of his contemporaries bore witness to the general esteem in which he was held. The criticism and doubts about his ability which came from every side after the disasters in America are in striking contrast to the opinions expressed before his departure from England. The worst said against either of the Howes before their appointment was that they were so reserved and taciturn that any accurate estimate of their characters was extremely difficult. Although this inclined some people to doubt whether the appointments would bring the favourable results desired by the ministry, nevertheless there were few if any who

[1] Fortescue, vol. 3, no. 1556.
[2] Ibid., no. 1563.
[3] Ibid., no. 1565.

doubted that the Howes were at least competent officers.

Sir William Howe was a man of large physique, about six feet tall, and sturdily built. He shared that swarthiness of complexion which gave his brother the nickname of 'Black Dick.' Today he might have been called a 'strong, silent man,' for he spoke but little and never in such fashion as to reveal to others his plans and intentions, unless such revelation was absolutely necessary. But, in spite of this inscrutability, he was considered a man of moderate opinions and sound common sense, and, wherever he commanded, was always popular with the troops. He was also thought to have the soldierly vigour needed to make moderate opinions effective in action. In short, much of his availability for the task entrusted to him came from the fact that he was considered a 'middle-of-the-road' man, combining moderate opinions, tactful nature, and the esteem of the Americans, with such military ability and character as would fit him for the effort needed to rewin the colonies.

That Sir William Howe was at an early date under consideration for this post is clear from a list of available names drawn up by the King. It also contained, among others, those of Clinton and Burgoyne but did not indicate upon which the final choice would fall.[4] Lord North was able, during January, to discover through an intermediary Sir William Howe's reaction to the prospect of a command in America. Sir Philip Skene wrote to the minister on the 23rd that he had seen General Howe and that it would be possible to persuade him to serve under Gage.[5] The Major went on to praise Howe, mentioning that he had served with

[4] Fortescue, vol. 3, no. 1569.
[5] *H.M.C. Mss. of Earl of Dartmouth*, vol. 2, p. 262.

him in many difficult situations and had 'found him unsurpassed in activity, bravery, and experience, and beloved by the troops.'

Meanwhile, the endeavour to secure Amherst for the chief command in America did not prosper. For a few days the ministers thought he was about to accept, but then, so rumour said, his wife dissuaded him.[6] Whatever the cause of Sir Jeffrey's refusal, it must have seemed to him very persuasive for he was reported to have been offered a peerage if he would take the command. The reason he assigned was his inability to bring himself to command against the Americans.

With Amherst definitely unavailable, the ministry decided to continue Gage in command but to send three major-generals to assist him. Howe, Clinton, and Burgoyne were chosen for the purpose. Walpole commented caustically upon the appointments:

The Duke of Richmond artfully in the Lords complained of the cruelty of sending Howe to command against Boston, when the first object he would behold there would be the monument they had erected to his brother, slain in the past war. Howe was one of those brave, silent brothers, and was reckoned sensible, though so silent that nobody knew whether he was or not. Burgoyne had offered himself to this service; but he was a vain, very ambitious man, with a half understanding that was worse than none; Clinton had not that fault, for he had no sense at all.[7]

Burgoyne recorded that Barrington told him the appointments were very much the personal decision of the King, who considered the available officers on their merits, and that the choice was made entirely on that basis.[8] The character of George III was such

6 Walpole, *Last Journals*, vol. 1, pp. 432-3.
7 Ibid., p. 433.
8 Fonblanque, *Burgoyne*, p. 122.

that it is not improbable that Barrington's account was in large measure accurate. But Burgoyne, although he was chosen for an American post on his supposed merits, might have risen higher if his own information was correct. He understood that Sir Gilbert Ellyot had suggested him for the chief command in America and that Howe and Clinton should be left at home.[9] Although that hope miscarried, Burgoyne did not despair of securing precedence over his two associates and suggested himself to Lord North for the command at New York. But he received no satisfaction on that score, although Germain, who still had some months to wait before he replaced Dartmouth, looked favourably upon his plea and expressed the belief that Howe's place was with the main body of the army, where his ability and reputation would go far to restore discipline and morale.[10] Burgoyne even went so far as to suggest to Howe himself that he would like to be employed at New York, but found that gentleman somewhat elusive in his reply and clear only in his own wish not to go to Boston. Of this sentiment Burgoyne wrote :

I knew the reason given publicly by all his friends for that wish was the obligation his family owed to the Bostonians, who had erected a monument to the late Lord Howe and particularly complimented the general. However, I very soon discovered that the secret and real reason was the low opinion he held of the commander-in-chief as a soldier.[11]

Burgoyne felt his disappointment all the more keenly from the fact that rumours had come to him that made him think he would be the recipient of the

9 Fonblanque, *Burgoyne*, p. 126.
10 Ibid., p. 126.
11 Ibid., p. 129.

royal favour.[12]   Furthermore, he was given to understand that Lord North and the rest of the cabinet
favoured his advancement.   But he also heard that
Howe's friends were diligently at work.   Their dili-
gence or influence finally carried the day for their
candidate.[13]

It has long been believed that the fact that the Howes
were descended illegitimately from George I exercised
some influence in their appointment, but this has never
been proved.   That the King felt some obligation toward Sir William Howe would appear from a conversation Burgoyne reported with Lord North.   Burgoyne
had complained of the limited opportunity left him by
his appointment as it then stood.   North sympathized
with his discontent and sought to turn him off with the
observation that it was thought proper to leave the
more definite allocation of duties to Gage, thus imply-
ing that Gage had decided how each of the major-
generals should be employed.   But Burgoyne, if we
can credit his account of the interview, was not to be
duped by so weak an excuse and so told Lord North,
who admitted that Burgoyne's suspicions were correct
and that the choice nominally attributed to Gage was
in reality dictated by directions from the home government.   He explained the course taken, so favourable
to Howe and disappointing to Burgoyne, on the
ground that some promise, he was not very explicit
about its nature, had been made early and very in-
advisedly to Howe.   Lord North represented the King
as rather embarrassed by this pledge but apparently of
the opinion that he was bound by it.[14]

That there was more to this explanation than a desire to smooth things over with Burgoyne would appear

12 Ibid., p. 130.
13 Ibid., p. 130.
14 Ibid., p. 132.

from a letter of the King to Lord North early in April
1775:

> I am sorry Howe seems to look so much on the com-
> mand in New York as the post of confidence, as I think
> Burgoyne would best manage any negociation; but a full
> conversation will send the latter in good humour, who at
> present feels a little hurt at not having been enough let
> into the views of government, and if he remains at Boston
> he may be able to suggest what falls in conversation to the
> Commander-in-Chief, which may prove of great utility.[15]

There is pretty clear indication here of a previous
pledge to Howe. It is only natural that many have
supposed the left-handed relationship explained the
promise, but it is not necessary to go so far. Famili-
arity with the manner in which favours were parcelled
out in the eighteenth century supports the belief that
Howe approached the government with some request
for employment, that his distinguished record and high
position commanded favourable consideration for his
request, and that he consequently received some sort of
promise which the King felt obliged to redeem.

We now come to a difficulty. If Sir William Howe
secured his American command in this quite ordinary
fashion, how are we to reconcile that fact with his well-
known letter to Mr. Kirk? Kirk was a member of the
constituency which Sir William represented in Parliament. The latter had stated to his constituents some
time earlier that he would not accept a command
against the Americans, for which attitude his previous
popularity with the colonists and more particularly
that of his slain elder brother gave ample excuse.
When it now became noised abroad that, after all, he
was to go to Boston in a position of great importance,

15 From Fortescue, *Correspondence of King George III*, vol. 3, no. 1640.
By permission of The Macmillan Company, publishers.

his previous statement was remembered and brought
a reminder from Kirk on 10 February 1775.[16]
Sir William replied on the 21st of February:

My going thither [to America] was not of my seeking.
I was ordered, and could not refuse, without incurring the
odious name of backwardness to serve my country in distress. . . I have been most highly complimented upon the
occasion, by those who are even averse to the measures of
the Administration.
Every man's private feelings ought to give way to the
service of the public at all times; but particularly when
of that delicate nature in which our affairs stand at the
present. . . One word for America. You are deceived if
you suppose that there are not many loyal and peaceable
subjects in that country. I may safely assert that the
insurgents are very few, in comparison with the whole of
the people.
There are certainly those who do not agree with a taxa-
tion from hence, but who do not wish to sever themselves
from the supremacy of this country. This last set of men,
I should hope, by their being relieved of the grievance,
will most readily return to all due obedience to the laws.
With respect to the few, who, I am told, desire to separate themselves from the Mother Country, I trust, when
they find they are not well supported in their frantic
ideas by the more moderate, which I have described, they
will, from fear of punishment, subside to the laws.[17]

What are we to make of this letter, and can it be
reconciled with the picture of Howe given by Burgoyne that shows him diligently in search of an American command? At first sight it appears impossible
and we seem compelled to convict Howe of lying to
Kirk, or Burgoyne of lying or of believing someone
else's lies. In view of the corroboration of Bur-

[16] Reproduced in the pamphlet entitled, *A Reply to the Observations
of Lt. Gen. Sir William Howe*, pp. 146-8. This pamphlet will hereafter be cited as *A Reply*, etc.
[17] Ibid., pp. 148-50.

goyne's story by the letter from George III to Lord North it is difficult to convict Burgoyne of falsehood or even of a very serious misinterpretation of what was told him. The case against Howe's honesty looks formidable, and we can appreciate the stimulus afforded by the incident to the suspicions of those who later suspected him of accepting the American command in order to render aid and comfort to the revolting colonists and through them to the Opposition.

But is not such an explanation a little hasty, especially when the general's conduct is capable of a different explanation? What more natural than that Howe, with a brilliant record and apparently with the best years of his career just ahead, should elicit from the government some promise of favour in any desirable appointments that might be made. Any embarrassment he may have felt from his previous statement to his constituents, should his appointment prove to be an American command, could be exorcised by his belief that such an appointment would prove primarily a task of negotiation. A man anxious for preferment, possessed of every reason for believing himself peculiarly fitted to carry out the combination of threat and promise that would be the task of a negotiator, would find it easy to convince himself that he was not accepting a command to wage war on the Americans in the ordinary sense in which he had indicated he would decline such an opportunity. Such reasoning would perhaps not satisfy a logician, but far less convincing arguments have satisfied men anxious to shine in this world. Howe evidently felt some embarrassment in accepting the command, as his letter to Kirk would show, but it seems likely that he really convinced himself that he was acting in logical and consistent fashion.

This view of the reasons that led Sir William Howe

to accept the American command receives support from an examination of the events that led, early in 1776, to the association with him of his brother, Admiral Lord Richard Howe, as naval commander and joint commissioner.

William Eden wrote to Germain on 3 October 1775 that Lord North had confided to him several months earlier that he thought the American difficulty could best be dealt with by giving some person a commission which would enable him to settle matters.[18] Eden wrote three weeks later that nobody could be found adequate to so great an office, unless Germain were willing to fill it, and that if he would not, the burden must be both divided and reduced.[19]

When George III opened Parliament in October 1775 he proposed to send commissioners to treat with any provinces in America that might be disposed to return to their allegiance. That the King agreed to this proposal with little confidence of its ultimate success is obvious from his correspondence with Lord North. Only a few weeks before he had made special note of a conversation with General Haldimand in which that officer had ridiculed the idea that anything less than a vigorous use of force could bring the Americans back to obedience.[20] The King had reached the same opinion at least a month earlier.[21] Walpole, writing at a later date, reported that the public was surprised and perplexed by the final decision to attempt a commission, some thinking it mere foolishness, others believing the ministers had become alarmed and were prepared to treat with the colonies.[22] But, he

[18] H.M.C. Mss. of Mrs. Stopford-Sackville, vol. 2, p. 10.
[19] Ibid., vol. 2, p. 12. Eden-Germain, 21 October 1775.
[20] Fortescue, vol. 3, no. 1697.
[21] Ibid., no. 1595.
[22] Walpole, Last Journals, vol. 1, p. 483.

went on to say, there was a secret motive, not known until afterwards, that made the whole plan ridiculous and contemptible.   Just what that was Walpole did not indicate definitely, but certain negotiations were going on between the ministry and Lord Howe which made it probable that he had them in mind when he made this allusion.

The negotiations concerned an appointment and the proper order of naval preferment.   Sir Charles Saunders, Lieutenant-General of the Marines, died at the end of 1774.   It appears that Lord North had previously promised Lord Richard Howe that when a vacancy next occurred in the office he would receive the appointment.[23]   But North was easy going and probably made the promise without much reflection.   At least, he soon forgot it.   This lapse of memory was to cause him considerable embarrassment for, upon news of Saunders' death. Lord Sandwich asked Lord North in a casual way whether he had any objections to giving Admiral Palliser the place.   Lord North, forgetting completely his earlier promise to Howe, replied that he had none.   Lord Sandwich thereupon took Palliser immediately to the King to kiss hands.

No sooner had news of the appointment become public than Lord Howe came to town to claim Lord North's promise.   They met in the House of Commons and Howe told North that next day he intended to see the King and, as a result of the broken promise, to resign all his offices.   He added that he felt sure his brother would take a similar step.   North, greatly upset, pleaded distraction with the affairs of America as the reason for his forgetfulness and urged Lord Howe to reconsider or at least postpone his intention.

23 Walpole, *Last Journals*, vol. 1, p. 483.

Germain joined them and added his pleas to those of North, with the result that Howe was pacified for the time being.[24]   It appears that, in order to carry his point, North promised Lord Howe that he would promptly be given some other employment perhaps even more lucrative than that he had originally been promised.

According to Walpole's information, North first attempted to persuade Forbes, the General of Marines, to resign his post to Lord Howe in return for a substantial pension.   Forbes, however, preferred the office he held and North was obliged to look elsewhere.   He then hit upon the naval command in America as the most convenient reward, although this had originally been intended for Admiral Shuldham, who was at the time the commander on that station.   Shuldham was a friend of Sandwich, who was thus 'punished for his dexterous industry.' [25]

But some difficulties still remained in the relations of Lord Howe and the government.   North was eager to let Shuldham down as easily as possible and proposed to give him a separate command on the St. Lawrence.   Howe resented this as disparaging to himself and also feared that it would lead Sandwich, whom he disliked, to refuse him proper support.   Consequently he indicated to North that he intended to demand an audience of the King on 2 February 1776.[26]   This news greatly frightened North for he feared that it meant Howe intended to resign his employments. Such a turn in affairs would have been embarrassing to the ministry, for news of the appointment of Howe had leaked out and had had a good effect on public

24 Ibid., p. 522.
25 Ibid., p. 522.
26 Fortescue, vol. 3, no. 1816.

opinion. North feared that if the appointment fell through the loss would be much greater than if it had never been considered.

Lord Howe actually saw the King at the time he intended but without the unhappy results feared by North. The King, aware of North's anxiety, wrote him promptly after the interview that matters were not as bad as he feared and that there were very fair prospects of bringing the affair to a successful conclusion, thanks rather to the obliging attitude of Lord Sandwich than to that of Lord Howe.[27]   Later in the same afternoon the King wrote again to North:

> By a conversation he [the King] had with Lord Howe today, he thought that he perceived him to be very uneasy at the apprehension that he should be thought to decline service, in a critical moment, and therefore hopes that there is not in his mind any determination to avoid the appointment.[28]

The King was prompt in undertaking the necessary arrangements and was able to write the next day to North:

> I have seen Lord Sandwich, and I think settled the command of the N. American fleet agreeably to Lord Howe's proposal to me yesterday, the mode of saving Lord Sandwich and Shuldham I think really without the least objection; if there had been any I should have jumped over it to settle this material affair. . . I out of delicacy to Lord Sandwich leave the expedients I have consented to to be named by himself to you.[29]

The same day the King received a note from Sandwich saying he had seen Howe and told him he should

[27] From Fortescue, *Correspondence of King George III,* vol. 3, no. 1817. By permission of The Macmillan Company, publishers.
[28] Ibid., no. 1818.
[29] Ibid., no. 1820.

have complete command on the St. Lawrence as well as in other parts of America and also have his promotion antedated, apparently to carry it back to the date on which the original promise of North should have been fulfilled.   With this assurance Howe seemed perfectly satisfied, not so much as asking what means were to be taken to satisfy Shuldham.[30]

If Walpole was right, there may have been other reasons than professional pique to tempt Lord Howe to refuse the American appointment.   The diarist believed that, in spite of the gesture of the commission, the court had no real intention of treating with the Americans, but planned instead to subdue them by force.[31]   This opinion receives at least partial corroboration from a letter of the King in the preceding November in which he wrote to North, 'I have always feared a commission as not likely to meet with success, yet I think it right to be attempted, whilst every act of vigour is unremittingly carrying on.'[32]   In the royal mind the commission was a slender hope, to be attempted because it was unwise to forego any possible avenue of success, and also because those in England who were lukewarm towards the government would feel that some measures other than mere force ought to be used.   Even at this early date the seeds of confusion and failure had been sown, for the government regarded the commission primarily as a sop, whereas those who undertook it thought of it as a vital part of the plan for pacifying the colonies.   The government and its agents had already begun to work at cross purposes.

Even in his own mind Lord Howe seems not to have

---

[30] Ibid., no. 1821.
[31] Walpole, *Last Journals*, vol. 1, p. 521.
[32] Donne, vol. 1, p. 293.

felt sure what measures ought to be adopted in America.[33] Less than a year before receiving the American command he had spoken in Parliament in favour of engrossing the bill against Massachusetts, declaring against the 'late pretended conciliatory bill' on the ground that it would be wrong to treat with America so long as that country was in rebellion.[34] Yet Lord Howe was certainly not the uncompromising advocate of force that this opinion might indicate. In fact, he seems to have varied his opinion from time to time, and in that variation, which was not peculiar to him or to his brother, is to be found an explanation of much that seems illogical or inconsistent in the action of the British government and its agents in those difficult months.

In view of the somewhat tortuous method by which the appointment of Lord Howe to the American command was accomplished, it is not strange that the public should have shown some surprise. It was reported that he had made a great many requisitions of the government, of which most remained secret.[35] The public astonishment is well expressed by a letter written at the time:

What makes this yet more extraordinary is that Lord Howe both hates and despises Lord Sandwich, and he has not spoken to Lord George Germain since the expedition to the coast of France in 1758, although these two men preside at the head of the two offices through which he must transmit all business.[36]

[33] Howe is said to have approached Franklin, when he first heard he might be appointed, to secure advice. They talked over the problem of conciliation but the stiff-necked attitude of the King, so it was reported, brought their plans to nought.

[34] Walpole, *Last Journals*, vol. 1, p. 441.

[35] *H.M.C. Mss. of Cornwallis Wykeham-Martin, Various Collections*, vol. 6, p. 314. Letter of Capt. J. Leveson-Gower to Capt., the Hon. Wm. Cornwallis, 27 February 1776.

[36] Ibid.

In a situation where so much depended upon a sympathetic understanding between the British government and the commanders of its armed forces, this personal friction was almost certain to bring unfortunate results.

Although it was settled early in the winter that Lord Howe was to have the naval command in America, together with a commission to secure peace, many important details of the plan had to be arranged in the weeks that followed, details that gave so much trouble that they at times threatened to upset the whole appointment. The first draft of the instructions for the commissioners did not at all satisfy Lord Howe. They were, in his opinion, much too harsh. He complained that they prevented him from negotiating a treaty until the preliminary conditions were entirely complied with, which he thought would mean that military operations must continue until the Americans had been driven to the back settlements or so beaten that they would be scarcely worth conquering. He added that he could not undertake the task upon such terms, especially as they were not in agreement with what he understood to be the government's intention when he accepted the command earlier in the winter.[37]

These objections, which were advanced in a letter of 26 March 1776, led the government to undertake to alter the commission in conformity with the Admiral's wishes. Howe wrote to Germain on April 1st, acknowledging that some of his objections had been met, but expressing himself as yet not satisfied; for it seemed to him that the declaring of peace and the granting of pardons were the only decisive measures the commissioners were empowered to undertake. He

---

[37] *H.M.C. Mss. of Mrs. Stopford-Sackville*, vol. 2, p. 25, Lord Howe-Germain, 26 March 1776.

was evidently irked by the idea that everything of real importance must be submitted to the ministry for final decision.[38]

In spite of the alterations that had been made, matters remained in a state unsatisfactory to both parties. The King opposed the granting of a freer hand to the commissioners and even hoped that Lord Howe could be persuaded to give up the idea of being a commissioner.[39] Thomas Hutchinson called upon Lord Howe on April 14 and found him in a rather uncomfortable frame of mind. Hutchinson noted in his diary, 'He seems unacquainted [about America]. He complimented me by wishing he had my knowledge. Matters don't seem to be yet settled.'[40] And D'Oyley told him three days later that it was still uncertain whether Lord Howe would go.[41]

The reason for the settlement of these difficulties in such fashion that Lord Howe finally went to America as commissioner was explained by Wedderburn in a letter written to Germain shortly before the solution was reached. He said he was sure Howe would have the commission because there was nobody else available and, 'the difficulty of breaking with him upon it is at least more pressing, if it is not as great, as the danger of entrusting the Commission to his judgment.'[42] The exact steps by which Howe was finally pacified and his objections met are not entirely clear, but Wedderburn's letter explains the substance and motive of the government's action.

It was even suspected at the time that the arrangements between Lord Howe and his superiors had not

38 *H.M.C. Mss. of Mrs. Stopford-Sackville*, vol. 2, p. 27.
39 Fortescue, vol. 3, no. 1849.
40 *Diary of Thos. Hutchinson*, vol. 2, pp. 21-22.
41 Ibid., p. 34.
42 *H.M.C. Mss. of Mrs. Stopford-Sackville*, vol. 2, p. 28, Wedderburn-Germain, 24 April 1776.

been entirely settled at the time he left for America. Walpole, after commenting on the threatening news from France, went on to say :

Peace, even before the news from France, had become the measure. They had hurried away Lord Howe out of town to Portsmouth the day before his brother's retreat from Boston was sure of being mentioned in the House of Commons, lest Lord Howe's want of sense should draw him into betraying secrets in defence of his brother — yet to that want of sense they trusted so momentous a negociation. They hurried him off with vast power, it is said, and with few instructions, hoping he would hazard a disadvantageous peace, and be liable to bear the blame. I have heard too, but I do not know if it is true, that he obtained a full pardon for whatever he should do, under the king's sign manual. If he did, some friend more shrewd than himself must have suggested that salvo.[43]

Although most of this was merely a sneer at Howe, it is sufficiently supported by other evidence to justify the belief that the government had little faith in the commission sent to America. Everything points to the conclusion that the commission was intended partly as a sop to those who thought some conciliatory effort should be made ; partly as an indulgence to Lord Howe, who would not otherwise accept the American command ; and partly as a forlorn hope. Even the choice of Lord Howe for any command in America seems to have been a somewhat accidental, not to say reluctant, decision on the part of the government. The ministers appear to have been brought to it by promises of preferment to Lord Howe which his political influence made it awkward to ignore and for the satisfaction of which the American command was at the time the only opening of an importance adequate to his rank. Then, to secure Lord Howe's acceptance

43 Walpole, *Last Journals*, vol. 1, p. 50.

and avoid the resignation that he threatened, the government was willing to draw up the commission in a form that seemed to concede his minimum demands. The concessions, however, were made grudgingly and without real belief in the value of the measures they authorized. Under the circumstances, the commission, as an instrument for pacifying the colonies and for ensuring successful co-operation between the home government and its commanders in America, was crippled at birth.

We must now turn to the second point to be examined in this chapter, namely, the adequacy of the preparations made by the British government for the war in America. It is a subject that requires care, for eighteenth-century standards of adequacy were different from our own. The obstacles in the way of adequate preparation, the shortage of recruits, the lack of funds, and the absence of the almost omnipotent power possessed by the modern state, were more serious than can easily be realized today. We must judge the efforts of the government of George III in the light of circumstances.

In addition to the practical difficulties peculiar to the time and situation, Lord North and his colleagues had to recognize political limitations upon their efforts. There is reason to believe that in the early weeks of the struggle the ministers felt very uncertain what effort they could afford to make in America. A passage in Walpole's *Last Journals* paints their embarrassment, although allowance must be made for his bias. Under the entry for 23 June 1775, he wrote:

Bad news poured in from America. . . The ministers were aground: they first thought of sending Hessians, Hanoverians, and even a large body of Russians—but found it would be too expensive or unpopular. They were offered three thousand Highlanders, but did not dare accept them.   At last they thought of recalling Gage and the troops, and it was said to be carried in council but by one voice that they should not.   At last, after several consultations, the ministers determined to prosecute the war, and sent to General Carleton at Quebec to march with six thousand Canadians to the back of the colonies.   Still they had little hopes of making any impression this campaign, but waited anxiously for the result of the general Congress, in hopes it would propose some terms of accommodation.[44]

The phrase, 'but found it would be too expensive or unpopular' furnishes the clue to the problem.   George III and his ministry were engaged in a domestic political contest of which the American crisis was an unwelcome sideshow.   A victory in America would have been useless if purchased at the expense of political defeat in Great Britain.   This fact limited, quite as effectively as any material circumstance, the amount of support the government could demand or secure from the country for supporting the war in the colonies.

After the outbreak of the conflict the ministry came rapidly to a realization that war in America presented a serious problem, although its members were not yet fully aware of the great proportions the conflict was eventually to assume.   A note of pessimism sounds through the early discussion of military measures.   A great military effort in America would have required the despatch of practically all the troops in the kingdom.   This in turn would have necessitated the raising of new units to replace those embarked for the colonies.   The British government usually turned to Ireland at such times, but Jenkinson was gloomy about recruiting prospects there.   He wrote to the King:

[44] Walpole, *Last Journals*, vol. 1, p. 467.

It is a point therefore worthy of the most serious consideration what probability there is of raising the new corps which are to replace the troops drawn from thence; for we have hitherto found by experience that the recruits raised in Ireland desert so fast while they continue in that kingdom, or in the neighborhood of it, that not above half of those who are enlisted are ever brought to the publick service: the recruiting funds of the regiments who have sent parties there have been exhausted; — and for the same reason we have been obliged to march the companies lately raised in Ireland from the western coast of this kingdom immediately upon their arrival.[45]

From other sources came further discouraging reports. In August 1775, North reported a conversation with Barrington, who was very pessimistic, so much so that North was induced to recommend to the King, over Barrington's objections, that the government should take advantage of the offer made by certain gentlemen to raise corps on their own initiative. Not only did North hope for some troops from this source, but he thought that the mere activity of these influential people would help the cause of the government by giving it the appearance of support.[46]

The King, however, did not entirely share his minister's discouragement, as he indicated in his reply to North's account of his conversation with Barrington:

I have read Lord Barrington's two letters which do not surprise me, he is diffident as to raising recruits, but that is as much occasioned by his wish to have the American war alone carried on by sea; I do not see the prospect so indifferent as he does, the best time for recruiting is not yet come; and the different arrangements now just set in motion must have a due time given them before any judgment can be formed whether the coming to the very disagreeable measure of raising new corps will be neces-

[45] From Fortescue, *Correspondence of King George III*, vol. 3, no. 1628. By permission of The Macmillan Company, publishers.
[46] Ibid., no. 1699.

sary; but in that case I shall never agree to disobliging the whole army by giving them to every young man that pretends he can soon compleat them; I know full well what little good arose from Charles Townshend's plan when the corps were compleated most of them were declared by the general who received them to be composed of men totally unfit to carry muskets.[47]

After a short discussion of the time needed for training before a new corps could be fit for service, the King continued:

The misfortune is that at the beginning of this American business there has been an unwillingness to augment the Army and Navy I proposed early in the summer the sending of beating orders to Ireland this was objected to in the cabinet . . . there is now every means using to compleat the old corps, and I cannot agree to putting additional irons in the fire.

A good deal may be read between the lines of this interchange of notes between the King and Lord North. North obviously felt discouraged and therefore was prepared to undertake a method of recruiting not consonant with the best military practice. The King did not despair so quickly, but his objection to the proposals of the minister was founded not so much on optimism as on a belief that their disadvantages were so manifest that it would be wiser to take any chance, however slim, of success through more normal methods.

But, in spite of pessimism, in spite of difficulties, the government early in 1775 prepared for vigorous action in America. At a meeting of the cabinet on June 15 extensive measures for augmenting the forces were adopted. Regiments in America were to be enlarged by drafts from Great Britain; Carleton was to be

[47] Ibid., no. 1702.

directed to raise two thousand Canadian light infantry; it was decided to endeavour to raise a body of Highlanders, and inquiry was to be made about the possibility of raising three thousand foreign troops.[48] Further measures of a similar nature were adopted a week later.[49]   On June 26 it was suggested that the keeping of twelve thousand men in Ireland was no longer possible, and consequently five regiments in the island were ordered sent to Gage.   Extraordinary means were to be taken to recruit the army, and it was the opinion of the cabinet that a force of not less than twenty thousand men, exclusive of irregulars, should be assembled in America for the next campaign.[50]

By the end of the summer the negotiations for foreign mercenaries had made considerable progress. The Empress of Russia was first approached and led the British government to believe for a time that it had found a certain source of supply.   Indeed, so copious at first appeared her supply of purchasable troops and so great her readiness to see them employed, that the modest hopes of early summer, the securing of three thousand mercenaries, rose quickly to a request for twenty thousand.   It was hoped that at least an equal number of British troops could be maintained in America with them.[51]

But these hopes were doomed to an early disappointment.   Dartmouth was obliged to write Sir William Howe on 27 October 1775 that the Russian negotiation appeared to be on the point of failure.[52]   This setback made it necessary to look elsewhere and the government turned to Germany.   Germain hoped on 5 Jan-

[48] *Dom. State Papers*, Geo. III, 11, Minutes of cabinet meeting at Lord North's, 15 June 1775.
[49] Ibid., 21 June 1775.
[50] Ibid., 26 July 1775.
[51] C.O.5/92, pp. 481-3.   Dartmouth-Howe, 5 September 1775.
[52] Ibid., pp. 539-52.   Dartmouth-Howe, 22 October 1775.

uary 1776 to be able to secure at least ten thousand troops there and was in fact negotiating for seventeen thousand. Within a few days the negotiations reached a successful conclusion and Great Britain was able to secure all the troops for which Germain had negotiated, several thousand more than he originally expected.[53] Walpole, who was no friend of the ministry, recognized the vigour and scope of the efforts made to send troops to America. He wrote in his Journals in January 1776:

Every effort was used in these islands to raise soldiers and sailors, but with indifferent success, and not at all in proportion to the extraordinary premiums given to particular favourites who offered or were invited to raise them. . . Lord Mansfield, Wedderburn, and the Scotch sounded high Lord George's spirit ; and nothing was talked of but conquering America in one campaign ; whilst indeed the more sober part of the ministers, who saw the wilderness and profusion of the expense, were apprehensive that, if the business could not be effected in time, the Administration would be blown up, finding themselves at a dead stand.[54]

And again :

The year began with mighty preparations for carrying on the war in America with vigour. Lord George Sackville Germain, who had been brought into power for that end, was indefatigable in laying plans for raising and hiring troops, in sending supplies and recruits, and more naval force.[55]

It seems clear that, whatever might have been the inefficiency of the government, there was no lack of effort.

Walpole also reported a division within the cabinet between those who followed Germain in urging force

[53] Ibid., pp. 555-9. Dartmouth-Howe, 27 October 1775.
[54] Walpole, *Last Journals*, vol. 1, p. 510.
[55] Ibid.

without stint and those with a greater propensity to peace. This produced, so he thought, a certain ambiguity in the public announcements of cabinet officers.[56] However that may have been, and however confusing this ambiguity may have been to the commander in America, contemporaries were nevertheless impressed by the vigour of the ministerial preparations for carrying on the war. Thomas Hutchinson wrote, 'In general it is agreed that the force for America is as great as has been desired by the commanders there. . ."[57] Yet in spite of it all, Hutchinson concluded with a pathetic confession of gloomy foreboding. 'I count the days, and absurd as it is so near the close of life, I can hardly help wishing to sleep away the time between this and the spring, that I may escape the succession of unfortunate events which I am always in fear of.'

As Hutchinson foresaw, in spite of the vigour of the government, the difficulties were great. The extent to which the ministry was prepared to go for even a few recruits may be seen in a letter of Lord North to the King:

Lord North begs leave to submit to his Majesty, whether an application may not be made to the East India Company to stop, or, at least, to diminish their recruiting for a short space of time. He fears that such an application would be unsuccessful but if they would desist from recruiting for the next four months, the army might gain a thousand men by it, especially if the persons now employed by the Company for enlisting were, during that time, taken into the service of the public.[58]

But after Lord North had received the royal permis-

56 Walpole, *Last Journals*, vol. 1, pp. 510-11.
57 *Diary of Thos. Hutchinson*, vol. 2, p. 6.
58 From Fortescue, *Correspondence of King George III*, vol. 3, no. 1708. By permission of The Macmillan Company, publishers.

sion to make this application, he was only able to secure from the Company a promise to restrict somewhat its recruiting.[59] This helplessness of the government in the face of a private company, even in wartime, testifies to the peculiar difficulties under which Lord North and his colleagues had to work. The despotic power of government which in modern times makes possible the complete subordination of a nation's life to purposes of state was not available to the rules of eighteenth-century Great Britain and we must bear that fact in mind when judging their efforts.

Confronted with such difficulties, had the government of Lord North been really supine, it might have abandoned positive measures for subduing the American colonies in favour of the purely naval pressure which Barrington advocated. But, in spite of earlier doubts about the prospects of the contest, the cabinet soon decided to make a strenuous effort by both land and sea. Lord North wrote the King on 12 November 1775 that the cabinet had decided the day before to submit to the King the necessity of a speedy augmentation of force and to recommend the securing of a corps of foreign troops. North justified these measures as necessary to avoid another defensive campaign which would create discontent at home and increase the risk of a foreign war.[60] Further light is thrown on the intensity of the effort to secure foreign mercenaries by a note from the King objecting to some of the proposals for securing troops in Germany, on the ground that they would violate the law of the land and turn him into a kidnapper which did not seem to him a very honourable occupation.[61]

[59] Fortescue, vol. 3, no. 1715.
[60] Ibid., no. 1760.
[61] Ibid., no. 1763.

At the same time everything possible was done to comb out from the troops then in Great Britain all those that could be spared for America. The letters between the King and Lord North show the extent to which the government ran the risk of assuming that peace would be maintained in Europe. Only five regiments were to be left in Ireland, a diminutive garrison for that troublesome island. It was even planned to remove all the British troops there and replace them by foreigners, but the Irish parliament vetoed that proposal. In England itself only four battalions were to remain. The hazard that the government accepted in order to reinforce the army in America was tremendous.

The King in particular did everything in his power to instil vigour into the administration. A letter to Sandwich in January 1776 reveals the intensity of his prodding. Sandwich had just written the King a letter excusing himself for certain delays, in which he dwelt upon the extraordinary demands to which his department had been subjected and upon what he had already achieved. The King replied:

> I trust your activity will instil that vigilance into the inferiors in your great department that no delay in sending out the succours in the spring will arrive in the short notice you have had; you call it unprecedented, the expression in ordinary times ought undoubtedly to be attended to, but when such acts of vigour are shown by the rebellious Americans, we must shew that the English Lion when rouzed has not only his wonted resolution but has added the swiftness of the race horse.[62]

The King mentioned the fact that the navy had disappointed the government by lagging behind the other departments in its preparations and continued:

[62] From Fortescue, *Correspondence of King George III*, vol. 3, no. 1810. By permission of The Macmillan Company, publishers.

I cannot too strongly inculcate the necessity of setting aside all official forms that in the least delay the engaging transports.

We cannot go into the detailed results of all these efforts and exhortations, for an adequate examination of the subject would require a volume in itself.[63]   We can, however, look ahead a little and see what sort of armament was provided for the American service in the summer of 1776.   Estimates differ somewhat as to the exact numbers sent to America, but we are well within bounds when we say that the British government had at least thirty thousand men under arms there.   This army, with the very extensive naval force sent at the same time, made one of the most powerful armaments that Great Britain had ever sent forth.   Sir William Howe, who would naturally have been the first to detect any inadequacy, was profuse, as will be seen, in his compliments to the ministry upon the success of its exertions.

Certain facts are clear.   The government at first felt uncertain about its ability to raise forces adequate to the emergency in America.   That much can be said, without accepting Walpole's story that a single vote in council prevented the abandonment of the war. But when the decision to prosecute the war had been made, the ministry, vigorously prompted by the King, showed unexpected energy both in securing troops abroad and in stripping the United Kingdom of all the troops that could possibly be spared.   These efforts were sufficient to place in the hands of the Howes in 1776 an array which supporters of the ministry claimed, with considerable justice, was the finest military and naval force ever sent out by a British government.

[63] See E. E. Curtis, *The Organization of the British Army during the American Revolution.*

Whatever mistakes may have been made then and later, the King and his ministers did not commit the blunder of allowing an unjustifiable optimism at the beginning of the war to tempt them into inadequate preparation. The opposite took place: early pessimism was followed by an effort far more adequate than any observer would have expected from the spirit and information prevalent early in the autumn of 1775.

CHAPTER V

THE BATTLE OF BUNKER HILL

Not long after Sir William Howe's arrival in America the battle of Bunker Hill provided him with an opportunity to show his talents. He was, of course, acting under the orders of Gage when he led the British troops on the 17th of June, but certain of his contemporaries believed that Howe's experiences on that day coloured his whole later conduct. Henry Lee wrote, 'The sad and impressive experience of this murderous day sunk deep into the mind of Sir William Howe ; and it seems to have had its influence upon all his subsequent operations with decisive control.'[1] Although Lee possessed no personal knowledge of the working of Howe's mind, he was a shrewd observer of the events in which he took part and his opinion is worthy of consideration. His explanation has the merit of appearing to furnish a natural explanation for much that has often been attributed to scarcely credible causes.

The main outlines of the battle and the events leading up to it are too familiar to need recapitulation. Much has been written by way of criticism of the British methods of attack. The ponderous advance in the face of entrenchments appeared almost criminally stupid to many critics and has been made the first count in their indictment of Sir William Howe.

---

[1] Henry Lee, *Memoirs of the War in the Southern Department of the United States*, vol. 1, p. 55.

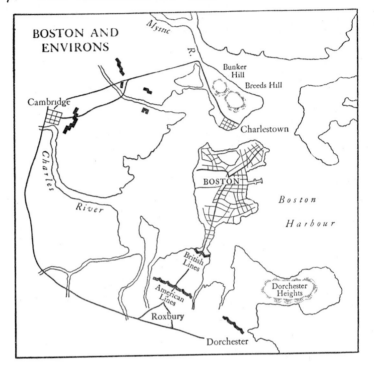

BOSTON AND ENVIRONS

It would certainly be unfair to saddle that much-criticized officer with the responsibility for the original error, that of not taking possession of Charlestown before the Americans could do so. Gage must bear the blame for that. The exact reason why Gage failed to occupy Charlestown and the hills above it is not clear. It has been suggested that he saw the position could not be maintained by the American troops because of the possibility of intercepting their communications across Charlestown Neck, and that hence he did not expect them to occupy it. Gage's failure to perform this manœuvre when the crisis arose does not, however, lend support to this speculation. Further doubt is thrown upon it by Clinton who believed that the discovery of the American design upon Bunker Hill was responsible for the abandonment of a plan to occupy Dorchester Heights.   He implied that the ultimate occupation of the Charlestown peninsula was intended, but that the move of the Americans forced Gage to place it before instead of after the plan for the advance upon Dorchester Heights.[2]   It appears, then, that the correct explanation is that the British had not got round to the job.

We also know very little about the reasons behind the orders issued to Howe when he was sent across the harbour to dislodge the Americans from their new entrenchments.[3]   Frothingham credits Gage with deciding against landing on Charlestown Neck because of fear of being caught between two fires, the American forces on the peninsula and those coming from Cambridge.[4]   That may be true, but if so it shows an exaggerated idea of the offensive capacities of the Americans.[5]   It might have been a dangerous move against

[2] Clinton, *An Historical Detail of Seven Years Campaigns in North America*, vol. 1, p. 39.   Hereafter referred to as Clinton's *Historical Detail.*
[3] Allen French, in his *First Year of the American Revolution*, pp. 209-210, says that the British knew of the American operations above Charlestown the evening of the 16th.   Howe approved operations at daybreak but Gage doubted the American intentions.
[4] Frothingham, *Siege of Boston*, p. 127.
[5] Harold Murdock, in his *Bunker Hill, Notes and Queries*, when speaking of the decision of the British council of war, says, 'The landing was to be made at Moulton's Point on the mouth of the Mystic, the most distant point from the redoubt, and the clear intent was to advance along the river out of range of that work with a view to occupying a position on the flank and well to the rear of its defenders.   Thus, it was probably argued, Clinton's principal aim might still be achieved' (pp. 11-12).
This is, however, all supposition.   No evidence is adduced to support it. Murdock criticizes the council of war for neglecting to provide naval support for the movement, but to me this seems to indicate that there was never any intention of making such a movement.
Murdock argues (pp. 21-2) that while Howe was preparing to advance cautiously near the Mystic, the provincials stopped the move by occupying the rail fence.   This caused Howe to change his plans and send for his reserve.   But Murdock says on p. 23, 'There is no evidence to show that the General requested or that the admiral offered any naval support in the Mystic to meet the new situation.'   This seems to me further proof that the flanking movement along the Mystic shore was never intended.

well-drilled European troops, but the inexperience and imperfect drill of the Americans would have greatly reduced the hazard. There were also rumours that it was the desire of the British commander not to make the Americans too desperate. The implication was that the threat of an attack, if made while the avenue of retreat remained open, would lead to an American withdrawal and thus enable the British to recover the position without cost to themselves.[6] The argument sounds rather too subtle.

In fact, there is no evidence that explains in precise and unmistakable fashion the reasons behind the British plan of attack at Bunker Hill. Of the familiar explanations, that of Frothingham sounds the most convincing, but it is not entirely so. The most striking fact about the strictly contemporary sources for the battle, that is, those written within a few hours or, at most, within a few days of the event, is that they say almost nothing about the reasons for the direction taken by the British attack. The official accounts merely mention that it was ordered and took place in about the fashion originally directed. Seemingly this material affords us little assistance in the solution of the problem.

Does not this silence in reality point toward the correct solution? If the interception of the Americans at Charlestown Neck had been the obvious course, or even a course which Gage and those near him believed would be thought logical, is it not likely that some pains would have been taken to defend the plan actually adopted? Instead there is every appearance that Gage felt his orders were so natural, so inevitable

[6] A criticism of Howe in the *London Chronicle* of 3 August 1779 signed T. P.

under the circumstances, that they required neither explanation nor defence.

It was, in fact, not so extraordinary that Gage should regard his action in this light. The age of the machine gun had not yet made frontal assaults the desperate measure they have become today. In the eighteenth century infantry were taught to advance well within range of the opposing infantry and then to halt and deliver a volley point blank. This custom, which today would be suicidal, was much less sanguinary than might be supposed. The muskets of the eighteenth century were so bad and the average infantryman so poor a shot that, except at a range of a very few yards, the fire of a line of infantry was extremely ineffective. So thoroughly understood was this fact that current military teaching regarded it as an advantage if your opponent could be induced to fire first, so that you might march in closer before delivering your return volley. It was assumed that the casualties from his original volley would not be sufficiently heavy to place you at any serious disadvantage.

So there was nothing repugnant to current military theory in the idea of the British troops marching up the not very difficult slope of Bunker Hill to receive a volley from the Americans posted behind rather rudimentary entrenchments. The British could not return the fire effectively, but that would scarce be thought a necessary preliminary to a bayonet attack on such poorly trained troops as the Americans. There would be a volley from the breastwork, a certain number of casualties, a rush before the defenders could reload, and the bayonet would finish off those who had the temerity to remain for a second shot at the attackers.

Had the Americans, in addition to their deficiencies in military organization and discipline, been no better marksmen than their opponents, these calculations would probably not have gone awry.   But the men who lined the parapet at Bunker Hill carried rifles, for the most part, instead of muskets.   Although considered unsuitable for normal military use, where the bayonet rather than the bullet was the decisive weapon, the rifle was vastly superior to the musket in precision. The men who used it on this occasion had acquired their proficiency in the hunting field, where accuracy was at a premium.   The contrast between a volley fired by such men, each of whom took careful individual aim, and one fired by European troops, who were content to level their muskets in the general direction of the enemy, was tremendous.

The British command apparently failed to realize this difference or believed that the individual excellence of the Americans as marksmen would be counteracted by the fright occasioned by the British advance.   The day of Lexington and Concord had shown the quality of American marksmanship.   But that had been a desultory action, with the Americans secure in the knowledge that the British sought only to get back to Boston as easily as possible.   Did it seem likely that the colonists would show the same persistence and accuracy of fire when actively attacked in a position from which retreat, unless made very promptly, would be next to impossible?   Troops that had stood several hours of galling fire on April 19th ought to be able to stand the few moments of it necessary to reach and overrun the American entrenchments.   The British apparently felt entirely confident of their ability to dislodge the Americans without serious difficulty by a routine assault.   This view receives support from an account of Bunker Hill written by Clinton in which he said, 'The general idea was the redoubt was only a redan. that the hill was open and easy of ascent and in short that it would easily be carried.' [7] He goes on to say that he took a more serious view of the quality of the American defences. However that may be, his description of the prevalent opinion that the American position could be carried without difficulty fits in perfectly with the analysis of the British plans already given.

If some deep strategical reason is needed to explain the British choice of methods, it may possibly be found in their belief that only by such methods could the Americans be brought to action. An attack upon Charlestown Neck must have become visible long in advance and have afforded the Americans time to retreat without fighting. In reading the despatches of the time one feels that at first the British command welcomed the chance for an engagement provided by the American venture upon Bunker Hill. There seems to have been a feeling that at last these annoying Americans had put themselves in a position where they could be brought to action on reasonable terms and had thus given the British an opportunity to relieve the irritating stalemate that had imposed itself upon the contending armies. A frontal attack might tempt the Americans to try their luck and perhaps lead them to delay their retreat until too late to effect it without disastrous loss. Thus a resounding victory might be won, something which would have an effect far superior to the dislodging of an entrenching party by a threat in their rear.

This seems the most reasonable explanation of the

[7] *Clinton Papers*, date uncertain. Apparently written soon after June 17.

conduct of the British operations, in so far as we need presuppose anything more than a perfectly routine reaction upon the part of the command. There can be no doubt that the British wanted to come to grips with the Americans on terms that would permit them to capitalize their normal advantages. The contemporary British discussions of what might be done by way of a sally from Boston all expressed regret that decisive attack, in the sense of a European battlefield, was impossible because the enemy could not be brought to bay. Regulars faced by irregulars always welcome eagerly any indication that their opponents can be tempted to oppose them in regular fashion. In the American advance upon Bunker Hill just such an opportunity appeared to present itself. What more normal, then, than an instant determination to attack in routine fashion and demonstrate the superiority of British troops in open battle?

It is not necessary to suppose that all this was thought out precisely. History is frequently falsified by supposing that its characters dissect their own motives with the precision that historians seek to attain for them. More often what historians label motives are but states of mind, irritation, or eagerness to do something for which one has been trained, and these more or less spontaneous reactions are often quite as influential as cool calculations. There is good reason for believing that such mental processes contributed largely to the planning of the action at Bunker Hill by the British command. They prompted a routine decision and prevented a close examination of the special features of the situation which alone could have warned the British of the sanguinary surprise awaiting them.

Since the principal criticism of the British manage-

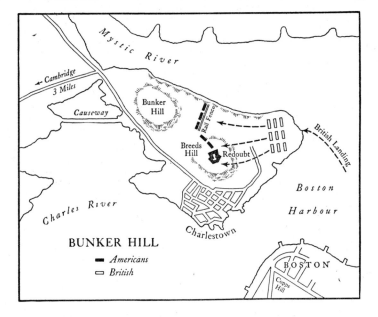

ment at Bunker Hill has been directed against the general plan of action, Gage even more than Howe must bear the blame.   Other criticisms, for which Howe must answer, have been brought against the management of the action after it had begun.   There is reason to believe that shot too large for the bore was sent to some of the artillery, but it seems unlikely that this mistake had any decisive effect upon the struggle, for the artillery played but a subordinate part.[8]   The tactical arrangement of the infantry assault has been criticized.   Some writers have suggested that the British ought to have advanced in small columns instead of in line, in order to present a smaller target and hasten the advance.[9]   Others have condemned the

[8] *A View*, etc., p. 73.   The latter part of this pamphlet contains a collection of the Fugitive Pieces that led to the Howe Inquiry.   It will hereafter be cited as *Fugitive Pieces*.
[9] *Fugitive Pieces*, p. 74.

overburdening of the troops with full campaign equipment and one critic has argued that it was a mistake to stop and deliver a volley against the entrenchment.[10]

On the whole these criticisms seem just, especially in view of what we now know.   But it must be remembered that those in command at the time thought they were doing a routine job and it was not to be expected that they would appreciate the need for departing from routine in the matter of detail.   There is no evidence to show that these variations from the normal were suggested to Sir William Howe at the time, nor is there any reason for supposing that he doubted the adequacy of the usual methods.   We may criticize him for lack of superior astuteness, but it was a fault apparently shared by all his military colleagues.

The further charge is made that Howe neglected to pursue the Americans with vigour and hence sacrificed the fruits of victory.   Even from American sources came criticism of this sort.   The account of the battle prepared by the Committee of Public Safety says, 'It was expected they would prosecute the supposed advantage they had gained by marching immediately to Cambridge—which was not then in a state of defence.'[11]   It was also contended that Clinton urged Howe to pursue the enemy, but that the latter refused to give orders for the move.[12]

We have an explanation from Sir William himself for this decision, the more significant in that it was written to his brother in England before criticism had become rife.   He wrote, 'The soldiers were so much harassed, and there were so many officers lost, that the pursuit was not followed with all the vigour that

[10] *Fugitive Pieces.*
[11] Frothingham, *Siege of Boston*, pp. 381-5.
[12] *Fugitive Pieces*, p. 74.

might be expected.' [13]   Even some who criticized the
general management of the action admitted that there
were reasons for not ordering a vigorous pursuit.[14]
So far as could be seen by Sir William Howe at the
time, the prospects of doing the enemy serious damage
by immediate pursuit were not great.   The scattered
groups of American survivors could hasten away from
the scene much more rapidly than the British could
follow, unless the latter were to rush ahead pell-mell,
without semblance of order.   There is no reason to
suppose that Howe was aware of the defenceless state
of Cambridge at the moment.   Even had he known
it, a decision to advance would have required great
boldness.   The British troops were fatigued and
shaken.   Few military units could lose nearly half
their effectives and still be in a condition to attempt
a further advance of considerable distance and uncertainty.   Furthermore, it would have been foolhardy,
on the basis of Howe's information, to have pushed
ahead with his weary forces through open country
where his flanks would have been vulnerable against
an opponent supposed to be superior in numbers.   An
extension of the attack on Bunker Hill into an advance
upon Cambridge was no part of the original plan and
the events of the day had diminished rather than increased whatever temptation there might have been to
undertake it.   Only an unusual opportunity would
have justified the risk of a hurried advance after
Bunker Hill.   Certainly Howe was not aware of its
existence and it is extremely doubtful whether it was,
in fact, awaiting him.

The rest of the summer was a period of stagnation.

[13] *H.M.C. Stopford-Sackville Mss.*, vol. 2, p. 5, General Howe-Lord Howe,
Charlestown, 22 June 1775.
[14] Criticism of Howe in the *London Chronicle*, 3 August 1775.

The Americans lay quietly outside the British lines, devoting their time to the development of their military organization and asking nothing better than that the British would leave them to the unmolested accomplishment of this task. Within the British camp there was an equal want of action. According to Burgoyne that quiescence was due, not so much to lack of bravery or decision on the part of Gage, but to conditions which he could not alter. In a letter to Lord Rochfort, Burgoyne described vividly the difficulties of conducting operations from Boston as a base.

Driven from one hill, you will see the enemy continually retrenched upon the next; every step we move must be the slow step of a siege; could we at last penetrate ten miles, perhaps we should not attain a single sheep or an ounce of flour by our laborious progress, for they remove every article of provisions as they go. . . Count our numbers, my Lord; any officer will tell you that in such a country, and against such an enemy, who in composition and system are all light troops, they are not more than requisite to secure our convoys and communications between the army and the great deposit of magazine; or if that difficulty were got over by a great and active genius, look into our state once more and you will find us totally unprovided with head waggons, hospital carriages, bat-horses, sufficient artillery horses, and many other articles of attirail indespensably necessary for an army to proceed by land to any distance.[15]

Burgoyne did not blame Gage for the dilemma, although he harboured no illusions as to that officer's abilities. He wrote to General Harvey that it was 'no reflection to say he is unequal to his present station, for few characters in the world would be fit for it. It requires a genius of the first class, together with

[15] Fonblanque, *Burgoyne*, p. 148.

a firm reliance upon support from home.'[16] And to Lord Rochfort he commented upon Gage, 'In the military I believe him capable of figuring upon ordinary and given lines of conduct; but his mind has not resources for great and sudden and hardy exertion, which spring self-suggested in extraordinary characters and generally overbear all opposition.'[17]

One suspects that Burgoyne had himself in mind when describing the commander of extraordinary ability, but his estimate of Gage and of the difficulties facing him came very close to the mark. This verdict agrees well with the character of the British command as illustrated at Bunker Hill and through the early part of the siege of Boston. Routine ideas controlled the conduct of affairs. Gage acted like a soundly trained tactician. Attacks were launched or action refused in accordance with patterns, capacities, and expectations learned on the battlefields of Europe. During the summer of 1775 the British declined to move because it had become apparent that normal tactical methods could not produce a favourable result, and their leaders failed to perceive any modification of routine that offered better prospects.

If it was Gage's first duty to avoid all risk of disaster, we can scarcely quarrel with his caution. Since we know the outcome of the war, we are tempted to say that Gage should have risked much in order to defeat the Americans before their organization was complete. Clinton believed that some vigorous move ought to be attempted and claimed that Howe agreed with him in a talk they had on the subject in August.[18] But at that stage of the struggle it was by no means evident

---

[16] Ibid., p. 140.
[17] Ibid., p. 149.
[18] Clinton's *Historical Detail*, vol. 1, p. 40 and also the Clinton papers, 19 August 1775, note of a conversation with Howe.

that extraordinary risks must be run by the British to give them any hope of success. Caught by the sudden flare-up of rebellion on a large scale, they had good reason for pursuing a policy of safety so as to add no burden of further loss to handicap the serious effort that must come in the following year. Gage was, without doubt, inclined by temperament to the adoption of such a routine policy, but it is very difficult to see that he sacrificed any prospects of success sufficiently brilliant to justify the scorn usually heaped upon him for his inaction.

The government in England, however, either failed to appreciate Gage's difficulties or felt that, even if the inaction of the summer of 1775 was unavoidable, he was not the proper leader for the vigorous attack planned for the following year. On 2 August 1775, Dartmouth wrote to Gage to inform him of his recall, glossing it over with the fiction that he was to return to England in order to give the government exact information about the situation in the colonies so that the proper steps might be taken to meet the crisis.[19] By the same ship Sir William Howe received a commission to command in Gage's absence, and that legal fiction continued throughout the winter. Not until April of the following year was Gage formally removed from his position and Howe and Carleton nominated to two independent commands in America.

19 C.O.5/92, pp. 427-30.

CHAPTER VI

THE SIEGE OF BOSTON

ON 10 October 1775 General Gage handed over the command of the British troops in Boston to Sir William Howe and shortly afterwards sailed for England, where it may be presumed he gave that advice and information for which the government was so eager that it could not continue him in command in Boston.

The man who succeeded him in command of the British forces had a distinguished record. Born into a family of soldiers and sailors, he had seen much service and had been present at one of the most stirring conquests of the century. He it was who had led the party that first scaled the Heights of Abraham and prepared the way for the unexpected appearance of Wolfe above Quebec. Since the Seven Years' War, Howe's most valuable service had been the organization of the British light infantry, for which his experience in the American campaigns had admirably fitted him. His appointment seemed to presage a happier day for the British arms in America.

The first chapter of Howe's command in America did not, however, proceed in accordance with the original plans of the British government. Dartmouth, before he turned over the reins of office to Lord George Germain, had sent instructions to America for the evacuation of Boston, since it seemed evident that nothing further could be gained by remaining in that place. But, when those orders reached Howe on No-

vember 9, he felt them impossible of execution.[1] The
lateness of the season forbade the attempt, for the
early winter gales might strike the coast at any time.
A graver difficulty lay in a lack of transports which
was so serious that an evacuation would have required
two embarkations. Approximately half the army
would have had to be carried to the new quarters and
then the ships would have had to return for the other
half.   Howe wrote that if this were done, 'more would
be hazarded than prudence could justify, especially as
I should in that case be dependent upon the return
of transports at a season when the navigation on this
coast, from the violence of the north winds, is so very
precarious.'[2]   In this opinion Clinton, Burgoyne, and
Percy agreed.

Nor did Howe feel that much was to be feared from
remaining in Boston. Nothing could be attempted
at any other place during the winter season, and he
felt no fear of an attack from the Americans. Nothing
would have suited the British better than such an
attempt by their opponents, for the superior discipline
of the British troops, fighting in prepared positions,
must have resulted in the bloody repulse of any assault that Washington might have been so foolhardy
as to launch against them. Only once, in fact, did
Washington seriously contemplate an assault, and then
only when the freezing of the Charles River gave an
opportunity for turning the British lines. But a council of war called to consider the proposal felt so much
less optimistic than Washington that the plan was
dropped.[3]

---

[1] *The Narrative of Lt. Gen. Sir William Howe in a committee of the
House of Commons*, p. 3.   Hereafter referred to as *Howe's Narrative*.

[2] C.O.5/92, pp. 641-50. Howe-Dartmouth, 26 November 1775.

[3] Ford's edition of Washington's writings, vol. 3, p. 429, Washington to
Governor Trumbull, 19 February 1776. This collection will hereafter be
referred to as Ford.

Any friction that might have developed between Dartmouth and Howe over the latter's failure to carry out the orders for evacuation was forestalled by the appointment of Germain to the Colonial Office. In England it was even rumoured that, owing to various slips, the order to evacuate Boston never reached Howe. This is clearly a mistake, in view of Howe's acknowledgement of receipt of the orders, but Thomas Hutchinson has a passage in his Diary which shows that the going astray of orders was not altogether unknown to government business at the time.

I was surprised to see Mr. P (ownall) and Mr. K (nox) looking over the Letter Book to see by what vessels the orders went. In my business as a merchant I never wrote a letter of consequence but I tracked the ship it went by from the hour she sailed, and was anxious to inquire by every opportunity after her arrival ; but the way here is to send letters from the office of the Secretary of State to the Admiralty, to go as soon as may be. Some little thing or other hinders the sailing of the ship, and the Admiralty do not consider, or perhaps do not know, the importance of the Secretary of State's despatches ; the ship lies five or six weeks, and the despatches answer to no purpose.— This shows the want of one great director to keep every part of the operations of government constantly in his head.[4]

Germain, either because of good sense or the fact it was not his own orders that had been disregarded, approved of Howe's decision not to evacuate Boston.[5] Perhaps Burgoyne, who arrived in England at this time, brought first hand information about the situation at Boston which prompted this approval. However that may be, Germain's agreement with Howe's course of action was so emphatic that he wrote that he would have approved even had adequate shipping

[4] *Diary of Thos. Hutchinson*, entry of 8 May 1776, vol. 2, pp. 44-5.
[5] C.O.5/93, pp. 1-20. Germain-Howe, 5 January 1776.

been available for evacuation in one embarkation.
Thus Howe, first of all by his own decision, but in the
end with the full consent of the government, was committed to standing a winter siege in Boston.

Although he has been criticized for this choice, it
is difficult to see how he would have bettered himself
by a removal.   Halifax, to which he finally withdrew,
would have been no improvement; it was bad enough
in the early spring.   Removal to New York or some
other place to the southward would have meant a
winter campaign, and eighteenth-century soldiers never
embarked willingly upon such a venture.   Furthermore, in the days of sail the danger attending coastal
navigation at that season of the year was very real.
The hazards of any move were great, the benefits uncertain.   In view of the fact that remaining in Boston, although it exposed the British troops to discomfort, secured them against any serious disaster and left
them intact for the next summer's campaign, we can
scarcely call Sir William Howe's decision erroneous,
except on the assumption that the British cause had
already fallen into such desperate straits as to justify
any risk.   Certainly nothing known at the time warranted such an estimate of the situation.

Since dissatisfaction with the inactivity of Gage was
said to have been the principal reason for his recall,
the change of command naturally aroused hope of
more activity.[6]   Things did, indeed, stir a little more
briskly, but the activity was directed towards strength-
ening the defences and improving the living conditions of the garrison rather than towards any plans for
aggressive action that might alter the balance of
forces.[7]   In reality, nothing could have been done that

6 Frothingham, *Siege of Boston*, pp. 250-1.
7 Ibid., pp. 252-3.

would have promised any return commensurate with the cost of the effort. Gage had described the difficulties of the situation very sensibly in his letter of August 20 to Dartmouth.[8] Bunker Hill had shown that the storming of the American lines which must precede any British advance would prove very costly. Yet that would be only the first of many difficulties. The army lacked transport for a rapid advance and the force that could safely be spared for such a thrust was too small to provide the troops needed for maintaining communications with Boston. In the regions that might be invaded, political conditions were such that the establishment of legal government would not endure even momentarily after the withdrawal of the troops. Whatever his inadequacies, Gage understood that the task of subduing the colonies demanded more than the marching of armies through the countryside, and that it was useless to set up loyal governments only to see them crumble as soon as the redcoats had turned the next corner in the road.

Sir William Howe had recognized the hopelessness of the British position in Boston when he recommended evacuation in his letter of October 9 to Dartmouth. But he felt unable to act until he had received authorization from England and that did not come until November 9, too late for the move to be made safely.[9] It seems unlikely, however, that Sir William Howe really entertained any hope of immediate evacuation, for obviously no answer to his suggestion could come until well into December. It was only the coincidence that Dartmouth had arrived at the same decision previous to the receipt of Howe's recommendation that brought authorization for evacu-

[8] C.O.5/92, pp. 525-7. Gage-Dartmouth, 20 August 1775.
[9] *Howe's Narrative*, p. 3.

ation as early as November 9.   Howe's opinion must
be considered either as an advance justification for
doing nothing at Boston or as an effort to save the
government from the mistake of trying to hold the
city during another campaign.

Although it is scarcely possible to doubt seriously
the correctness of Howe's belief that nothing decisive
could be done at Boston, because of the lack of definite objectives and the strength of hostile sentiment in
the locality, he has nevertheless been criticized for
not attempting various raids against the Americans in
order to wear them down and keep them in a state of
apprehension.   Such efforts, however, must always
have ended in a retreat to Boston and thus have had
at least the appearance of an American victory.   They
would have cost heavily in casualties and the rigour
of the season would have impaired the health of the
survivors.   Not improbably the British loss would
have been as great as the American and their propor-
tionate loss much greater.   As Percy put it, 'Our army
is so small that we cannot even afford a victory.'[10]
Activity that involved heavy losses without hope of
important advantage might have compromised the
prospects for the next campaign.

Although probably nothing better could have been
done under the circumstances, the winter spent by
the British in Boston was far from pleasant.   Physical
trials and tribulations crowded upon each other.   The
winter had scarcely begun before smallpox made its
appearance.   It is interesting to note that the men
were not ordered, but urged, to submit themselves to
vaccination.[11]   The bitter cold brought a serious fuel

---

[10] *The Percy Letters*, pp. 58-9, Percy to General Harvey, July 28.
[11] *The Kemble Papers, Proceedings of the New York Historical Society*,
1883, vol. 1, p. 269.   Howe's order of December 5.

shortage. In the emergency men were sent to cut up wharves, houses, old ships, and the city trees.[12] Unauthorized foraging for fuel became widespread, so much so that general orders were issued threatening with instant death any soldiers caught pulling down fences or houses without authorization. The shortage drove hundreds of civilians away from the city.[13]

As is always the case when a body of troops must be kept under discipline while suffering from inaction and physical discomfort, difficulties were experienced in preserving military order. Plundering began to grow, although Howe was rigorous in his endeavours to suppress it.[14] At best it was never easy to prevent irregularities among troops of that day. The problem was complicated by the great numbers of camp women who were almost compelled to eke out a living by petty plunder. Special orders had to be issued prohibiting their presence at fires.[15] Measures were also necessary to guard against the temptation to laxity and unreadiness occasioned by the military stagnation. Officers and soldiers off duty were forbidden access to the works facing the Americans. The troops there had been so hospitable to visitors that it was necessary to order specifically that civilians should be kept out.[16] There was the usual difficulty with alcohol, leading to efforts to suppress unlicensed dramshops. Although difficulties arose on every side, the evidence seems to show that Howe handled the problems of discipline and administration in very creditable fashion.

But even with the best of management, the winter

12 Frothingham, *Siege of Boston,* p. 282.
13 Ibid., p. 281.
14 *Kemble Papers,* vol. 1, p. 254.
15 Ibid., vol. 1, p. 254.
16 Ibid., p. 279.

was trying to officers, rank and file, and inhabitants alike. Howe had at first endeavoured to keep the inhabitants in the city, even to the point of threatening those attempting to escape with severe punishment and those who got away with forfeiture of goods.[17] But before the winter was far advanced he began to see an advantage in the disappearance of some of the city's population. At first, departure was authorized only by special permission, but before the end of the year additional facilities were offered and several hundred people took advantage of them.[18]

To make conditions more annoying, the British suffered from inadequate knowledge of the situation and activities of the enemy. This handicap was felt from the very beginning of the siege. Burgoyne wrote to Lord Rochford, complaining that the niggardliness of the Treasury had been so great that 'we are destitute not only of cattle and magazines of forage, but of the most important of all circumstances in war or negociation — intelligence. We are ignorant, not only of what passes in congresses, but want spies for the hill half a mile off.'[19] The deficiency felt thus early plagued the British more or less throughout the entire war. So marked was it at Boston during the winter of 1775–76 that the morale of the rank and file suffered to some degree, as reflected in the rumour that no despatches or other information had been received from England since October.

But the greatest difficulty the occupants of Boston, both civil and military, had to face during the winter was a shortage of supplies. Before the middle of December the scarcity had become acute.[20] The strin-

[17] Frothingham, *Siege of Boston*, p. 260.
[18] Ibid.
[19] Fonblanque, *Burgoyne*, p. 149.
[20] Frothingham, *Siege of Boston*, p. 280.

gency, especially in supplies for the army, had existed in some measure since the early days of the siege. As far back as the middle of May the contractors had begun to fall short of their promised deliveries. In flour they were nearly a million pounds short, and in other things in similar ratio.[21] By that time, in most essentials of diet, the supply on hand was not adequate for more than three months and in some articles for much less. As the summer wore on and the number of troops in Boston increased, the reserve grew less, so that early in October the provisions on hand would not suffice for more than twenty days and some things were almost entirely lacking.[22]

A variety of difficulties brought about this shortage. The investment of the town naturally shut off the normal supply of provisions from the countryside.[23] Administrative difficulties, red tape of one sort or another, added to the scarcity. At one time Gage sent two ships to Quebec to fetch supplies, intending thereby to facilitate the work of the contractors and save them expense. But upon their return the contractors' agent at Boston refused to receive them, on the ground that they had been consigned to the general.[24] On another occasion two vessels bound for Europe were brought in, but the agent refused to purchase the contents of one because he thought the price too high, and the captain of the other refused to sell because unauthorized to do so by the owners. When five ships with flour did arrive early in October, most of their contents was found to be in such poor

---

21 C.O.5/93, pp. 105-113. Memorandum of failures of contractors in victualling of the troops at Boston. Entry of 16 May 1775.

22 Ibid., pp. 110-111. Supply failures memorandum, entry of July 16 and of August 29.

23 Ibid., pp. 105-113. Entry of May 16.

24 Ibid.

condition that the flour had to be made into biscuits immediately to save it from decay.[25]

The shortage of supplies, inevitably acute because of the natural difficulties, was made more distressing by the existing system which left the supply of provisions in the hands of contractors. Not only did they fail in their assignments, but, as has been illustrated above, they often refused, because of red tape, stupidity, or a desire to save themselves a few pennies regardless of the fate of the army, to avail themselves of such opportunities as they had for carrying out their contracts. Fortunately the army did have one recourse to which it could turn in times of great emergency. The Commissary-General was able, upon such occasions, to furnish the army for a time with provisions belonging to the Crown, largely secured from supplies remaining on board the transports after their voyage from Europe.[26] Commanders who had to struggle with such a tangled system deserve a little extra indulgence.

Gage, before giving up the command, made what efforts he could to alleviate the shortage. Early in October no less than thirty-eight transports were out in search of forage and fuel.[27] Their return was anxiously awaited, for the season was already late for successful foraging. By the middle of November it had become obvious that, unless additional supplies could soon be secured, the town must be evacuated by March at the latest.[28] The situation filled the British officers with gloom for there seemed little prospect of an early change. Such stray provision ships as attempted to get into Boston ran a great risk of being

25 Ibid. p. 111, entry of October 2.
26 C.O.5/93, p. 113. The supply failures memorandum.
27 Ibid., pp. 587-98. Gage-Dartmouth, 7 October 1775.
28 Ibid., pp. 695-702. Howe-Dartmouth, 2 December 1775.

picked up by an American privateer and several of them actually suffered that fate.[29]   The operations of these privateers, sometimes carried on almost within sight of the town, added to the gloom.   Hope of supplies from Europe was nearly abandoned, as the winter had set in with great severity and made it probable that the ships had been obliged to bear away to the West Indies, where they must almost certainly remain until spring.[30]

On December 14 Howe confessed to the government his great anxiety about the situation.[31]   Nor were his difficulties confined to the supplying of his troops.   Many civilians had to be assisted, either by reason of various useful services they performed or because they were well disposed toward the British government.   Neglect of these people would have prejudiced future attempts to win popular support.[32] Howe worried greatly about the American privateers which put out from inlets that could not be reached by the ships of the fleet.   Admiral Graves believed that these pests could not be ferreted out without the aid of a considerable landing force and Howe felt unable to spare enough troops for the purpose.[33]   Sir William sent the prisoners taken from one privateer to England, hoping that the uncertainty about their fate would deter others.   'Besides,' he wrote, 'I could wish a distinction made between prisoners taken on shore and on sea, which last mode of war will hurt us more effectually than anything they can do by land during our stay at this place.'[34]

[29] B.M.Add.Mss. 21,680, ff. 53-6.   Maj. Hutcheson-Haldimand, 12 December 1775.
[30] Ibid., 21,680, ff. 53-6.   Maj. Hutcheson-Haldimand, 12 December 1775.
[31] C.O.5/93, pp. 21-3.   Howe-Dartmouth, 13 December 1775.
[32] Ibid.
[33] Ibid.
[34] Ibid., pp. 29-31.   Howe-Dartmouth (private), 14 December 1775.

The middle of December saw some slight relief. Four store ships arrived from London, followed soon after by six more from the Bay of Fundy, which brought a supply of forage.[35]   But by the middle of January the situation had become critical once more. Ten days later the skies brightened, for some of the store ships from Europe arrived, and the besieged felt that after all the government had not forgotten them.[36] Rumours also came of abundant salt provisions at St. Eustatius which led the General to send an armed transport to fetch them.[37]   Captain Payne, sent out to try to find provisions in the West Indies, discovered that the conjectures about the fate of the provision ships expected from England had been correct.   He found twenty-six of them at Antigua, whither they had been driven by the weather.   Most of them were badly damaged.   Some had been obliged to jettison the greater part of their cargo and in others the cargo had rotted.[38]

As it was, with these few arrivals at crucial moments, the British in Boston just managed to make both ends meet, although not without being severely pinched at times.   While at first sight it appears surprising that any army supported by such a navy as Great Britain's should suffer from shortage, the government felt it had taken every possible measure to keep the army supplied.   Robinson wrote to Howe that the country was nearly exhausted of ships which could be spared from trade and that the price of tonnage had risen to the exorbitant figure of twelve and six a ton.   He comforted the general, however, with the assurance that before the first of September 1776 enough pro-

---

[35] B.M.Add.Mss. 21,680, ff. 72-73. Maj. Hutcheson-Haldimand, 25 December 1775.
[36] Ibid., ff. 77-80. Same to same, 16 January 1776.
[37] C.O.5/93, pp. 47-50. Howe-Dartmouth (private), 19 December 1775.
[38] Memorandum in C.O.5/93, pp. 265-9.

visions and supplies of all sorts would be despatched to keep the army in comfort until May 1777.[39]

It does seem that, on the whole, the shortage from which the British army suffered while at Boston was due more to nature and the influence of a cumbersome system than to any shortcomings of individuals or cabinets. The tempestuous weather that drove the supply ships to the West Indies was inescapable. The difficulties with the army contractors were probably no worse than those experienced by almost every military commander of the day.

Whatever the responsibility for this shortage, there is reason to believe that it had more than a momentary influence upon events. The correspondence of Sir William Howe during the succeeding years shows repeatedly that his embarrassment at Boston made a deep impression upon him. His exaggerated anxiety always to be perfectly supplied before beginning any operation and his preoccupation with the problem of merely keeping his army in being are certainly traceable in some measure to his recollection of the winter of 1775–76. As he was criticized more frequently for caution of this sort than for timidity in tactics, it seems likely that the difficulties over supplies at Boston had a more lasting influence upon Sir William Howe than his experience upon the slopes of Bunker Hill.

Among other features of the siege of Boston it is interesting to note that Howe was already endeavouring to raise Loyalist troops. Although the immediate situation of the British offered little temptation to prospective recruits, Loyalist faith in the ultimate triumph of the government was sufficient to bring a certain amount of success to Howe's efforts. A general

39 *H.M.C., American Mss. in the Royal Institution*, vol. 1, pp. 46-7. John Robinson-Howe, 24 January 1776.

order of the month of November mentions three Loyalist companies that had been formed.[40]   Early in December some Irish merchants were armed as the Loyal Irish Volunteers, and Colonel Gorham stated that he had some three hundred men in his command, the Royal Fencible Americans.[41]   Although the exact number of Loyalist troops raised is very uncertain, enough was done to constitute a quite creditable showing under the circumstances.

During most of the winter the British position in Boston was safe from all danger except hunger.   The city was then on a peninsula, joined to the mainland by a very narrow and highly fortified neck of land and overlooked only by two hills of any military consequence.   One of these, Bunker Hill, had been held by the British since the preceding June and was not difficult to protect, since it could be reached only by a narrow causeway.   The other, to the southward, was Dorchester Heights.   This overlooked both the town and the British lines protecting the town, but remained unoccupied.

It is said that in June, just after Bunker Hill, an attempt to occupy the height was considered, but was rejected on the ground that there were not sufficient troops to overcome the resistance that might be expected and at the same time leave an adequate garrison in the city.   Clinton places this projected occupation at an earlier date, before Bunker Hill, and attributes the abandonment of the enterprise to the appearance of indications that the Americans were about to move on Charlestown.[42]   The British argued, so Kemble reported, that the Americans could be dislodged from

[40] Frothingham, *Siege of Boston,* p. 279.
[41] Ibid.
[42] Clinton's *Historical Detail,* vol. 1, p. 39.

Dorchester Heights by artillery action from within the lines should they attempt to seize the hill.[43]

The British nevertheless felt uneasy about the height, for on February 13 they made a scouting raid, but failed to find any American preparations for fortifying the position.[44] Howe wrote to Clinton that this raid was carried out as a consequence of information he had secured of the enemy's intention to occupy the heights as soon as the season permitted.[45] It was therefore not altogether a surprise when on the morning of March 5 the British observed that fortifications had been thrown up on the hill during the night, works which, although obviously not complete, would be so within a short while if left unmolested.

Whatever may have been the effect of Bunker Hill upon the mind and nerve of General Howe, he gave no evidence of fright upon this occasion: instead he promptly ordered an assault upon the American position, to take place the next morning. Howe himself planned to lead the attack from one side, while a diversion was to be made at the same time against the Roxbury Lines.[46] It is interesting to notice that the troops were given orders not to load.[47] Bunker Hill had apparently taught the futility of musketry volleys against entrenched opponents.

But the assault never took place. A storm came up which by nightfall had made the bay unsafe for the small boats that were to be used to carry the troops to the point of attack.[48] During all the following day and night the storm continued, and, with the leisure thus given, the Americans were able to complete and

[43] *The Kemble Papers*, vol. 1, p. 44, entry of 22 June 1775.
[44] Ibid.
[45] Clinton Papers, Howe-Clinton, 21 March 1776.
[46] *Kemble Papers*, vol. 1, p. 71. Entry of 5 March 1776.
[47] Ibid.
[48] Ibid.

strengthen their defences. By the time the waters of the bay were once more practicable for small boats, Howe felt that conditions were substantially altered and that the completion of the American defences left little prospect of carrying the position except at prohibitive cost, if indeed it could be carried at all.[49] Washington was of the same mind, for he greatly regretted the British decision not to attack.[50]

With the abandonment of the assault on Dorchester Heights, the effect of the American move upon the British position in Boston demanded immediate consideration. Sir William Howe's situation had become very difficult. Rumours of lack of news from England had damaged the morale of the troops and the fleet and army complained of each other.[51] After long months of uncomfortable inaction, the prospect of a further and very serious embarrassment could not be viewed lightly. So, on the seventh of March, an army council convened which agreed with Howe that evacuation was the most desirable measure. Howe explained the situation in a letter to the government.

The enemy, by taking possession of and fortifying the commanding heights of Dorchester Neck, in order to force the ships by their cannon to quit the harbour, has reduced me to the necessity either of exposing the army to the greatest distresses by remaining in Boston, or of withdrawing it under straitened circumstances. The importance of preserving this force when it could no longer act to advantage did not leave any room to doubt of the propriety of its removal.[52]

We are still left wondering why Howe did not secure Dorchester Heights before the Americans occu-

[49] C.O.5/93, pp. 173-82. Howe-Dartmouth, 21 March 1776.
[50] Ford, vol. 3, pp. 450-1. Washington-President of Congress, 7 March 1776.
[51] Frothingham, *Siege of Boston,* p. 301.
[52] C.O.5/93, pp. 173-82. Howe-Dartmouth, 21 March 1776.

pied it, and why the latter delayed their occupation so long. Possibly the winter weather is the explanation, although that requires the improbable supposition that the season had moderated sufficiently by the first week in March to facilitate operations. A more probable interpretation is available. Frequently in military operations a point of vantage is left unoccupied by both sides because its value, in view of the existing condition and numbers of each army, seems rather less than the effort necessary to secure and maintain it. Such situations arise most often where both armies are occupying positions rather too extensive for the available numbers. Where such a condition does exist, an important position may be left open for some time, until one side or the other becomes convinced that its possession is worth the cost and the risk.

Until March 1776 Dorchester Heights presented such a situation. Occupation of the heights by the British would have demanded of them a further dispersion of a force they already felt to be inadequate. Possession of the heights was not necessary to protect the town from assault, nor would the occupation do the Americans any harm. It had value only in view of the possibility that the Americans might place artillery on it which would make life in Boston exceedingly uncomfortable. The Americans, on their side, hard pressed to hold their army together and suffering acutely most of the winter from shortage of military stores, especially from lack of powder, had no desire to provoke an action.[53] So a situation arose in which, for a considerable period, both parties, so far as they

---

[53] Allen French, in his *First Year of the American Revolution*, p. 656, says that Washington was kept from occupying Dorchester Heights by the difficulty, when the ground was frozen, of fortifying it adequately in one night.

could see, stood to gain by leaving the position unoccupied.

Such a balance, however, cannot last indefinitely.
One side or the other will finally decide that the potential advantage is worth the cost and will occupy
the position. It was almost inevitable that in this
particular case Washington should be the first to move,
for Dorchester Heights had offensive possibilities for
him, whereas it was useful to Howe only in order to
prevent the Americans from annoying the town of
Boston. The weather intervened to prevent the contest which this break in the equilibrium would nor-
mally have entailed. Howe evacuated rather than
waste men on a risky assault. As he knew he must
evacuate before summer anyway, he could scarcely
justify the sacrifice of several hundred men to gain a
relatively more comfortable possession of the city for
a few weeks longer.

Another example of tacit understanding in war presented itself during the evacuation of Boston. The
British could not depart without giving Washington
ample warning and thereby affording an opportunity
for an American attack at the moment of embarkation. But Sir William Howe held a hostage in hand
in the shape of his ability to work irreparable damage
to the town before he left. The facts are that Washington permitted the British to embark without
molestation and that the British left the town undam-
aged, except for such minor damage as was done by
wanton individuals. This has led to a story that a
definite bargain was reached between Washington and
Howe. But the best evidence points to a contrary
belief. That steps were taken by some of the inhabitants to secure such a bargain seems nearly cer-

tain.[54] Howe gave them to understand that he would leave the town unharmed if he was not molested, although he gave no formal promise. This statement was reported to Washington, who said that, since it was only very informal, he could take no notice of it. But he did, in fact, act as if an understanding existed. Both parties had as much to lose as to gain. To destroy the town would have brought little comfort to the British, whereas an attack by the Americans would have been embarrassing. To the Americans an attack on Howe's rearguard could not have yielded a really important success, whereas the destruction of Boston, except for unavoidable cause, might have outraged important supporters of the Revolution.

News that Boston was to be evacuated naturally brought consternation to the Loyalist inhabitants, who saw themselves and their property left to the mercy of revengeful rebels. Howe recognized that something must be done for them, but the doing it was a very awkward business, since there was scarcely sufficient transport for the troops.[55] Nevertheless, great efforts were made to accommodate both the persons and goods of the Loyalists. Unfortunately, the people thus favoured failed to co-operate very well and Howe was compelled to abandon some of the machinery of administration he had designed for the purpose.[56] Under the circumstances, however, everything that could have been done for the Loyalists seems to have been done.

Howe was later charged with having left a rich supply of stores in Boston, which the Americans were

[54] Frothingham, *Siege of Boston*, pp. 303-04. See also Winsor, *Narrative and Critical History*, vol. 6, p. 158.
[55] C.O.5/93, p. 190. Transport memorandum.
[56] Dom. State Papers, Geo. III, 18. The Howe Inquiry.

able to appropriate.[57] But the evidence does not show that he left anything which, in view of the conditions, he might reasonably have been expected to carry away. On the whole, the evacuation seems to have been well managed, although there was at times a good deal of disorder on the part of individual soldiers, especially drunkenness and the indiscriminate destruction of such things as furniture.[58] Finally, at the end of the operation, departure was delayed three days by unfavourable weather, so that the last troops did not get away until the seventeenth of March.

Once on board the transports, the British lay out in the bay several days and alarmed Washington, who thought he smelt some shrewd design which they meant to execute before they left.[59] But nothing more sinister was intended than the achievement of some sort of order out of the chaos of embarkation before sending the crowded ships to sea.

The choice of Halifax as a destination brought criticism upon Howe. He ought, it was said, to have taken his troops immediately to New York or to some other likely place from which to begin operations. But Howe felt Halifax was the only place where the army could remain safely for the moment, although he was aware, when writing from Nantasket on March 21, that it was 'stripped of provisions during the winter and afforded few conveniences for so numerous a body.'[60] Active operations at this time, however, he felt to be impossible.

I am justly sensible how much more conducive it would be to His Majesty's service if the army was in a situation

[57] Dom. State Papers, Geo. III, 18. The Howe Inquiry.
[58] *Kemble Papers*, vol. 1, p. 72, entry of 9 March 1776. Also Maj. Hutcheson-Haldimand, 24 March 1776, B.M.Add.Mss. 21,680, ff. 94-7.
[59] Ford, vol. 3, pp. 493-4. Washington-Joseph Reed, 25 March 1776.
[60] C.O.5/93, pp. 173-82. Howe-Dartmouth, 21 March 1776.

to proceed immediately to New York; but the present condition of the troops, crowded in the transports, without regard to conveniences, the inevitable dissortment of stores, and all the incumbrances with which I am clogged, effectually disable me from the exertion of this force in any offensive operations.[61]

He also remarked that his last despatches from England were of October 22nd.

Thus ended the siege, or as it might better be called, the investment of Boston. Had the British been determined to hold the town, the Americans could not have taken it. Had Howe wished to break out into the country, it is almost certain that he could have done so. But he would have had nowhere to go. The investment took place because for the moment the British had nothing better to do. They were not in a position to advance on New York, nor did they see anything to be gained by marching around eastern Massachusetts. Howe's actions rested upon the fundamental idea that it was his business to hold his army together, to keep it in as good condition as possible, and then to use it as the nucleus for the enlarged force which would be given him for decisive operations during the next campaign.

If his prospects were sufficiently promising for the next year he can scarcely be blamed for playing safe. In a sense the British forces in America suffered during all of 1775 from the effects of a surprise, the sudden breaking out of rebellion in the spring. Although trouble was by no means unexpected, the exact manner and time of the outbreak took the initiative away from Gage. When Howe assumed the command in October it was too late in the season to redress the situation by important changes in plan. The risk

61 Ibid.

of moving the army from Boston at that time of year could have been justified only by the securing of some precious advantage which a few months' delay would lose. It seems unlikely, even with our present knowledge of what was to follow, that the British sacrificed any decisive advantage by remaining in Boston during the winter. To Sir William Howe, with such information as he had available, delay merely meant that by the next summer the British force would receive an increase of such magnitude that there seemed little likelihood that the strength of the Revolution could keep pace with it. His immediate task appeared to be the avoidance of any mistake that would compromise the prospects for the coming season.

Under the circumstances, ought Howe to have done more than he did to annoy and damage the Americans outside of Boston or to attempt to win back the immediately surrounding region to the Crown? Perhaps a more vigorous commander would have done more on general principles, in order to keep the enemy guessing and disturbed, and to preserve the morale and confidence of his own men. But, aside from that, it is difficult to see what could have been achieved. The rebellion had gone so far that a restoration of royal government over an area of fifty miles round Boston would have been far from decisive. The attempt to effect it might have led to a succession of experiences as costly, both morally and physically, as the day of Lexington and Concord. In truth, it was not within the power of Howe to end the revolution then and there, or even to work it very serious harm.

Nevertheless, one cannot make light of the moral loss resulting from a passive policy. Howe was criticized at the time for his inaction. One must not take too seriously most of the criticism that floats round an army, but if it has at the time an appearance of being justified, it may in the long run affect the general morale. Granted that Howe could have accomplished nothing decisive, would it not have been better to do something at least for the sake of effect, even if the effect was only on his own mind? He showed throughout his command a growing pessimism, a feeling that military achievement, no matter how brilliant, would bring by itself no decisive results in the struggle. It is quite possible that Howe, by permitting himself to accept an awkward situation at Boston, without even a show of attempting to do more than endure it, contributed to the development of a pessimistic frame of mind both in himself and in those about him which influenced his and their actions in the later stages of the war. It is impossible to pronounce definitely, but it seems probable that this was the case.

CHAPTER VII

THE PLANS FOR 1776

THE spring of 1776 marks the beginning of a new stage in the War of the American Revolution. In a sense, all that had gone before was preparatory, the impromptu result of the fact that hostilities happened to break out where and when they did. The year 1775 had shown the Americans that they could organize a resistance to the Crown; it had shown the British that the defeat of the revolt would require extensive preparations and careful planning. This preliminary stage, in which neither side felt prepared to attempt anything decisive, passed with the evacuation of Boston. Only the results of the next campaign could show whether American resistance, once organized, would be able to stand in the face of British might, now aroused to the fact that a real war was to be faced.

There was never any serious question on the British side that the campaign must be begun from some spot other than Boston. Long before the evacuation of the city, British military opinion had expressed itself almost unanimously against the suitability of Boston as a base of operations. Percy, in July 1775, regretted that the army had not taken advantage of the Hudson River rather than remain in Boston without magazines and surrounded by a country, 'so penetrated by hills, woods, and ravines, as makes it the most favourable spot in the world for the irregular and undisciplined

troops of the rebels.'[1]   The following month Clinton
expressed the same view when he urged upon Gage
the advantages of New York where, since it was the
episcopal part of America, the friends of government
would certainly be most numerous.[2]   Gage, before he
gave up the command, recognized fully the need of
a better base, of 'some province where you can be
secured, and from whence you can draw supplies of
provision and forage.'[3]

Howe, at the time he took over the command, held
exactly the same opinion and explained to the government that it was useless to attack the Americans from
Boston :

> They would have every advantage in the defence of it
> on their side, being indefatigable in the raising of field
> works, which they judiciously suppose must wear us down
> by repeated onsets; Whereas they are so numerous in this
> part of the country, that they would not feel the loss they
> might sustain, in the least degree of proportion with us.
> Neither could we prevent them from having supplies of
> all denominations from the southern colonies, or even
> preserve the communications between the army and this
> town without difficulty.[4]

With this opinion no one of any importance disagreed.
Since Boston was unanimously condemned as a focus
of operations, our attention must now turn to the development of the plans finally adopted for the coming
campaign.   The germ of the strategy both for 1776
and 1777 can be traced back to the period before
Concord and Lexington.   In a letter of 15 April 1775
Dartmouth suggested to Gage that certain regiments
originally intended for Boston could be diverted to

---

1 *The Percy Letters*, pp. 52-3.   Percy-Gen. Harvey, 28 July 1775.
2 Clinton Papers, Clinton-Gage, 7 August 1775.
3 C.O.5/92, pp. 585-9.   Gage-Dartmouth, 1 October 1775.
4 C.O.5/92, pp. 621-30.   Howe-Dartmouth, 9 October 1775.

New York, where the friends of the British government believed the presence of such a corps would prove helpful, and where, disposed along the line of the Hudson, it would isolate New England from the rest of the colonies.[5] The later plans of Burgoyne and Germain added nothing materially new to this concept, except a variation in the method of approach. In view of the controversy that arose about the campaign of 1777, it is well to note that in this early hint of it the fundamental thing was the holding of the line of the Hudson in order to separate the colonies.

This idea was not original with Dartmouth. The internal evidence of the letter in question shows pretty clearly that the suggestion came from several quarters, particularly from supporters of the Crown in New York. The memory of the French and Indian War was sufficiently vivid to prevent any neglect of the strategic possibilities of the Hudson and there is pretty clear indication that military men in England recognized fully the importance and possibilities of the region without the need of a reminder from the colonies.[6]

Gage pointed out, in the letter cited on a previous page, that the deficiencies which made Boston unsuitable as a base of operations would not be felt in New York. He also advised placing some troops in Rhode Island as a threat to the southern New England coast.[7] Sir William Howe, several weeks before he took over the command at Boston, shared Gage's opinion and proposed that an army of fifteen thousand men attack New York from the sea, while four thousand regulars,

[5] C.O.5/92, pp. 197-221. Dartmouth-Gage, 15 April 1775.
[6] Ibid., pp. 397-410. Dartmouth-Gage, 2 August 1775.
[7] Ibid., pp. 585-9. Gage-Dartmouth, 1 October 1775.

Canadians, and Indians operate from the side of Canada, and five thousand troops remain to hold Boston. He remarked that he felt himself unequal to directing such a plan and urged the appointment of a viceroy with unlimited powers in order to co-ordinate these several operations.[8] Howe also advised, significantly, that if the government could not furnish these forces, which he judged to be the minimum necessary, it ought to withdraw entirely from the colonies and leave them to quarrel with each other until they felt ready for terms with the mother country. Thus early we see him of the opinion that if the government could not make an effort of a certain calibre, it were better to make no effort at all.

Meanwhile Dartmouth weighed in his mind various ideas suggested to him by the military men in England and finally put them together in the form of an inquiry sent to Gage.[9] He began with the admission that there was little chance of doing anything more in the current year. For the next year the questions were : first, should the whole force be devoted to pushing the war in New England ; secondly, would it not be better to seize New York immediately, at the same time holding Boston with the smallest force capable of keeping the city and launching various diversions from it ; and thirdly, would it not be wise to embark the army and indulge in various descents upon the coast, which would at least make possible a gathering of supplies. But, if none of these suggestions attracted him, Gage was to consider whether, should Boston prove untenable, it would not be well to remove the army to Halifax and Quebec until the events

[8] *H.M.C. Mss. of Mrs. Stopford-Sackville,* vol. 2, p. 9. Lord Howe-Germain, 25 September 1775. Lord Howe reported his brother's opinions to Germain.

[9] C.O.5/92, pp. 397-410. Dartmouth-Gage, 2 August 1775.

of the winter should point out the proper plan for the next summer.

Dartmouth indicated pretty clearly his own preference and the reasons for it:

> A variety of cogent reasons occur in favour . . . of the possession of New York. For if . . . we could recover the attachment and fidelity of that province, as many judicious and well informed persons think we may, it would . . . not only be of great weight in the general scale of advantage, but might also increase our strength by the junction of numbers which would show themselves upon the least appearance of protection.[10]

Dartmouth showed clearly his belief that the reduction of the colonies depended upon more than military force, that one of the most important uses of force was to make it possible for the friends of the government to assist the army in restoring the country to obedience. We cannot tell, however, just what proportion of the work Dartmouth hoped would be done by the Loyalists.

By the early days of October Howe's own ideas had taken more definite shape.[11] He had come to the conclusion that the strength of the army would not be adequate to hold both Boston and New York, and found Gage, Clinton, and Burgoyne in agreement with him. Hence he suggested an army of twelve thousand men to attack New York. After the taking of the city the army would devote its immediate attention to opening communication with Canada. Five battalions, he thought, would suffice to hold New York during this operation.

Then, with these preliminary manœuvres completed, the real centre of rebellion could be attacked:

[10] C.O.5/92, pp. 397-410. Dartmouth-Gage, 2 August 1775.
[11] Ibid., pp. 621-30. Howe-Dartmouth, 9 October 1775.

The accomplishment of the primary object for opening the communication being obtained by the two armies [he had suggested an army of 3,000 to operate from Canada] and secured by proper posts, in which operation the reduction of the rebels in the province of New York must in some measure be included, these corps might take separate routes into the province of Massachusetts Bay, as circumstances may arise.[12]

The plan here suggested assumed conditions different from those found by Howe when he approached New York in July of the following year. He evidently expected little formal resistance from the American armies in New York. He was to brush them aside quickly in order to get about the serious business of organizing the posts along the Hudson, preparatory to an advance into New England. Howe apparently believed that organized resistance was largely localized round Boston, and that it must diminish greatly if operations were removed from that locality. If the rest of the colonies could be quarantined by holding the Hudson, the infection might be cured by a methodical reconquest of New England.

Howe went on to urge the superior merit of Rhode Island over Boston as a base for diversions against New England, arguing that a body of troops left in Boston could do no more than defend the city, whereas in Rhode Island they would so threaten Connecticut that the forces of that colony would have to be kept at home for defence. Here again he seems to have had in mind a war of militia wherein the major effort of each colony would be devoted to the defence of its own soil. At the close of his letter Howe urged that the troops be sent so that he might begin his campaign in the later part of April and that great advantages

12 Ibid., pp. 621-30. Howe-Dartmouth, 9 October 1775.

might be gained if five thousand men could be added to the twenty thousand that Dartmouth expected to supply.

Such were the early ideas of the British government and Sir William Howe about the campaign of 1776. Certain features of these plans ought to be kept in mind. First of all, the suitability of New York as the principal scene of operations was appreciated very early and by a great many individuals. Secondly, the use to be made of New York was twofold: the Hudson was to be held, in an effort to isolate New England; and potential Loyalist sentiment was to be encouraged by the presence of British troops. Thirdly, the manner, as well as the object, of the campaign ultimately undertaken by Burgoyne was plainly considered. Fourthly, and perhaps most important of all, little allowance seems to have been made for a really formidable permanent army in the hands of the Americans. Not that the British authorities expected to meet no field army at all; but they seem to have expected it to lose a large proportion of its numbers if compelled to operate in areas not especially favourable to the Revolution. Thus the districts of divided sentiment might be captured rather easily and the obstinately rebellious areas left until the work of reconquest had gathered speed and weight.

Mention has been made before of the fact that no plan of operations could be counted a good plan that demanded a larger force than the government was able or willing to supply. It is important for us to know how many troops Sir William Howe thought he needed for his campaign; whether he conveyed his wishes unambiguously to the British government; whether that government indicated it would be able to supply him in the fashion desired; and whether it did, in fact, do so.

The first indication of the numbers Sir William Howe thought necessary to the task ahead came to the British government indirectly. Lord Howe wrote to Germain in the last week of September 1775, over a fortnight before the latter succeeded Dartmouth, that he had received two letters from his brother in America, the latest written August 20, urging the need of transferring the war to New York and indicating the numbers necessary for a successful offensive campaign in that quarter.[13] The General proposed a force of 15,000 men for New York; 4000 regulars, Canadians, and Indians for an advance from Canada; and 5000 men for holding Boston,—24,000 in all. Nothing, in his judgement, could be done with smaller numbers.

When Sir William Howe wrote directly to the government a few weeks later he lowered his demands somewhat. He contented himself with a request for 12,000 men for use at New York, and abandoned the plan to hold Boston.[14] Having decided by the end of November to occupy Rhode Island as well, he asked for 5000 men, in addition to the 12,000 he intended to use at New York.[15] Nothing was said in this letter about a Canadian expedition. Sir William thought that, with such reinforcements as could be sent to augment the formations he already had, a supplement of 4000 Russians would bring his numbers to the point necessary for effective action. It is interesting to notice that he expected to meet an American army

---

[13] H.M.C. Mss. of Mrs. Stopford-Sackville, vol. 2, p. 9. Lord Howe-Germain, 25 September 1775.
[14] C.O.5/92, pp. 621-30. Howe-Dartmouth, 9 October 1775.
[15] Ibid., pp. 641-50. Howe-Dartmouth, 26 November 1775.

of about 10,000 at Rhode Island and one of 20,000 at New York and that he expected to be obliged to begin operations at the latter place by a siege. Apparently he felt confident of success if he were not at a greater numerical disadvantage than two to one.

These ideas of the late summer and autumn of 1775 underwent no radical change during the winter. Writing, as he still supposed, to Dartmouth on 16 January 1776, Howe said:

> With a proper army of 20,000 men, having 12,000 at New York, 6,000 at Rhode Island, and 2,000 at Halifax, exclusive of an army for the province of Quebec, the present unfavourable appearance of things would probably wear a different aspect before the end of the ensuing campaign. With fewer troops the success of any offensive operations will be very doubtful, the enemy possessing advantages that will not be readily overcome by a small force; neither is their army by any means to be despised, having in it many European soldiers, and all or most of the young men of spirit in the country, who are exceedingly diligent and attentive to their military profession.[16]

This is substantially a repetition of earlier requests, with some alteration of detail, and must have appeared so to the government in London. But two features of the letter merit attention. First, Howe tended to push his demands for troops beyond the figure in his first letters to the government, although no higher than in the private letter to his brother. Just why this original disparity existed cannot be determined certainly, but the evidence seems to justify certain inferences. The letter to his brother probably represented the real wish of Sir William, a private opinion that need not commit him formally, but which he could feel certain would be communicated to someone

---

[16] C.O.5/93, pp. 65-74. Howe-Dartmouth, 16 January 1776.

in authority. The earliest of his formal requests probably represented the largest force he hoped to get
under existing conditions. Thus a divergence appears between the numbers he felt free to demand
and those he really thought necessary. He recognized that the apparent circumstances of his situation
did not warrant as extensive an effort by the government as he felt inwardly to be needed. This feeling
that the problem was more formidable than appearances indicated or than the government was willing to
recognize grew on Howe and, as we shall see, played
a very important part in shaping his later actions and
attitude.

The second point to notice is his tribute to the
military worth of the American troops. Sir William
never shared the contempt felt for them by some of
his colleagues. But his earliest plan of campaign
showed little respect for the ability of the Americans
to oppose him with a regular field army. The letter
of January 16, however, indicated a marked modification of his original opinion. Now he dwelt on the
military virtues of his antagonists and hinted that,
even with the reinforcements asked for, he must expect to undergo the hazards of a regular campaign
against a competent adversary. Washington's army,
rather than scattered local resistance, began to loom
up as the hardest nut to crack. This shift in emphasis,
if carried far, meant a radical alteration of the problem facing the British command. We shall have to
notice later how far this change of view developed and
to what degree Howe accommodated his plans to this
alteration of his original estimate.

The success of the British government in securing
several thousand Hessians enabled Germain to inform
Howe that his requests for reinforcements could be

met. Germain wrote definitely at the end of March that over twelve thousand Hessians were intended for the army under his command.[17] He also gave notice of the approaching shipment of over three thousand Highlanders and of the probability that the southern expedition under Clinton would soon join Howe. Thus the government made it clear, many weeks before the campaign could open, that the forces available for offensive operations would be, not merely as great as requested, but appreciably greater. Only in the lateness of their arrival did they in any way fall short of the General's hopes.

Meanwhile, as the winter dragged on and Howe had time to cogitate over his problems, his ideas gradually developed, usually in the direction of greater respect for the obstacles ahead of him. In January he commented on the attack of Clinton and Parker on South Carolina :

But I am free to own my opinion to your Lordship which has been to leave the southern provinces in the fullest persuasion of their security until the rebels should have been defeated on the side of New York, which event appears to me more clearly than ever of so much consequence that our utmost strength should be exerted to accomplish it before designs of less importance are taken up inconsistent with the general plan of operations for the ensuing campaign, and it is to be presumed the southern rebels would have been less able to defend themselves, had they not been roused up by the conduct of their governors, who have not, I fear, the means of suppressing them.[18]

Howe then went on to describe the pernicious effect of such diversions upon his own prospects :

[17] C.O.5/93, pp. 137-51. Germain-Howe, 28 March 1776.
[18] Ibid., pp. 65-74. Howe-Dartmouth, 16 January 1776.

These drains, added to that to the southward, from whence I can promise myself little assistance to the main army, will reduce the expected strength for the campaign so considerably, that if a respectable supply of troops from Europe does not arrive soon in the spring, another defensive campaign, I conclude, will be the consequence. For by the want of a force to act early, the rebel army will have full time to entrench in every strong position their commanders may fix upon, in which case, tho' we should get possession of New York without resistance, we must not expect to carry their entrenched camps without considerable loss; whereas on the contrary the army, at the opening of the campaign, being in force, would probably by rapid movements bring the rebels to an action upon equal terms, before they could cover themselves by works of any significance.[19]

These two excerpts from Howe's letters furnish additional evidence that he had by January 1776 divested himself of any belief that he might easily brush aside the formal resistance awaiting him at New York. What he had originally regarded as but a preliminary to the real work of pacification now threatened to consume the entire summer. Yet this increase in the importance of the American army did not seem to Howe to indicate that its defeat would suffice to end the rebellion without the necessity of a piecemeal pacification of the country. He thus saw himself faced with the dismal prospect of spending the summer in defeating the formal resistance of the enemy, without at the end having done more than clear the way for the laborious business of pacification.

In the passages quoted may also be seen the reflection of Howe's experience at Boston. He dreaded lest his campaign at New York develop into another impasse such as that then facing him in Massachusetts. He felt it imperative to get the jump on the enemy

[19] Ibid.

before the latter could plan and prepare defensive positions of the type that had immobilized the British in the first year of the war. Otherwise nothing could be accomplished. Howe was gradually bringing himself to a frame of mind where he believed British success depended upon a very narrow margin of time and force, failing which he must drastically curtail his plans and expectations. It must be admitted that his recent experiences gave him some warrant for this belief, but at the same time his attitude led him into the danger of concluding too easily that circumstances were hopelessly unfavourable to the accomplishment of his designs.

Howe gave evidence of just such a state of pessimism in a letter to Germain sent from Halifax.

The scene here at present wears a lowering aspect, there not being the least prospect of conciliating this continent until its armies have been roughly dealt with ; and I confess my apprehensions that such an event will not be readily brought about, the rebels get on apace, and knowing their advantages in having the whole country, as it were, at their disposal, they will not be readily brought into a situation where the King's troops can meet them upon equal terms. Their armies retiring a few miles back from the navigable rivers, ours cannot follow them from the difficulties I expect to meet with in procuring land carriage. It cannot be denied that there are many inhabitants in every province well affected to Government, from whom no doubt we shall have assistance, but not until His Majesty's arms have a clear superiority by a decisive victory.[20]

There is nothing novel in the statement that the American army must first be defeated decisively. The startling thing is the admission that it may not prove possible to do so.

[20] H.M.C. Mss. of Mrs. Stopford-Sackville, vol. 2, p. 30. Howe-Germain, 26 April 1776.

The final plans for 1776 involved no serious alteration from Sir William Howe's original concept.   Howe
wrote to Germain on April 25 to say that he had news
that Washington had gone with the bulk of his forces
to New York.   The Americans were also fortifying
Rhode Island, but this caused him no serious apprehension.

New York being the greater object of the two, and the
possession of it more extensive in its consequences, as well
as more conducive to the credit of His Majesty's arms, will
be my principal aim when enabled to proceed thither by
a sufficient supply of provisions, since both services cannot be undertaken with the present force, and it is become
highly necessary that the first exertion of the army should
be directed to the most important purposes, to check the
spirit which the evacuation of Boston will naturally raise
among the rebels.   In this disposition it is probable that
the leaders, urged by the people and flushed with the idea
of superiority, may be the readier brought to a decisive
action, than which nothing is more to be desired or sought
for by us, as the most effectual means to terminate this
expensive war, and I have the greatest reason to be sanguine in my hopes of a success from the present health
and high order of the army.   If this cannot be effected
before the reinforcements arrive from Europe, it is most
likely that they will act upon the defensive, by having
recourse to strong intrenched situations, in order to spin
out the campaign if possible without exposing themselves
to any decisive action.[21]

This letter, at first sight, contradicts the pessimism of
the one cited just previously, which was written a day
later.   The reservation in the last sentence makes the
difference less sharp, but a real difference remains and
indicates a tendency in Howe to oscillate between pessimism and an occasional mood of cautious optimism.
Such a quality, altogether human, is nevertheless

[21] C.O.5/93, pp. 277-84.   Howe-Germain, 25 April 1776.

worthy of note, for the temperamental reactions of commanders, both in the heat of battle and through the long months of a campaign, greatly influence the ultimate result.

Howe's last word to Germain about his plans before leaving Halifax, sent on May 12, indicated no modification of his earlier schemes, except that he proposed to occupy Rhode Island as soon as the situation in New York was well in hand. He stressed the idea that the British army must avoid another defensive situation such as had plagued it at Boston, and expressed the hope that the northern army might make its way to the Hudson and join hands with his own force.[22]

Germain expressed warm approval of the many plans elaborated or suggested by Sir William Howe ; and in reality they were many, not in substance, but only in detail. He asked only one modification, but that was of considerable importance. On May 3 he wrote :

> The plan you propose, for attacking New York as soon as possible, is becoming that spirit and vigour with which you always act, but as such large reinforcements are going to you, I wish they may arrive before the time of carrying it into execution, that your forces may be so increased as to render your success more certain.[23]

The delay in the beginning of the campaign thus rested upon a direct order from Germain. In obeying it Howe was compelled to sacrifice the opportunity he so much stressed, of attacking the Americans before they could be prepared to oppose him behind a succession of fortified posts. His dread of being compelled to face such tactics must be remembered when examining his later conduct.

So far as can be discovered, no friction existed in

[22] *H.M.C. Mss. of Mrs. Stopford-Sackville*, vol. 2, p. 31. Howe-Germain, 12 May 1776.
[23] C.O.5/93, pp. 231-39. Germain-Howe, 3 May 1776.

the spring of 1776 between Howe and Germain. Germain felt entirely satisfied with Howe and the latter expressed himself as thoroughly content with the preparations made by the government for supporting the coming campaign. He wrote to Germain on June 8:

> I cannot take my leave from your Lordship without expressing my utter amazement at the decisive and masterly strokes for carrying such extensive plans into immediate execution as have been effected since your Lordship has assumed the conducting of this war, which is already most happily experienced by those who have the honour of serving here under your guidance.[24]

After all allowance for the flattery of official correspondence, it seems safe to say that Howe felt satisfied with the support he had received. His plans had required generous support, but the government had given him even more than he had asked.

Thus, during the winter of 1775-76 there occurred a gradual and not altogether clear change in Sir William Howe's estimate of his situation. He at first seemed to contemplate a piecemeal pacification, in which the preliminary defeat of formal resistance would be quickly and easily accomplished. Then he revised his ideas and concluded that the defeat of the main American army would prove difficult and not altogether certain of accomplishment in a single campaign. By spring he had reached a position where he apparently still believed the ultimate work of pacification must be piecemeal, but thought that the necessary preliminary to it, the defeat of the American field army, would probably tax the utmost strength of his forces. Only in a very fortunate conjuncture of circumstance did he see any hope of relief from his

24 Ibid., pp. 429-31. Howe-Germain, 8 June 1776.

dilemma, except that at the very end of the spring he did for a moment appear to hope that the Revolution might collapse after the defeat of the main army of the Americans and that American overconfidence might afford an opportunity for such a stroke. Yet it is doubtful if, even then, he thought such a development at all likely. More and more he seemed to grow convinced that the difficulties facing him were immense and that no success was within reach which would, in the near future, bring a final end to the Revolution.

CHAPTER VIII

THE BATTLE OF LONG ISLAND

SIR WILLIAM HOWE had originally hoped that the forces for the campaign would be available as soon as warm weather appeared, since he attached great importance to beginning operations before the Americans could complete their preparations. But a letter from Germain brought word that the government wished him to wait for reinforcements before attempting anything, and we have no reason to believe that Howe himself contemplated a serious attack with the troops available at Halifax.

Conditions at Halifax did not facilitate an early opening of the campaign. The British were eager to get away, for they found it very difficult to support so large an army in the town and never had more than a slender margin of supplies.[1] But this shortage acted also as an inducement to delay, for as a consequence it was impossible to put the army and its supplies in good order for the campaign or to equip the fleet in the manner required for the sailing of the expedition.[2] As late as May 23 departure was held up by lack of provisions and, although preparations were under way that presaged an early move, many officers felt uneasy about the amount of good campaigning weather that was slipping by without use.[3] Not until June 11 did the army finally leave.

[1] B.M.Add.Mss. 21,680, ff. 100-103. Maj. Hutcheson-Haldimand, 24 April 1776.
[2] Ibid., ff. 105-110. Same to same, 12 May 1776.
[3] Ibid., ff. 111-16. Same to same, 23 May 1776.

This was the first and most serious of the delays that prevented action against the Americans until August. Who was to blame? Some have criticized Howe for not moving to New York at once and have implied that he could have secured the city without serious difficulty had he landed there early in the spring.[4] But Howe's instructions from Germain to wait for reinforcements were definite, and Howe himself had frequently indicated that he could do nothing in an offensive way until the troops he had at Boston were considerably augmented. The mere possession of New York City was not the objective of the campaign and Howe had no intention of again possessing a city, only to be shut up in it without means of further effective action. Better accept a shortened campaign than experience another Boston. Sir William felt in no mood in the spring of 1776 to accept big risks, nor did the situation, so far as could be seen, require it.[5]

Must we then blame Germain and the British government for the delay? We cannot saddle Germain with the entire responsibility because he ordered Howe to wait for reinforcements; for Howe, if left to himself, would most certainly have done the same. To both it appeared that failure was much more likely to come from haste and inadequate preparation than from lack of time for active campaigning, a not unreasonable view at the time. If Germain is to bear any peculiar share of the blame it must be on the ground that he was responsible for the tardiness of the reinforcements. The answer to this question is to be found in the chapter on British preparations. We need not reconsider it in detail here, but it seems that the British government, at least in so far as Germain's office was con-

[4] Channing, *History of the United States,* vol. 3, p. 229.
[5] C.O.5/93, pp. 421-26. Howe-Germain, 7 June 1776.

cerned, did about as well as could have been expected.
The task of securing additional troops was very formidable and the Hessians did not arrive in England until
late. If incompetence is to be imputed, it must be
to Sandwich and the Admiralty, as evidenced by the
impatience of the King with that department. But
it seems very doubtful whether greater efficiency there
would have made possible the arrival of Howe's reinforcements before the Americans were ready to give
battle. True, Washington did rejoice that the British
delay gave him time to advance his works ; but, in view
of their small value when the storm struck, the extra
effort appears to have been of little worth.[6] However
the thing may look in retrospect, both Germain and
George III professed to be entirely convinced of the
adequacy of Howe's reasons for delaying so long at
Halifax.[7]

Howe landed the troops brought from Halifax on
Staten Island on July 2, but not until August 22 did
his army begin its advance by the landing on Long
Island. Sir William pointed to his critics that this
delay was in conformity with the instructions of the
government.

Our operations were not expected to commence before
the arrival of the troops from England or of General Clinton's army from Charles-Town. General Clinton arrived
on the first of August. Nine days only were allotted for
the refreshment of the troops after the great length of time
they had been on board their transports, and for making
all necessary arrangements.[8]

It is perhaps debatable whether the troops needed
nine days rest. A despatch from Lord Howe to the

[6] Ford, vol. 4, pp. 234-5. Washington-Schuyler, 11 July 1776.
[7] C.O.5/93, pp. 451-4. Germain-Howe, 22 August 1776.
[8] *Observations upon a Pamphlet entitled Letters to a Nobleman*, pp.
47-8. Hereafter referred to as *Observations upon a Pamphlet*.

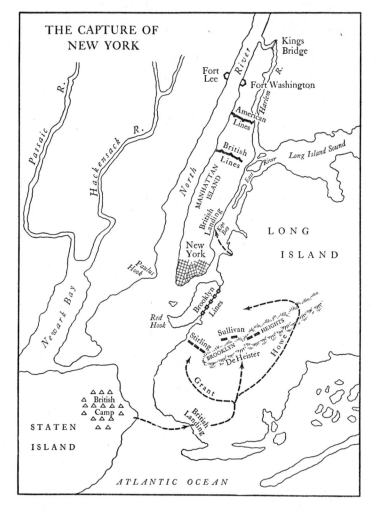

Admiralty makes it plain that the possibility of landing the troops on Long Island directly was considered,
but rejected on at least the ostensible ground of their
need of refreshment.[9]   Others than Howe felt a period
of recuperation after a fourteen weeks voyage to be

[9] Admiralty 1/487, pp. 839-45. Lord Howe-Admiralty, 29 June 1777.

desirable.[10] Nor can we dismiss as worthless Sir William's excuse of the excessive heat to justify the inaction of the troops that had landed earlier on Staten Island.[11] Troops accustomed to the relatively cool weather of northern Europe needed to be acclimated before they were ready to withstand the heat of an American summer.

But one cannot feel entirely satisfied with these explanations. Lord Howe arrived with the Hessians and the Guards, but also with the commission to negotiate peace. We know that in the days intervening between his arrival and the landing on Long Island endeavours were made, which will be described later, to approach the American authorities with an eye to negotiation. We also know that the troops from Europe arrived in good condition and could have, had it been necessary, gone immediately into action without suffering any dangerous handicap. It is difficult not to believe that the military arguments for delay were appreciably reinforced by the desire of the two brothers to try the effect of their commission to negotiate. Possibly the bloodshed of an assault on New York might be avoided. Even the complete failure of negotiations would at least assist the British commanders to discover the exact degree to which they must rely upon military force.

How far the political supplemented the military motive in prompting delay is beyond exact estimate. This uncertainty is not, however, vastly important, for the nine days that elapsed were in no sense decisive. They provided the Americans neither with time for any substantial improvement of their defences nor

[10] B.M.Add.Mss., 21,680, ff. 141-4. Maj. Hutcheson-Haldimand, 14 August 1776.
[11] *Howe's Narrative*, p. 4.

with any indication of the exact direction of the British assault.[12]

The main features of the battle of Long Island, which followed the final concentration of the British forces, are so familiar to students of the American Revolution that a detailed examination of them is unnecessary. The conduct of the British command just before and during the action, however, merits a few remarks. Whatever may have been the wisdom of waiting until August 22 before landing on Long Island, the time was utilized to work out to perfection every detail of the movement. A letter from Major Hutcheson in the Quarter Master's department describes the activity of the British in building flat-bottomed boats, sufficient for landing six thousand men in a single move, and so carefully designed that each was provided with a hinged front that could be let down to serve as a gangplank over which the men and guns could go ashore as soon as the bow of the boat touched the beach.[13] Meanwhile the secret of the time and place of the intended landing was most effectively guarded by the high command.[14]

The landing, which took place on August 22, showed in its smoothness of execution the careful preparation that had preceded it. The small craft containing the troops moved forward in regular divisions, closely protected by the ships of war.[15] Although thus elaborately prepared for any contingency, the British in fact found nothing to oppose them. Possibly, under the circumstances, the elaborate care seems unneces-

---

[12] Ford, vol. 4, pp. 364-5. Washington-Gov. Trumbull, 24 August 1776.
[13] B.M.Add.Mss. 21,680, ff. 133-8. Maj. Hutcheson-Haldimand, 14 August 1776.
[14] Ibid., ff. 141-4. Same to same, 14 August 1776.
[15] Admiralty, 1/487, pp. 119-25. Lord Howe-Admiralty, 31 August 1776.

THE BATTLE OF
LONG ISLAND

sary, but there is no evidence that it caused any delay, and the neglect of it might have been costly.

A purely naval measure was attempted in conjunction with the landing on Long Island. On the day before the battle was fought, Lord Howe ordered some ships to attempt to move up the river towards the town of New York, to act as a diversion.[16] There is no indication in his explanation of the move that he planned to sever communications between Long Island and the city, although the Americans suspected that to be his intention. Whatever the plan, the British

16 Ibid.

failed to accomplish it, for the wind shifted to the northward and the ships could not get up.

The battle of Long Island, on August 27, was a very brief, simple, and decisive affair. The Americans had posted themselves along some heights southeast of Brooklyn, with their right flank resting upon the sea. But their left flank was in the air. Sir William Howe detected the weakness of their position and decided to turn the exposed flank, while making a spirited diversion against the enemy right and centre in order to hold his opponent. Unfortunately for the Americans, their arrangements for reconnoitring the unprotected area to their left were inadequate and unlucky; and the British column, which had set out during the night, worked its way far round the American flank before its presence became known to the colonial command. The result was the complete overthrow of the American defence. The troops in position on the heights saved themselves from capture only by instant retreat, and suffered heavy loss in the confusion of the move.

In view of the later disputes over the adequacy of the numbers provided by the government for operations in America, the numbers engaged in the battle of Long Island are worthy of notice. Lord Howe wrote the Admiralty that he put ashore an army of fifteen thousand at Gravesend Bay, and on the 25th of August landed an additional corps of Hessians.[17] It is perfectly clear that Sir William Howe had all and more than the fifteen thousand men he had told his brother the previous summer would be needed for operations around New York.

The overwhelming success of the British at the battle of Long Island has sometimes been used to support an indictment of the general conduct of Sir Wil-

17 Admiralty 1/487, pp. 119-25. Lord Howe-Admiralty, 31 August 1776.

liam Howe. The critics argue that a man able to direct so brilliant an action as that on Long Island must be, when he cares to exert himself, a brilliant commander. The contrast between Long Island and the disappointments to come is used to prove that only a lack of genuine desire to win could explain the later failures.

The argument is a specious one at best. Even had Howe been a genius, it would not have been reasonable to expect him to shine with equal brightness upon all occasions. To argue that, because Howe at certain times showed to much less advantage than upon others, he therefore intended to let victory escape him, is as sensible as to argue that Frederick the Great intended to lose at Kunersdorf, or Napoleon at Leipzig. There are additional objections in the case of Sir William Howe. Is there any reason to suppose that his plan of battle on Long Island manifested such genius as to render his later failures incapable of rational explanation? Long Island was a great British success, but not a success that was due to great genius. Howe had decidedly superior forces and employed them in obvious fashion, to outflank an opponent who had carelessly exposed himself to such a move. It was a thoroughly competent plan, nothing more. Under the circumstances both a genius and a soldier of ordinary ability would have done the same thing. The incident proves nothing more than that Howe knew how to do a workmanlike job in a relatively simple situation.

Although Howe's critics had nothing to complain of in the handling of the actual battle and, in fact, took great pains to praise it in order the better to emphasize his later faults, an incident occurred shortly after the conclusion of the fighting that was used as one of the major reasons for casting suspicion upon the integrity of his conduct. To cover the landing place that enabled them to communicate with New York the Americans had erected in Brooklyn a fortified line of over a mile in length. The fugitives from the battle fled precipitately into these lines, hard pressed by the pursuing British. Presumably, if the lines had not existed or could have been carried without delay, practically all of the survivors of the battle would have been compelled to surrender, for only the presence of the fortifications enabled the defeated Americans to delay their opponents long enough for the organization of the retreat across the East River.

What happened when the British approached the lines was recorded very briefly by Sir William Howe in his description of the day's fighting:

These battalions . . . pursued numbers of the rebel . . . so close to their principal redoubt and with such eagerness to attack it by storm, that it required repeated orders to prevail upon them to desist from the attempt. Had they been permitted to go on, it is my opinion they would have carried the redoubt, but as it was apparent the lines must have been ours at a very cheap rate by regular approaches, I would not risk the loss that might have been sustained in the assault.[18]

So the idea of assaulting the lines was abandoned and preparations were begun for regular approaches, which, however, were made unnecessary by the American evacuation two days later.

Stedman, who served under Howe, and wrote his *History of the American War* a few years later, made some interesting observations on this subject.

In reviewing the actions of men, the historian is often at a loss to conjecture the secret causes that gave them

[18] C.O.5/93, pp. 515-21. Howe-Germain, 3 September 1776.

birth. It cannot be denied that the American army lay almost entirely at the will of the British. That they were suffered to retire in safety, has by some been attributed to the reluctance of the Commander-in-Chief to shed the blood of a people so nearly allied to that source from whence he derived all his authority and power. We are rather inclined to adopt this idea, and to suppose motives of mistaken policy, than to leave ground for an imagination that the escape of the Americans resulted from any want of exertion on the part of Sir William Howe, or deficiency in the military science. He might possibly have conceived that the late victory would produce a revolution in sentiment capable of terminating the war without the extremity which it appeared to be, beyond all possibility of doubt, in his power to enforce.[19]

This interesting theory, which pictures a deliberate decision not to push British advantages ruthlessly, in order that the Americans might have time to recognize the handwriting on the wall and make a relatively painless submission, has been used also to explain later events. It has the attractiveness of a certain subtlety and derives some support from the indubitable fact that the Howes believed that the task of reconquering America demanded something more than military victory.

Howe's critics were not slow to make the most of the incident of the Brooklyn lines. One of them wrote :

There is scarce an instance to be found of a defeated army flying precipitately into their own trenches, ever defending them against a victorious army of near double their number.

But did we ever hear of a great and victorious army 's being stopped in the midst of a conquest, for forming regular approaches against the ditch of a line, which was three miles long and only three or four feet deep ? Did not the rebel fugitives run over the ditch and the breast-

19 Stedman, *History of the American War,* vol. 1, p. 199.

works . . . and could not the British troops as easily have followed them? [20]

He then went on to compare the Brooklyn lines with other positions successfully stormed, such as Fort Washington. Other criticisms were in the same vein, ridiculing the idea that the British could have been stopped or made to suffer heavy losses had they launched an immediate assault.

Howe, at a later date, sought to explain the paragraph in his despatch which admitted that the lines could probably have been rushed. He argued that he inserted it primarily as a tribute to the spirit of the troops, and that it was a wrong inference to suppose that such an action would have led to the destruction of the American army. [21] He then elaborated his argument in a passage that requires close examination.

The facts are these : — the rebels had a body of men posted in front of the lines, to guard against an attack from Flat-Bush, and from the lower road upon their right. These troops were defeated with considerable loss. The remainder of the corps was posted behind the lines, the main army being then on York Island : so that admitting the works to have been forced on the day of the action, the only advantage we should have gained would have been the destruction of a few more men, for the retreat of the greatest part would have been assured by the works constructed upon the heights of Brooklyn, opposite to New York, and their embarkation covered by a number of floating batteries.

On the other hand, the most essential duty I had to observe was, not wantonly to commit His Majesty's troops, where the object was inadequate. I well knew that any considerable loss sustained by the army could not speedily nor easily, be repaired. I also knew that one great point toward gaining the confidence of an army (and a general

[20] *Fugitive Pieces*, p. 80.
[21] *Howe's Narrative*, p. 4.

without it is upon the most dangerous ground) is never to expose the troops where, as I said before, the object is inadequate. . . The loss of 1,000 of perhaps 1,500 British troops, in carrying those lines, would have been but ill-repaid by double that number of the enemy, could it have been supposed they would have suffered in that proportion.[22]

There is much that requires explanation and excites wonder in this passage. Why did Howe think that, even after a successful assault, the lines upon the Heights of Brooklyn would still suffice to protect the American embarkation? Why did he believe that the only advantage that could be won would be the destruction of a few more of the enemy?

Howe appears to have believed that the capture of the point assaulted could harm only those in the conquered work; in other words, that the assault would be an end in itself, a minor tactical success without strategic consequence. Is there any justification for this view, or was it an afterthought of Sir William, possibly the result of a faulty recollection of the exact circumstances of the American position?

By referring back to his original despatch, we find some reason for believing that Howe actually did hold the view he later ascribed to himself. It was the 'principal redoubt' which he forbade his troops to storm. It was that point which he thought they could have carried, and he expressed no opinion as to the ability of his troops to force the entire line of fortifications.[23] The vulnerability of one redoubt did not necessarily make the entire position untenable. Neither in the exact wording nor in the general tenor of his despatch was there any indication that the General saw the possibility of achieving a success that would destroy all

[22] Ibid., p. 5.
[23] C.O.5/93, pp. 515-21. Howe-Germain, 3 September 1776.

that remained of the American force upon Long Island.

What light do other witnesses shed upon the problem? The witness most favourable to Howe was Captain Montressor, himself an engineer. Much of his evidence at the Inquiry dealt with the wisdom of attempting to storm the lines. He was with Howe the entire day and asserted that the General approached near enough to the lines to judge of their strength. He described the lines as well built, entirely complete, proof against cannon, and surrounded with formidable abbatis.[24] It was true he had never seen a case where it was held necessary to approach such lines by the siege method, but believed the attack on Ticonderoga in 1758 had failed for want of such a precaution. He also testified that there were no fascines available for filling the ditch, nor any scaling ladders or other apparatus for an assault.

Other evidence justified Howe on the ground that, whatever the actual strength of the lines, he was unable at the moment to determine how great it was. General Robertson said:

I marched at the head of my brigade to a place near the enemy's lines. I went to the situation where I thought I could best see without leaving my brigade far, and I could not make any judgment of the strength of the enemy's lines from any place I could see them. This made me wish that the Grenadiers would not go on. . . I imagine that the General called back the troops because he was unable to form a just estimate of the force of the lines.[25]

Yet Robertson was, on the whole, a witness unfavourable to Howe. He admitted that it was learned later that the lines were weakly manned, but held that Howe could not have known it at the time, and that, with

24 Dom. State Papers, Geo. III, 18. The Howe Inquiry.
25 Ibid.

the information available, storming seemed to him a very improper measure. Cornwallis was also questioned about the lines, but dodged any direct answer as to the propriety of storming them, saying only that he had never heard it suggested that they could be carried by assault.[26]

Clinton, in his *Historical Detail,* defended Howe's action. He admitted that he wished Howe had gone on, but said further:

I do not mean, however, by this to insinuate that Sir William Howe was in the least wrong in not doing so. On the contrary, I am persuaded that he acted from intelligence, and had I at the time possessed the same information he was master of, possibly I should like him have judged it prudent to wait for the less hazardous certainty of regular approaches. Nor can any after knowledge of the fallacy of that information invalidate the propriety of his conduct under it.[27]

Clinton observed further that Howe could not have known, what was later discovered, that the Americans did not have over eight hundred men to man the lines.

To what conclusion do these opinions point? Much depends upon how serious a task Howe deemed an assault upon the lines to be. The evidence at first sight appears contradictory. Montressor said that Howe could see how very formidable the lines were. Robertson said it was impossible to know, from such survey as could be made hastily on the spot, whether an assault was feasible. Clinton was convinced that Howe had what was to all appearances reliable information that an assault would be dangerous. But the contradiction is not so great as it might

[26] Ibid.
[27] Clinton's *Historical Detail,* vol. 1, p. 60.

seem. The difference amounts to this: Montressor thought it evident that the lines were very strong; Robertson thought that they might well be so for all that could then be determined; Clinton thought that Howe had adequate reason for thinking them so. Present information shows that the lines, although defective in many ways, probably had an outward appearance of great strength.[28]

Yet Howe, at this time, believed that the troops, if permitted to go on, could have carried the redoubt. If at first sight he appears condemned out of his own mouth, second thought makes it incredible that he would admit freely such a belief had he suspected it would be used so vigorously against him. We are forced to the conclusion that he saw nothing in the decision but what would meet general approval. It seems probable that, uncertain as he was of the exact nature of the fortification facing him, he felt doubtful whether an assault of the redoubt, even if successful, would bring the decisive results which, in the light of later knowledge, it seems likely would have attended it. Nor could he know how small was the force available to resist his assault. He was almost certainly unaware that Washington had sent less than half his army to oppose the British on Long Island and doubtless supposed there was a force behind the Brooklyn lines nearly as numerous as that he had just defeated in the open field. He saw the victory offered him as only the achievement of a limited objective, an honourable and spirited feat of arms, but one which would exact a considerable toll in casualties and do little to advance his strategic plans. It was natural that he should feel proud of the ability and willingness

[28] H. P. Johnston, *The Campaign of 1776 around New York and Brooklyn*, p. 214.

of his troops to attempt this feat and at the same time
feel pleased that his own restraint and sense had refused them permission to waste themselves on an
attack that appeared to offer little but glory.

Such an explanation of his view tallies with common
sense. It is impossible to believe that Howe was so
witless as to announce willingly to the world that he
had forfeited a brilliant strategic opportunity. If he
did miss such an opportunity he certainly was not
aware of it at the time. Possibly a commander of
genius, or intuition, might have gone ahead and taken
the chance. But Howe was no genius; only a well
trained officer, schooled in correct and prudent conduct. Viewing the situation as he did, he probably
acted according to his lights. A man of his training
would have taken great risks only where the obstacles
to ultimate success were so serious as to offer little
prospect of victory by safer methods. Since we know
that Howe failed, it is easy to argue that he ought to
have taken greater chances. But, at the time, he proceeded upon the reasonable assumption that the elements of permanent strength in the contest were mostly
on his side and felt that they would bring him victory
if he made no serious blunder.[29]

At times, it must be admitted, Howe seemed possessed of a different spirit, a feeling that the British
outlook was very unpromising. But in action he seems
always to have clung to the theory that success could
only be secured by taking no unnecessary chances.
Doubtless these points of view conflict; extreme caution is seldom adequate to success when the odds
against victory are formidable. In this inconsistency
lies perhaps one of the chief reasons for Howe's failure.
His variation and conflict of moods led him into an

[29] *Howe's Narrative*, p. 7.

uncertainty of attitude which prevented his making the most out of whatever plans he might adopt. Such perplexities are not rare : many a military commander has met failure because at crucial moments he was seized with doubts of the validity of the assumptions upon which his plan of campaign was based. Throughout the war Howe never permanently abandoned the rational conclusion at which he had arrived early in the contest, that a cautious use of Great Britain's advantages ought to bring victory. But from time to time, and with increasing frequency as the war dragged on, he was assailed with doubts as to the possibility of ultimate success ; and this pessimism sometimes led him, since he believed that prudence alone could win, to a greater caution than even routine practice would have required. Such a conflict in his own mind, and not treachery or sheer incompetence, explains what may appear to us now as missed opportunities.

With the British committed to carrying the Brooklyn lines by regular approaches, the Americans took early advantage of the respite afforded them to elude the danger that threatened. Two days after the battle, on the night of the 29th of August, they silently evacuated the lines and, aided by fortune and their own care and energy, ferried themselves across to Manhattan Island, leaving the British to discover several hours later that the bird had flown. Howe was criticized for letting the Americans get away thus cheaply. His opponents argued that, had he been alert and had he taken adequate measures to keep informed about the actions of the enemy, he might have attacked them at the moment of their retreat.

Persons familiar with actual warfare realize, however, that it is not always an easy task to discover immediately that the enemy has evacuated his lines.

Witnesses who testified before the Inquiry believed that adequate measures had been taken to secure information.[30] The weather gave important assistance to the Americans. During the early part of the retreat a violent northeaster was blowing. It hampered the Americans by limiting them to the use of rowboats, but it assisted them by deadening the sound of their movements and by persuading the British that no retreat would be attempted under such conditions. That this belief was not entirely unwarranted is shown by the fact that the withdrawal across the river during such weather has always been accounted a remarkable feat.[31] The wind did not last all night, but was replaced by a fog just before dawn, which furnished additional protection against discovery.

A more serious charge of neglect has been brought against Lord Howe for his failure to move ships up into the East River in order to cut off the retreat from Long Island. According to one critic:

I asked a warm friend of the Admiral's why his Lordship did not bring his heavy ships against the batteries on the East River, and cut off the rebel retreat, as well as risk his frigates to no purpose in the North River? The reply was the Admiral did not chuse to risk H.M. ships. Thus his Lordship will not risk H.M. ships; the General will not risk H.M. men; for these reasons the rebels escaped, and the rebellion continues.[32]

This is a possible explanation of the Admiral's inaction. There was undoubted risk in sending sailing ships up the East River when both shores were in possession of an enemy. The tide runs strongly in the channel and the ships must either dominate the cannon on shore or be destroyed by them.

[30] Dom. State Papers, Geo. III, 18. The Howe Inquiry.
[31] Johnston, *Campaign of 1776*, pp. 221-2.
[32] *Fugitive Pieces*, p. 77. Letter from New York, 9 March 1777.

But this evidence charging Lord Howe with excessive caution is only hearsay. More convincing testimony makes it appear that other considerations prompted him. It will be remembered that on the day of the battle of Long Island an attempt to move the ships up towards the city was thwarted by a contrary wind. No explanation comes from the British side of what the ships were doing between the day of the battle and the American retirement. But the council of war of the American army that decided to order a retreat from Brooklyn felt apprehensive about the danger of being cut off and noted, in its report to Congress, 'The enemy appeared to be endeavouring to get their ships into the East River to cut off communication with New York, but the wind as yet had not served them.' [32] Nor, as we know, did it serve them on the day of the retreat. In the face of this evidence it seems abundantly clear that, regardless of whether Lord Howe was prepared to risk his ships or not, the direction of the wind during the crucial days when a considerable section of the American army was isolated on Long Island was such as effectively to block an attempt to use the fleet to intercept the American retirement. [34] The sailing ship of those days simply could not beat up against the wind in such narrow waters.

On the whole, the charge of rank incompetence and inertia levelled at the Howe brothers in connection with the American retreat collapses. Lord Howe was effectively prevented from interfering with the retirement. For Sir William Howe to have blocked it would have required more than extreme energy; it would have required some measure of luck. In this

[33] Johnston, *Campaign of* 1776, p. 214.
[34] Ibid.

case, thanks to the weather, the luck was on the American side. The worst that can be said against the British commanders is that they did not display more than average initiative and perspicuity.

In passing judgement upon the battle of Long Island it must be remembered that the task of the Howes was more than that of defeating an army; it was the subduing of a rebellious country. As General Robertson told the Inquiry in 1779, when asked if the force sent out in 1776 was adequate to put down the Americans, 'I never had an idea of subduing the Americans — I meant to assist the good Americans to subdue the bad ones.'[35] Sir William Howe, reasoning along similar lines, hoped that a successful military advance would lead large numbers of the inhabitants to declare for the government. All his information during the early weeks of the summer led him to expect such a result, and he waited anxiously for the arrival of his brother with power as commissioner in order that an attractive offer might be made to those who waited only some adequate inducement to declare openly their support of the Crown.[36] Even before the landing on Long Island, Loyalists had come in driblets with tales of others ready to accept royal protection as soon as the army should move forward.[37] The landing, however, brought fewer declarations than had been expected, less than a hundred by the eve of the battle.[38] But after the British victory Lord Percy sent home very favourable reports of the attitude of the inhabitants, as well as of the effect of the action upon the American army. He wrote:

[35] Dom. State Papers, Geo. III, 18. The Howe Inquiry.
[36] C.O.5/93, pp. 433-7. Howe-Germain, 7 July 1776.
[37] B.M.Add.Mss. 21,680, ff. 141-4. Maj. Hutcheson-Haldimand, 14 August 1776.
[38] Ibid., ff. 147. Same to same, 26 August 1776.

Whole regiments, we are informed, have deserted from them at New York, and in short they are in the greatest state of confusion. They feel severely the blow of the 27th, and I think I may venture to assert, that they will never again stand before us in the field. Everything seems to be over with them, and I flatter myself now that this campaign will put a total end to the war.[39]

But this enthusiasm was not shared by the Commander-in-Chief. On September 2 Sir William wrote to Germain that there would probably be another campaign before the rebellion could be quelled.[40] It is very difficult to say whether pessimism or a sense of realities dictated this judgment. The rapid measures necessary to seize the opportunity described by Percy would scarcely have been consonant with the prudent plans of Howe. Although he had from time to time insisted upon the importance of an early start in the campaign, he never indicated that he intended to *brusquer l'affaire*. At no time did the situation seem to him to warrant such daring. Instead, right up to the moment of the American retreat, he showed his opponent the respect merited by an able enemy in good condition, an enemy capable of penalizing severely any false move by an adversary. If we accept Howe's estimate of the worth of the Americans, it is difficult to quarrel with his belief that the prudent execution of his plans would require another campaign. He had been disappointed in the tardy opening of the campaign, and he had reconciled himself to results considerably short of original expectations. He seemed dimly conscious of the danger that slow, methodical progress would perhaps overstrain govern-

[39] *Percy Letters,* pp. 67-70. Percy-Duke of Northumberland, 1 September 1776.
[40] C.O.5/93, p. 511. Howe-Germain, 2 September 1776.

mental patience, yet it still seemed to him so clearly the correct course that he showed no inclination to deviate from it. Probably both theory and temperament reinforced each other in this particular.

Some critics have argued that Howe ought never to have landed upon Long Island but ought, instead, to have sailed up the North River and landed in Westchester, thus cutting off New York at a blow. Such a move, however, could not have been carried out without giving the Americans time to evacuate the city. It would not have tempted them to open battle, the thing desired above all others by the British, and it presented inherent difficulties of its own. By landing on Long Island Howe secured, in fact, an opportunity for battle under as favourable conditions as could reasonably be expected.

Of the operations as a whole, this much may be said: they produced less decisive results than might have been secured had the British been favoured with better intelligence, better weather for the movement of their ships, and a commander more willing to take chances. But the prudence shown by Howe was in accord with good military practice and there was no convincing reason why he should throw normal routine to the winds, at least none of which he was aware at the time. As we view matters in retrospect, it may appear that his pessimistic foreboding lest the government would not support him adequately in the methodical and expensive measures he thought necessary ought to have prompted him to greater boldness, in order, if possible, to reach a decision with the forces he had. But his fear of limited support, if it had any effect, seems to have inclined him to a greater measure of the caution which eighteenth-century military ideas imposed upon the commander of a costly professional army. In making his openings he showed himself a capable leader, although not so brilliant as sometimes supposed. In using them Howe was unimaginative, but justified by contemporary practice.

CHAPTER IX

THE WORK OF THE HOWES AS COMMISSIONERS

IN accepting the naval command in America, Lord Howe did not intend that he and his brother should be confined to naval and military means alone for reducing the revolting colonies to obedience. He definitely informed Germain in March of 1776 that he could not accept a commission that so limited his method of action.[1] Sir William Howe, as well, intended that negotiation should form an integral part of his plan of operations. As he explained later:

I have heard it said, that my civil commission was inconsistent with my military command,— and that my mind was more intent upon bringing about a peace by negotiation than by force of arms. Sir, thinking it my first duty, I certainly should have preferred the former mode of conciliation and my brother and I for that purpose did go to the utmost verge of our very limited commission and instructions. But our proceedings in the character of commissioners never for one moment suspended our military operations.[2]

This intention, of joining an offer of peace to the threat of war, was not an original idea with either of the Howes. Lord North confided to Eden many months before the commission was publicly proposed that he thought the American business could best be accomplished in that fashion.[3] The idea was so nat-

[1] H.M.C. Mss. of Mrs. Stopford-Sackville, vol. 2, p. 25.
[2] Howe's Narrative, p. 32.
[3] H.M.C. Mss. of Mrs. Stopford-Sackville, vol. 2, p. 10. Wm. Eden-Germain, 3 October 1775.

ural that, like the plan for seizing the line of the Hudson, it seems impossible to attribute it to any one mind. The scheme did, however, probably appear much more important to the Howes than to most persons; for, as Wedderburn observed, Lord Howe would not have been anxious about his instructions unless he intended to follow them.[4]

The instructions took final shape on May 1. A summary of them will be useful. First of all, the commissioners were empowered to grant pardons, excepting any persons they might think desirable. They could grant the King's peace and remove the restrictions upon trade, but before doing so they were to exact reasonable assurance that there would be no revival of the revolution. As a guarantee of this they were to require the dissolution of all revolutionary bodies, the disbanding of all revolutionary troops, the surrender of all forts and posts, and the restoration to office of the regular authorities. Nor were they to exercise their power of removing restrictions until the local assemblies expressed their intention of returning to obedience. The commissioners were instructed to enforce these stipulations rigidly and not to deviate from this course except by special authorization from England.[5]

Certain promises they were empowered to make, although so many qualifications hedged them round that the qualification seemed to bulk almost as large as the promise. A resolution of the House of Commons of 20 February 1775 promised that no colonial tax would be levied, beyond what was needed for the regulation of trade, provided the colonies would contribute an

---

[4] *H.M.C. Mss. of Mrs. Stopford-Sackville,* vol. 2, p. 28. Alex. Wedderburn-Germain, 24 April 1776.
[5] C.O.5/177, pp. 1-14. Copy of instructions to the Howes.

adequate sum for defence and the expense of civil government. The commissioners were to confer with any colony willing to accept these terms, in order to work out the details of the arrangement. This feature of the instructions seems to have been due largely to the representations of Lord Howe.[6]

But the liberty of action of the commissioners under this clause was curtailed by certain restrictions. Before an arrangement with any colony could be concluded, the Loyalists were to be compensated for the damage they had suffered. No treaty could be made except with persons duly elected after their colony had already received the King's peace.[7] The colonies, in raising the revenue contemplated under the proposed scheme, were not to be allowed to tax imports from Great Britain nor exports from their own shores which were used in British manufacture. Another restriction commanded the commissioners to prepare the way for reform of the colonial governments in order to ensure stricter observance of proper subordination toward the home government. But, worst of all, a blanket reservation was included:

It is our will and pleasure that in the discussion of any arrangement that may be brought forward into negociation . . . you do not pledge yourselves in any act of consent and acquiescence that may be construed to preclude our royal determination upon such report as you shall make to us.[8]

This was an effective check upon the more general authorization which empowered them to take measures, where necessary, not covered in their specific instructions.

[6] *H.M.C. Mss. of Mrs. Stopford-Sackville*, vol. 2, p. 25. Lord Howe-Germain, 26 March 1776.
[7] C.O.5/177, pp. 1-14. Copy of instructions to the Howes.
[8] Ibid. Also in B.M.Add. Mss. 34,413. ff. 29-34, the Royal Warrant; ff. 45-51, the actual instructions.

The request that the alteration of the charters of Rhode Island and Connecticut, which the Crown thought necessary, should be made known in detail to the commissioners and that they should be empowered to declare these colonies at peace if they complied, was substantially met in an additional instruction of May 6.[9] But it was done with the reservation that the commissioners were not to enter into any conference with either of these colonies until they could be expected to submit, or unless failure to do so would hurt some general peace negotiation.[10]

These instructions, in the form that Lord Howe finally carried them to America, were some improvement on the first draft, which had, in his view, restrained him from entering into any sort of treaty until all the preliminary conditions had been met.[11] But the improvement was not very great and the instructions were disappointing to the two men who had to execute them. Sir William spoke later of 'our very limited commission and instructions.'[12] In the correspondence between Lord Howe and the government during the spring of 1776, when the details of the commission were being thrashed out between them, the government was obviously unwilling to go beyond what was absolutely necessary to persuade Lord Howe to undertake the American command. The government seems never to have had more than an outside hope that anything would be accomplished by the measure. The King wrote in the preceding autumn,

[9] For Lord Howe's request see the uncalendared Germain papers owned by the late Mr. Wm. L. Clements. Lord Howe-Germain, Grafton Street, 1 April 1776.

[10] C.O.5/177, pp. 15-18. Additional instructions to commissioners. Also in B.M.Add. Mss. 34,415, ff. 52-3.

[11] H.M.C. Mss. of Mrs. Stopford-Sackville, vol. 2, p. 25, Lord Howe-Germain, 26 March 1776.

[12] Howe's Narrative, p. 32.

'I have always feared a commission not likely to meet with success, yet I think it right to be attempted, whilst every act of vigour is unremittingly carried on.'[13] The instructions to the Howes seem drawn more in the spirit of the King's pessimism than in the hope that they would achieve anything.

The instructions really offered very little to a commissioner seeking to use the olive branch. Since the Americans had to make a formal renunciation of rebellion and to surrender all means for maintaining it before receiving the benefits of the slender concessions offered, they could scarcely have been expected to accept such a proposal until it had become obvious that complete defeat was the only alternative. In other words, the offer would facilitate and render less expensive the completion of the war, but only after British victory had become certain.

Lord Howe, upon his arrival in America, lost no time in undertaking the work of the commission. While still off Massachusetts Bay, he drew up two documents for that purpose. The first was a declaration announcing his power as commissioner and emphasizing his authority to grant pardons. It said nothing about the rest of his instructions, the restrictions upon his right to declare the King's peace and the various demands that would be made of the colonies before they would be permitted to resume normal civil government.[14] The second document was a circular to the provincial governors informing them of his arrival and of his commission, and asking them to promulgate the above-mentioned declaration in such a manner as to give it the utmost publicity.[15] Although devious

---

[13] Donne, vol. 1, p. 293.
[14] C.O.5/177, p. 37. Declaration of Lord Howe, 7 June 1776.
[15] Ibid., pp. 33-4. Lord Howe to provincial governors, 20 June, 1777.

means were prepared to ensure the circulation of these declarations, the Americans apparently made no effort to suppress them and they became generally known almost at once. The Congress even took the trouble to publish the declaration, believing it would be more damaging than helpful to the British cause, since it showed that Lord Howe's powers were inadequate for the conclusion of a satisfactory reconciliation.[16]

On July 14 the Howe brothers took another and more specific step toward negotiation. They issued a joint declaration and sent a copy to Washington by flag of truce.[17] The officer who carried it was, however, detained in the harbour by the Americans while Washington consulted with his officers about the propriety of receiving the letter, since it was addressed to 'George Washington, Esq. etc. etc.'[18] It was their unanimous opinion that Washington could not receive a letter unless sent to him in his official capacity; so Colonels Reed and Knox met the British officer and said they knew no such person in the army as the gentleman whose name was on the envelope.

The Howes at first felt inclined to let the matter rest, but a few days later changed their minds and tried another method of approach.[19] Sir William's adjutant-general, Lt. Col. Patterson, was despatched with directions to see Washington personally, if possible; and he succeeded in doing so.[20] He began by endeavouring to explain away the miscarriage that had attended the attempt to deliver the letter of the 14th, saying that the 'etc. etc.' was intended to cover all of Washington's titles. Washington observed it might as well mean

[16] Ibid., pp. 43-6. Howe and Howe to Germain, 11 August 1776.
[17] Ibid.
[18] Johnston, *Campaign of 1776*, pp. 97-9.
[19] C.O.5/177, pp. 43-6.
[20] Johnston, *Campaign of 1776*, pp. 97-9.

anything. Patterson then informed Washington of
the Howes' authority as commissioners, of their great
desire for an accommodation, and said he hoped that
his visit might be considered a preliminary to further
negotiations. Washington professed himself lacking
in authority in such matters, but observed that Lord
Howe seemed to have nothing to offer but pardon,
which the Americans did not need. As Patterson
turned to go, he asked Washington if he had any message for the Howes. Washington replied that he had
nothing but his compliments.[21] Thus ended the first
direct attempt to use the powers of the commission.
It seems very unlikely that the effort occasioned any
serious delay in military operations. The delay that
occurred is to be explained by the causes mentioned
in the previous chapter.

It is uncertain just how much the Howes hoped to
secure from their attempt to approach Washington.
Possibly they expected no great success until military
events should have demonstrated to the Americans the
advantages of negotiation. Soon after the battle of
Long Island a much more persistent endeavour was
made to get in touch with the American authorities,
and to discover, if possible, whether anything could be
done to settle the dispute by conciliation. Even before
reaching New York, Lord Howe had planned a more
personal approach to the task than that embodied in
his general proclamation. He had written a letter to
Franklin, with whom he had become acquainted during the latter's stay in England and with whom he had
then discussed the difficulties between the colonies and
the mother country.[22] The letter contained no specific
proposals, but only an expression of Lord Howe's hope

21 Ibid.
22 Parton, *Life and Times of Benjamin Franklin*, vol. 2, p. 137.

that he might prove of service in promoting the achievement of lasting peace. One sentence from it seems to indicate that the Admiral took a mercantilist view of the causes of the conflict.

But, if the deep-rooted prejudices of America, and the necessity of preventing her trade from passing into foreign channels, must keep us still a divided people, I shall, from every private as well as public motive, most heartily lament that this is not the moment wherein those great objects of my ambition are to be attained.

One other feature of the letter ought to be noticed: it was not the letter of a confident man. Lord Howe apparently expected his efforts to fail. This is an early manifestation of the tone of pessimism which permeated, with increasing insistence, the activity of the Howe brothers in America. It is not to be confused with a desire not to succeed; but this inclination to look upon the dark side of things may very well, at crucial moments, have tipped the balance between a bold grasping of opportunity and a failure to do so. The battle of Long Island seemed to provide an opportunity for the more direct approach to conciliation which Lord Howe had in mind. The American cause had been staggered by the military defeat it had suffered. The faint-hearted were in a mood to accept the chance of an easy retreat from the dangers of continued resistance. The fortune of battle had given the Howes the exact agent they sought for the opening of negotiations. Among the American officers captured on Long Island was Major-General Sullivan. In the eighteenth century, capture, to an officer of high rank, meant the obligatory acceptance of enemy hospitality rather than incarceration. Between captor and captive, under such circumstances, there was frequently a good deal of social intercourse, so that it was only natural that Lord Howe should get into conversation with General Sullivan and that their talk should turn upon the issues of the conflict.

From this conversation Lord Howe learned certain things which led to his next move as commissioner.[23] Sullivan informed him that the American leaders understood the commissioners were restricted to the granting of pardons and the declaring of peace and lacked authority to discuss grievances. Lord Howe replied that the commissioners would be glad to discuss means for removing sources of dispute, and stated, somewhat ambiguously, that 'the redress of grievances might be the happy consequence.' Sullivan appears to have concluded from this statement that the Howes possessed greater powers than the Americans had at first believed. He thereupon offered to go to Philadelphia and correct the mistaken impression there. This he was allowed to do.

Sullivan succeeded in persuading Congress to take steps to discover just what powers the Howes possessed. A resolution was passed September 5 providing for the sending of a committee to discover whether Lord Howe had any power to treat with persons representing the Congress and, if so, what proposals he had to make for negotiations. The resolution stipulated specifically that Congress could not consent to its members treating with Lord Howe in their private capacity. The negotiation, if it were to take place at all, must be with the Revolution as an organization.[24]

Sullivan returned to British headquarters on September 9 and brought news of the approaching arrival of the delegation from Congress. Lord Howe was dis-

---

23 C.O.5/177, pp. 75-9. Lord Howe-Germain, 20 September 1776.
24 Ibid., p. 81. Lord Howe sent Germain a copy of the resolution of Congress.

appointed to discover they were not coming with power to treat, but only for the purpose of securing information about the extent of his own authority and intentions. Nevertheless, after a consultation with his brother, he decided it was best to receive them.[25] The Howes thought it important to dispel the idea that their powers were limited to granting pardons after unconditional surrender, since the continuance of such an impression would only make the Americans desperate and destroy any possibility of negotiation.

The evening of the same day brought a communication from the committee, which was composed of Franklin, John Adams, and Rutledge, saying they were ready to meet Lord Howe at any appointed place on the eleventh. The interview was held on Staten Island, opposite the town of Amboy. Sir William was that day occupied with military duties, so that the Admiral met the commissioners alone.

Lord Howe came immediately to the point and explained his powers and what he hoped to accomplish. The information he gave his interrogators is fully described in his own account of the conference.

I acquainted them that the King's desire to restore the public tranquillity and to render his American subjects happy in a permanent union with Great Britain had induced him to constitute commissioners upon the spot, to remove the restrictions upon trade and intercourse, to dispense the royal clemency to those who had been hurried away from their allegiance, to receive representations of grievances, and to discuss the means whereby that mutual confidence and just relation which ought to subsist between the colonies and the parent state, might be restored and preserved. I also gave them to understand that His Majesty was graciously disposed to a revision of such of his royal instructions as might have laid too much re-

25 Ibid., pp. 75-9. Lord Howe-Germain, 20 September 1776.

straint upon their legislation, and to concur in a reversal of any of the plantation laws by which the colonists might be aggrieved; that the commissioners were earnest on their part to prevent the further effusion of blood, and to proceed upon all such measures as might expedite the accomplishment of the purposes of their commission; that they were willing to confer with any of His Majesty's subjects, and to treat with delegates of the colonies, legally chosen, upon all matters relating to grievances and regulations; but that, for very obvious reasons, we could not enter into any treaty with their Congress, and much less proceed in any conference of negociation upon the inadmissible ground of independency; a pretension which the commissioners had not, nor was it possible they ever should have, authority to acknowledge.[26]

This did not contain much promise for the representatives of Congress. Any negotiation with the colonies as a whole, or on any terms other than an unrestricted return to the British allegiance, was clearly beyond the power of the Howes. One cannot but feel that Lord Howe painted a rather sanguine picture of what he would be able to do towards redressing American grievances. He had no real power. Everything that he might agree upon with the Americans required reference back to England before it had any more validity than a suggestion. One wonders if Lord Howe really expected, under existing conditions, to be able to secure substantial concessions from his government. Perhaps the most striking thing about his discourse to the committee of Congress was what he left out. He made no mention of the fact that his instructions stated explicitly that Great Britain, before restoring civil government to the colonies, would demand guarantees against a recurrence of revolutionary violence, and that, in the cases of Rhode Island and

26 C.O.5/177, pp. 75-9. Lord Howe-Germain, 20 September 1776.

Connecticut, those guarantees must take the shape of fundamental alterations of their charters.

Even without this knowledge, the Congressional commissioners gave Lord Howe no reason to hope for success from his efforts.[27] They stated very positively that the colonies would not agree to any peace that did not recognize their independence, and argued that Great Britain would derive more benefit from a friendly America, with whom she might ally herself, than from a group of dependent and dissatisfied colonies. Such talk was obviously of no use in forwarding the purpose Lord Howe had in mind; so the conference quickly came to an end.

After this demonstration of the futility of attempting to negotiate with Congress, the Howes felt their only chance of success lay in a direct appeal to the people. On September 19 they issued a proclamation warning the Americans against the misfortunes that the stubbornness of their representatives would bring down upon their heads.

The King being most graciously disposed to direct a revision of such of his royal instructions as may be construed to lay an improper restraint upon the freedom of legislation in any of his colonies, and to concur in the revisal of all acts by which his subjects may think themselves aggrieved, it is recommended to the inhabitants at large, to reflect seriously upon their present conditions, and expectations, and to judge for themselves whether it be more consistent with their honour and happiness to offer up their lives as a sacrifice to the unjust and precarious cause in which they are engaged, as to return to their allegiance, accept the blessings of peace, and to be secured in a free enjoyment of their liberty and properties, upon the true principles of the constitution.[28]

[27] C.O.5/177, pp. 75-9. Lord-Germain, 20 September 1776.
[28] The Shelburne Papers in the Wm. L. Clements Library. A Declaration signed by both the Howes, Sept. 19, 1776.

This declaration offered nothing more than was offered to the committee of Congress. There was the same assurance of the good intentions of the British government, expressed as favourably as the terms of the commission would permit, but necessarily lacking any promise of specific concessions. The emphasis upon the consequences of continued resistance is the only difference, and that merely one of degree.

The Howes' commission failed to make any impression upon the revolutionary authorities. Did it have any more success with the rank and file of the army or with the general run of the inhabitants? Some of the Howes' critics, who were anxious to prove that the brothers had not taken full advantage of their opportunities, tried to adduce evidence to show that the American determination to resist was seriously shaken by the prospect of conciliatory offers from the government. But the evidence was mostly hearsay, such as, 'A man who was in the rebel orderly room told me that he saw General Read, the rebel adjutant-general, come into the room and said this report had like to have disbanded their army.'[29] We need clearer evidence than this to establish the effectiveness of the proclamation. Everywhere the authorities showed themselves hostile to the offer. Congress felt so confident that the Americans would find nothing in the proposal to attract them that it hastened to publish Lord Howe's declaration to Franklin's committee. It thought that the only danger lay in an ignorant supposition that the commissioners might have greater powers than they actually had.

From the very beginning the Howes were disappointed in the results of their efforts.[30] Even in mo-

---

[29] Dom. State Papers, Geo. III, 18. The Howe Inquiry.
[30] C.O.5/177, pp. 43-6. Howe and Howe to Germain, 11 August 1776.

ments when the colonists seemed most likely to be persuaded by the military situation into accepting offers of conciliation, and when in the logic of events they ought to have been, their compliance fell short of expectations. The declaration of September 19 appeared at what should have been a propitious moment, immediately after the capture of New York. Yet the Howes reported pessimistically to Germain:

> As this declaration is published while the rebel army, as well as the province, is labouring under disappointment and many sufferings occasioned by the rapid and successful progress of His Majesty's forces, we are not without hopes of its producing some good, although we do not yet perceive any symptom of that disposition to allegiance, and submission to legal government, which would justify us in expecting to see the public tranquillity soon restored.[31]

So little evidence was there then, and for many weeks thereafter, of any disposition to accept the offers of the commissioners, that the Howes took no further step towards offering terms until the last day of November. They then issued a proclamation which, after the usual exhortation, offered absolute pardon to all who, within sixty days, subscribed to the declaration of allegiance.[32] Again the military situation seemed favourable to any attractive offer, and the proffered pardon was as extensive as it could well be, since it was extended to everyone. The Howes wrote to Germain that they trusted the King would approve of this lenity, since their primary purpose was to restore peace and tranquillity. But the note of pessimism was still present. Certain inhabitants of New York had petitioned that the King's peace be restored to the city.[33] That measure the brothers felt unable to adopt:

[31] C.O.5/177, pp. 75-9. Howe and Howe to Germain, 11 August 1776.
[32] Ibid., p. 97. Proclamation of the Howes, 30 November 1776.
[33] Ibid., pp. 89-92. Howe and Howe to Germain, 30 November 1776.

When we consider how small though important a part of this extensive province is yet professedly in allegiance, we cannot with any degree of propriety declare the whole at peace ; and to open the trade of this province partially, even could any trade now be carried on, would, in the present situation of affairs, be productive of no good effect, and might introduce such abuses as would defeat the intention of the prohibitory act.

Had they done otherwise the government would almost certainly have disapproved. Even the first pardon offer failed to meet the approval of Germain, who wrote :

It is poor encouragement for the friends of Government . . . to see their oppressors without distinction put upon the same footing with themselves, . . . This sentimental manner of making war will, I fear, not have the desired effect.[34]

Germain approved in general, however, the first steps taken by the commissioners.[35]

Although the story of the further efforts of the Howes to utilize the powers of their commission belongs, in point of time, to later chapters, it will perhaps make the picture clearer if it is inserted here. The first results of the offer of pardon on November 30 aroused sanguine hopes, so much so that the brothers thought for a moment that almost the whole of New Jersey had submitted or would do so shortly.[36] Many people of importance in Pennsylvania had also come in. Yet, in spite of the promising beginning, they did not feel convinced that the proclamation would lead to the general submission for which some friends of government had hoped. But it certainly produced

[34] *H.M.C. Various Collections*, vol. 6, p. 128. *Mss. of Miss Eyre Matcham*, Germain-Wm. Knox, 31 December 1776.
[35] C.O.5/177, pp. 63-6. Germain-Lord Howe, 7 October 1776.
[36] Ibid., pp. 115-17. Howe and Howe to Germain, 22 December 1776.

some effect, for the revolutionary authorities showed more signs of worry about the influence of the British offers at this time than at any other. Washington issued a counterblast, in the form of a proclamation, calling upon all who had received pardons from the British to repair immediately to American headquarters to surrender them and to take an oath of allegiance to the American cause, or else to withdraw themselves and their families within the British lines.[37]

If Washington felt disturbed by the numbers who accepted pardon, Germain showed equal concern over the effect of the offer. He was eager that all those who had not submitted within the allotted sixty days should be visited with the punishment which, in his eyes, their crimes merited and which ought to be inflicted upon them as an example for the future.[38] Before long he became impatient to receive the returns of those who had made their submission.[39] Germain seemed to envisage the task of reconciliation, not as a gesture and a persuasion which might change the attitude of the whole American people towards the British government, but as an offer to individuals which was to whittle away the support of the revolutionary cause. He did not look to see the revolutionary government, as a whole, come to terms with Great Britain, but to see its supporters flock in as individuals.

The Howes, on the other hand, although fully aware that their powers only permitted the dispensation of royal grace to individuals, apparently thought of its effect as something which should prepare the way for coming to terms with the revolutionary movement as a whole. It must be noticed, however, that they never

[37] C.O.5/177, pp. 135-8.
[38] Ibid., pp. 109-13. Germain to Howe and Howe, 14 January 1777.
[39] Ibid., pp. 123-4. Same to same, 3 March 1777.

showed any very great confidence in the ability of themselves or their commission to accomplish this object.
Such an outcome was rather at variance with the idea
which, more than any other, seemed to dominate their
strategy, the concept of a slow, methodical reconquest
of one area after another. Both in the strategy of
negotiation and in the strategy of war they seem to
have vacillated between sweeping measures, designed
to accomplish their objective by jarring loose the key-
stone of the arch of revolution, and measures based
upon the supposition that the revolution must be
destroyed stone by stone.

By the end of March the Howes spoke with even less
optimism about the results of the offer of pardon.[40]
They reported that not a single major figure of the
revolutionary party had availed himself of it, although
many of inferior rank had done so. The conclusion
was inescapable that the continued resistance of the
leaders proceeded from other causes than despair of
pardon for acts already committed. The commissioners felt concerned at Germain's indication that they
were to withhold the general pardon after the sixty
days were up, since a case might arise in which the
withholding it would prevent a speedy termination of
the war. The Secretary was, however, still willing
that every appearance of leniency should be retained,
and authorized the Howes to use the general pardon
if they thought necessary, although he warned them
against being too soft hearted.[41]

During these winter months the Howes apparently
made another effort to open negotiations with the
Americans, although the history of it is a little obscure.
Charles Lee, who was then a prisoner with the British

40 Ibid., pp. 147-8. Howe and Howe to Germain, 25 March 1777.
41 Ibid., pp. 151-6. Germain to Howe and Howe, 18 May 1777.

army, wrote to Congress on February 9 asking that body to permit two or three of its members to visit him.[42] The Howes offered to provide safe conducts and Lee promised very salutary results from the visit, although he did not specify what they were to be. Although Washington favoured granting the request and was seconded by opinion in his army, Congress decided against it. Greene feared that the rejection of the proposal would make Congress appear unnecessarily obstinate and determined upon securing the full measure of its demands, even at the cost of ruining the people. He argued that, had not Franklin and his committee met the Howes the preceding year, the public would have always believed a safe accommodation might have been secured.[43] But the Congressional point of view, as expressed by Adams, was that the proposed interview was merely an artful stratagem of the Howes to distract and divide the Americans, to blunt the shafts of the opposition in England, and to induce foreign nations to believe that a conclusion of the struggle was imminent. Nor could he see that the former conference had done the Americans anything but harm, both in England and in France.[44]

This difference of opinion within the American ranks throws a good deal of light on the situation. Obviously there existed in the army a feeling that, if a genuine accommodation could be secured, it ought at least to be considered. Looking at the difficult, if not quite desperate, situation of the Americans, Washington and Greene failed to see sufficient prospect of ultimate victory to justify a public refusal to consider what the Howes had to offer. One cannot but won-

[42] Moore, *Treason of Charles Lee,* p. 104.
[43] Ibid., p. 105.
[44] Ibid.

der what might have been the effect had the commissioners possessed something really attractive. The
difference of opinion between Congress and the army
officers seems to show that the idea of ending the Revolution through the use of an offer of conciliation was
perhaps not so hopeless as the actual history of the
negotiations might indicate. But, in the form in
which they were finally authorized to negotiate, success was beyond the reach of the Howes until the
Americans had been so beaten that supporters of their
cause would be ready to abandon it in return for
personal pardon.

Such a limited commission was clearly not the original idea of Lord Howe, and possibly he ought not to
have accepted it. But he was eager for employment
and felt a genuine desire to be the means of ending
the Revolution in a way satisfactory to both parties.
Aware that his personal standing with the Americans
marked him as a suitable negotiator, he apparently
convinced himself that certain minor alterations in the
original form of his instructions would provide a loop-
hole for the initiation of the more extensive negotiations which he envisaged. Not infrequently men have
accepted office upon terms that did not meet their real
wishes, and have succeeded, through shrewd management and good fortune, in circumventing the limitation and accomplishing their original purpose. The
Howes appear to have had some such hope in mind.

But the obstacles to success proved too formidable.
Wishing to negotiate broadly, their only opportunity
of doing so lay in the use of one or two loopholes in
rather narrow instructions. They could not, more-
over, escape the fact that they were not allowed to
treat with the existing revolutionary authorities, and
the Americans naturally felt disinclined to disband

their government in the uncertain hope that the government in London, to which everything had to be referred for confirmation, would accept such measures as the Howes might recommend or agree to.   In placing a hope in conciliation, the Howes had in mind measures very different from those intended by Germain and the British government.   They undertook a task for whose successful accomplishment their instructions allowed them insufficient latitude.   They soon became aware of this fact and the disappointment and discouragement they felt probably rendered their commission less effective than it might have been in accomplishing the limited purpose intended by the government.   Certain it is, that the failure contributed to the growth of pessimism about British prospects which increasingly weighed upon the minds of both the Howes, and particularly affected the military judgement of Sir William.

CHAPTER X

THE CAPTURE OF NEW YORK AND THE WESTCHESTER CAMPAIGN

With the American army badly shaken by the battle of Long Island, the next step for the British was to drive it out of New York. Many people expected the advance to begin immediately, within three or four days at most.[1] They therefore felt much surprised when the days went by and no attack was made. From the American withdrawal at Brooklyn on the night of the 29th of August until September 15 the British made no evident move to molest their opponents.

The critics of the Howes naturally made capital out of this delay. Even after eliminating partisanship, this inaction presents a puzzle, especially since it was generally believed in the British camp that the American army was in great confusion both of spirit and material. It almost appears as if the British command had intended to give the enemy a chance to withdraw without fighting and without loss.

But before accepting this view we must inquire whether military reasons, or some reason of state not apparent to the casual observer, can explain the mystery. Sir William Howe insisted that the time before the landing on Manhattan Island was spent in necessary preparations for that move.[2] Circumstances justified careful preparation. The Americans were

[1] B.M.Add.Mss. 21,680, ff. 148-9. Maj. Hutcheson to Haldimand, 1 September 1776.
[2] *Howe's Narrative*, p. 5.

known to have erected fortifications upon the island which the landing force would have to overcome. Sir William Howe evidently believed that a very considerable part of the American army had not been engaged on Long Island and hence would not share the confusion and loss of morale to be expected in the troops who had participated in the engagement. It was somewhat hazardous to assume that the Americans were incapable of spirited resistance.

The very nature of the operation presented serious physical difficulties. A large river had to be crossed under fire and an attack launched against entrenched positions immediately after landing. Success could not fairly be anticipated without careful planning and meticulous attention to detail. An improvisation might have succeeded but would have been too risky, except as a means of utilizing a great but fleeting opportunity.

Was there anything in the situation to justify the risk of a hasty advance? The British were not menaced by an awkward position from which only audacity could rescue them. Excuse for haste could have been found only in the existence of a precious opportunity which would not wait for methodical preparation. It is just possible that such an opportunity existed in the material and moral confusion among the Americans after the battle of Long Island and that a prompt assault upon Manhattan Island, if successful, might have led to the collapse of their army. But we cannot be certain that this would have been the result, any more than could Sir William Howe. The only thing sure was that unprepared action entailed a serious risk for the British. If they could hope for eventual success by less daring methods, and at the time such hope

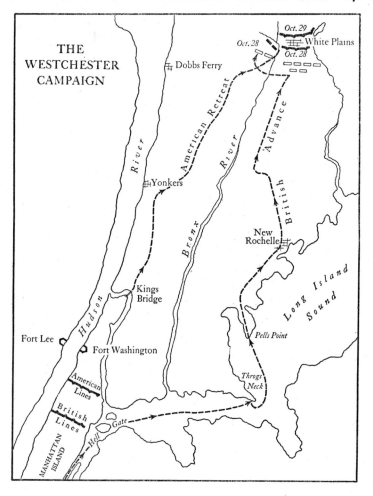

THE
WESTCHESTER
CAMPAIGN

seemed justified, the argument for caution was very
persuasive.

Did the British delay the attack upon New York
longer than necessary to prepare adequately for the
movement? One possibility is that the advance was
postponed until Lord Howe could have his interview

with the committee of Congress. It is at least a coincidence that Sullivan's trip to Philadelphia, the decision of Congress to send a committee, and the actual interview all took place during this period of inactivity. Suspicion is heightened by the fact that just at this time there was a gap of ten days between two important moves essential to the attack upon New York. Small boats had to be moved up the East River to a point opposite that chosen for attack. Part of this flotilla was sent up on the night of September 3, but the remainder was not sent until September 12 and 13.[3] Does Sullivan's trip explain the interruption of this work?

Certain facts of chronology make it seem unlikely that the preparations were interrupted in the hope they would not be needed. The first movement of boats up the East River took place the night of September 3. The resolution of Congress which authorized Franklin and his fellow committeemen to meet Lord Howe was passed on September 5. It is scarcely possible that the adoption of the plan suggested by the conversation with Sullivan, the trip of that officer to Philadelphia, the debate in Congress upon the propriety of the meeting, and the final passage of the resolution could have taken place within less than forty-eight hours. It took Sullivan four days from the time of the passage of the resolution to get back to the British lines.[4] Obviously the first movement of small boats was undertaken after the Sullivan negotiation had been begun and the interruption of this phase of the British preparations cannot be ascribed to hope that further military effort would prove unnecessary.

[3] Johnston, *Campaign of 1776*, p. 230.
[4] C.O.5/177, p. 81.

There would, in fact, have been no logic in a suspension of British preparations in order to wait and see what Sullivan accomplished, for the Howes never felt sanguine of achieving anything from the meeting with the Congressional committee. We must seek some other explanation for the interval between the first and later movements of the boats up the East River. It may be found almost certainly in purely material factors, in the relationship between the tides and the hours of darkness at that season of the year.[5]

The tide that flows in the East River is so strong that movements of boats of any kind, before the days of power, could not be carried out directly against it. Safety from bombardment compelled the British to move their small boats at night. Hence, this important phase of the work of preparation could be carried on only when the in-coming tide and the hours of darkness approximately coincided.

On September 3 the sun rose almost exactly at 5:30 and set at 6:30. By the 12th of the month there was an increase in the period of darkness of only a little over ten minutes at each end of the night, so little that, for convenience, it may be ignored. On September 3 the tide in the East River began to flow northwards at 10:30 in the evening and turned southwards at a quarter to four in the morning, thus giving over five hours of darkness in which tidal conditions were favourable for moving small boats upstream. But the

[5] The times for the tides in New York harbour were taken from the *New York Gazette* and *Weekly Mercury* for 1776 which, however, only gives high water at the Battery. Owing to the intricacies of the channel round New York, the time for the turning of the tide at any particular spot may vary considerably from that at the Battery. Hence it was necessary, through the use of the tidal currents charts of the Coast and Geodetic Survey, to work out the tidal conditions in the East River along the stretch which the boats covered. These conditions are so complex that there is a considerable variation in tidal chronology between the Manhattan shore and the Brooklyn shore up which the boats went.

lapse of as little as two days changed the situation. By the fifth the tide did not turn northward until after midnight. Since dawn began to appear before five o'clock, the time available was too short for safety, in view of the possibility of unexpected delay.

Conditions grew increasingly unfavourable during the next few days for movements on that particular tide, since the period of available darkness decreased by almost an hour every night. Further movements had to wait for the other tide which, in course of time, became favourable for a move in the early evening. An examination of the tidal tables shows that by the twelfth conditions were just barely favourable. On that night the work was resumed, and was carried through to completion on the following night. Not a day sooner was there enough darkness before the tide turned southward to enable the boats to be brought up. Even on the 12th the margin of safety was so small that only an eagerness to hasten arrangements can explain the decision not to wait a day or two longer.

Thus in the crucial matter of bringing up the small boats for the use of the landing party it seems practically certain that tidal conditions in the East River, rather than any choice of the Howes, led to the delay in attacking New York. That view is reinforced by a letter Sir William Howe wrote to Clinton on the first of September. He stated that he was about to begin preparations for taking New York and added that he would try to get some boats up the river that night if wind and tide permitted.[6] He was perfectly aware that wind and tide must be favourable before anything could be done. A year later Clinton ex-

6 The Clinton Papers, Howe-Clinton, 1 September 1776.

plained a delay in his expedition against the Highlands by the necessity of waiting until the tides were
suitable.[7]   In Howe's case the proper conjunction of
tide and darkness required exactly the delay which
British operations underwent.

While waiting for the boats to be brought up, the
British made careful preparation for the attack.   They
took possession of several small islands in the river,
after brief contests, in order to mask as long as possible
the exact direction of the real assault and to assist it
when made.[8]   The ships were moved about in the
river in order to give the appearance of threatening
various points and a battery was erected on one of
the islands near Hell Gate.   It has usually been supposed that this battery was intended to deceive the
Americans into thinking an attack was planned at
that point.   Clinton says, however, that an attack was
really intended but was abandoned because of the
strength of the American fort on the Manhattan shore
and because the pilots objected to taking the covering
ships into the dangerous currents of Hell Gate.[9]

Although preparations were begun well in advance,
it seems probable that the exact detail and first objective of the attack were not settled until shortly
before the advance took place.   Clinton says that he
advocated striking directly for Kings Bridge but that
those who wished to occupy New York carried the
day.[10]   Sir William Howe wrote Clinton on the 14th,
expressing a wish to talk over with him the idea of
landing at Kipp's Bay.[11]   The plan was evidently still

[7] *Ibid.* A memorandum by Clinton written in October 1777 about
his recent operations, to be shown only to particular friends.
[8] *The Boston History,* vol. 2, p. 137.
[9] Clinton's *Historical Detail,* p. 61.
[10] Ibid., p. 61.
[11] Clinton Papers, Howe-Clinton, 14 September 1776.

tentative. Clinton opposed landing the entire force there on the ground that the move would be too exposed, but his objections were overruled.[12]

The attack the next day was begun by embarking the troops in an inlet screened from observation from the Manhattan shore. Then, according to Clinton's note in his copy of Stedman's history, a feint was made which drew the Americans from their entrenchments and sent them scurrying to the point that appeared threatened.[13] The ships thereupon bombarded the vacated trenches and prevented the Americans from reoccupying them. Clinton, in his *Historical Detail*, however, described this valuable preliminary success of the British as a lucky accident rather than a design. As this is much the fuller account, this version must be accepted.[14] According to it, when the flotilla of small boats moved out into the river it was seen that the tide was flowing so rapidly that the boats, in crossing, would be carried above the intended landing point at Kipp's Bay. Clinton therefore ordered them to tie up alongside the transports and wait for the slack. The Americans thereupon concluded that they planned to wait for the ebb in order to land lower down at Stuyvesant Cove and, consequently, hurried away to man the entrenchments prepared at that point. When they discovered their mistake they tried to hurry back, but were prevented from taking the direct route by the fire from the ships. Before they could complete the detour, the landing had been effected. Very possibly this mischance helps explain the collapse of the morale of the American troops which proved so helpful to the British and brought forth the wrath of Wash-

---

[12] Clinton's *Historical Detail*, p. 61.
[13] Stedman, *American War*, Clinton's copy, vol. 1, p. 204.
[14] Clinton's *Historical Detail*, p. 62.

ington. The resistance was feeble and the British soon effected a complete conquest of their objective.

This brilliant start was followed by an incident from which has grown a romantic legend that has often been cited as proof of the incapacity of Sir William Howe. At the time the landing took place a considerable body of Americans were still on lower Manhattan Island, although the larger part of the army had retired to the northern end. It seems quite possible that a prompt British advance across the island, which is not over two miles in width at this point, would have cut off this group. But the British failed to advance promptly and the Americans, by marching hastily northward as closely as possible to the western shore, just managed to escape capture. Tradition has it that a Mrs. Murray, whose family name is now attached to the hill where once stood the country residence of the Murrays, saved the Americans by a subtle stratagem. This lady is said to have made use of her social graces to entertain and detain General Howe at tea. While he and Mrs. Murray exchanged compliments over the tea-cups, all action by the British army was suspended and thus the Americans escaped. It makes a plausible and attractive story.

The only difficulty is that the evidence for it is very inadequate. It is possible that Mrs. Murray did offer some form of hospitality to the British commander, but there is no proof that her hospitality prevented the capture of the Americans. The best evidence about British actions after the landing comes from Clinton.

It happened unfortunately too that much time was lost before the second embarkation landed (it being some hours after the first) ; as by our striking immediately across the Island great numbers of the enemy must have been taken prisoners; but my orders being to secure the Inclenberg, I did not think myself at liberty to attempt it before Sir William Howe joined us; and indeed I do not know but had we made such a move even then we should have cut off many of them who had not yet got over the River or to Kingbridge.[15]

This paints a picture rather different from that of the Murray tradition. Howe had expected serious resistance from the Americans and felt that the original landing party would have its hands full in occupying and retaining the Inclenberg, the commanding point of the ground near the landing place. When it had been reinforced by the second embarkation it would then be safe to consider what further moves might be attempted. He feared that boldness on the part of the original landing party might result in a reverse that would compromise the further development of the British plans. Hence the whole scheme was designed, not to cut off an enemy in full flight, but to secure, in the face of what was thought would be serious resistance, a position that would make possible the bringing over of the rest of the British army in safety.

Under those circumstances Clinton, whose force had the best chance of doing serious damage to the Americans, felt that obedience to the plans of his superior compelled him to halt after attaining his original objective. Although he later recognized that an opportunity had been lost, it is by no means certain that he was aware of it at the time. He apparently thought it would be hazardous to push ahead before the arrival of Sir William Howe. By the time Howe arrived the best of the opportunity had disappeared. In expressing a belief that even then the move should have

[15] Clinton's *Historical Detail*, p. 63.

been made, Clinton apparently had in mind only the rounding up of stragglers, not the capture of any considerable disciplined unit.

Thus the explanation of the escape of the Americans lies not in any stratagem of Mrs. Murray, but in the nature of the British plan and, back of that, in the assumptions upon which it was founded. Sir William Howe was prepared for a stubborn struggle and his whole scheme was devoted to getting his army across the river without the disaster which, in the face of real opposition, might well have resulted from any blunder or imprudence. An immediate opportunity to intercept a portion of the American army was unexpected and it is not altogether certain it was known even to Clinton, the man on the spot. By the time the carefully planned British advance had been completed and it had been discovered that the vigorous resistance expected was not to materialize, most of the opportunity for damaging the enemy by rapid movement had in all probability passed. It certainly must have appeared so to the British, for they could scarcely have believed that the enemy would offer so little resistance if he had much to lose by prompt British success. Perhaps Howe ought to have thrown a force across the island on the off chance of accomplishing something; but, in failing to do so, he did not neglect a perfectly obvious opportunity to do his opponent decisive harm.

Howe's critics have not contented themselves with pointing out lost opportunities on the day of the landing, but have condemned the entire plan of attacking Manhattan Island directly. They argue that he ought to have moved first into Westchester County and thereby have blockaded Washington and his entire army in New York. According to Clinton such a step was recommended to Howe. He himself suggested landing a force at Spuyten Duyvil. Howe, he thought, seemed inclined to adopt it, but eventually decided not to do so.[16] He surmised that the decision not to make a move into Westchester was due to the imperative need of securing New York as a base for the fleet.[17] The activity of the British army during the days after the capture of the city, which will be described shortly, tends to support Clinton's interpretation.

It is, in addition, highly questionable whether a movement into Westchester County would have brought the decisive results claimed for it by Howe's critics. An advance in that direction would have taken time and Washington could almost certainly have slipped away before the jaws of the trap snapped shut. Left with no alternative but a hurried retreat or disaster, Washington would have had neither temptation nor opportunity to offer the British the battle that their commander desired. If the campaign was to become a game of tag, the Americans, with their lighter equipment and unencumbered by the traditions of leisurely movement dominating European armies, would have escaped the British every time. Undoubtedly Howe could have forced the Americans to abandon New York immediately by landing in Westchester, but it was not his purpose to send his opponents skipping nimbly out of harm's way. He had to tempt the Americans to stand and give battle. They would not do so if it were obvious that defeat must mean annihilation. In the face of the utter improbability of being able to move his army across the west-

---

[16] Clinton's *Historical Detail*, p. 56.
[17] Stedman, *American War*, Clinton's copy, vol. 1, p. 208, Clinton's note.

ern end of Long Island Sound and across several miles of country afterwards in time to intercept the Americans, Howe's best chance for decisive victory lay in offering his opponent an apparently fair opportunity for successful resistance. He could then trust to the superior discipline and skill of the British troops to turn the contest into a decisive triumph. It might be hoped that Washington, after accepting such an offer of battle, would not be able to extricate himself without disastrous loss. The landing on Manhattan was just such a plan and probably came nearer to luring the Americans to disaster than any landing in Westchester County could have done.

From September 15 until October 12 the British remained in New York. No serious engagement took place except the battle of Harlem Heights, which was little more than an unusually obstinate skirmish and had no significance beyond the fact that the creditable performance of the American troops did something to restore the morale of the Revolutionary army. Washington's troops remained in their fortified position on the northern end of the island. As the Americans had a narrow front to defend, supported by prepared positions, Howe felt little temptation to repeat the experience of Bunker Hill.

Howe has been severely criticized for spending almost a month without making any further advance. There is, however, no mystery about the reasons for the delay. It was due to two causes. The first was the need for consolidating the British position in New York in order that the army might pass the winter there in safety and comfort. Clinton's comment points clearly in this direction and the character of British activity during the period supports that view. Most of the time was spent in forming redoubts across the island in order to protect the British camp.[18] Howe expressly declared that the time was spent in activity of this sort, and also in getting possession of Paulus Hook across the river in New Jersey, a post necessary to make the harbour safe for the shipping.[19] Work of this sort takes time, especially when the army concerned has but recently disembarked after a long sea voyage. The second reason was that some time was spent in making inquiries about the nature of the country in which operations would take place after the enemy had been manoeuvred out of his position at King's Bridge.[20]

But these reasons, genuine though they were, do not quite explain the extent of the delay. Although it was certainly highly important not to leave the British base at New York inadequately protected while the main army was campaigning elsewhere, it is difficult to believe that a move could not have been made safely before October 12, had a fair opportunity for achieving something decisive presented itself. A third reason prompted Sir William Howe to delay. He had come to the conclusion that nothing decisive could be accomplished during the limited amount of favourable campaigning weather that remained.[21] Ten days after the capture of New York he wrote to Germain that he looked upon further progress in the campaign as very precarious and that no dependence could be placed upon Carleton's approach from Canada. Hence he believed he ought to take no risks. 'I have not the smallest prospect of finishing the contest this campaign, nor until the rebels see preparations

---

18 Wilkin, *Some British Soldiers in America*, p. 187, letter of G. Harris.
19 *Howe's Narrative*, pp. 5-6.
20 Ibid., p. 6.
21 Ibid.

in the spring that may preclude all thoughts of further resistance.'[22] Furthermore, he had not found the disposition of the inhabitants in the country so far traversed nearly so friendly as he had been led to expect.[23] All in all, he saw no immediate prospect of decisive military or diplomatic success.

Howe's despatches for this period merit close attention. He had led his army to victory on Long Island and had captured New York City in easy fashion. Yet he felt discouraged. He concluded that there was little hope of further important progress that year. If that view was correct, there was logic in his decision not to risk anything for the sake of small and uncertain advantages.

But why did Howe feel discouraged? Success had attended all his military efforts. Victory had not brought, however, the more extensive results which he had expected. He had hoped that a few rapid blows would wreck the morale and organization of the American army and possibly lead to its disintegration. Or, it would be more accurate to say, as he looked over events in retrospect he convinced himself that such had been his expectation. A careful reading of the despatches and a close examination of the details of British operations will show that, in truth, Howe never felt really convinced that decisive success was within reach. Logic told him it was, but something more deeply embedded in his mind than logic told him it was not. We can see that, even when making plans on the assumption that rapid military triumph would cripple the entire revolution, he felt inwardly fully as much inclined to the belief that the revolu-

<hr>

[22] *H.M.C. Mss. of Mrs. Stopford-Sackville*, vol. 2, p. 41, Howe-Germain, 25 September 1776.
[23] *Howe's Narrative*, p. 5.

tion, if conquered at all, must be reduced in a deliberate, piecemeal fashion, one region after another, and only as many regions in a single campaign as could be secured and held without serious risk. The second idea was logically inconsistent with the first, and Howe's temperamental inclination to accept it certainly rendered the carrying out of his ostensible plan less vigorous and effective than would have been the case had he felt complete confidence in it. Half convinced, from the very beginning, that the seemingly logical results of the plans he adopted would not actually materialize, he refused, when his fears were in some measure realized, to see in further rapid campaigning any prospect of results more gratifying than those which had already fallen so far short of expectations. Believing as he did, he had a certain logic in his refusal to run risks for the sake of advantages which his recent experience convinced him would not prove decisive.

In spite of this frame of mind, Howe had considered briefly the possibility of a prompt advance. He wrote to Clinton on September 25:

I rather think they [the Americans] are making a movement to the eastward for the security of their left flank with perhaps a large detachment, but if it should prove to be from intelligence of Genl. Burgoyne's approaching Albany it may occasion our moving without waiting for our expected reinforcements.[24]

As no evidence appeared to confirm his suspicion, Sir William decided to wait until every preparation was complete. Even the formation of plans took time. Clinton wrote, 'It took us some time to determine the means of doing it [dislodging the Americans from their position] by a move to the continent.'[25] One

[24] Clinton Papers, Howe-Clinton, 25 September 1776.
[25] Clinton's *Historical Detail*, p. 64.

plan proposed by Clinton was dropped because Lord Howe said the ships could not lie at the point chosen for a landing. Lord Howe's own scheme was abandoned because it required a landing within three miles of the American force, while the ships must lie three-quarters of a mile offshore and the army could only land at certain tides. The plan finally adopted, that of landing at Frog's or Throg's Neck, originated with Sir William Erskine.[26]

The idea of the manoeuvre, as described by Howe to Germain, was simple :

> The very strong positions the enemy had taken on the island and fortified with incredible labour, determined me to get on their principal communication with Connecticut, with a view to forcing them to quit the strongholds in the neighborhood of King's Bridge, and, if possible, to bring them to action.[27]

It is worth notice that the principal purpose of the move was to compel the Americans to retreat from their fortified positions. To bring them to battle was desirable, but secondary, and it appears not to have occurred to Howe that there was any possibility of moving rapidly enough to pin his opponent between the army in the field and the garrison in New York.

The British advance took the Americans by surprise. Only the day before, Greene had written that their army was so well fortified and so thoroughly out of reach of the British ships that they had nothing more to fear that season.[28] This confident belief that they would be free from molestation could not have existed had the Americans thought that a move into Westchester by the British would place them in dan-

---

26 Ibid., p. 65.
27 C.O.5/93, pp. 589-604. Howe-Germain, 30 November 1776.
28 E. F. de Lancey, *The Capture of Mt. Washington the Result of Treason*, p. 13.

ger of immediate disaster. Greene seems to have felt that any move Sir William Howe might make would be so easy to parry that the British commander would not regard it worth while to attempt anything.

On the night of October 11 the British troops embarked in small boats and moved forward through the dangerous channel of Hell Gate, where the expedition ran into fog. Lord Howe, with magnificent determination, persisted in going ahead and the difficulties of navigation were surmounted without loss.[29] The decision to land on Throg's Neck led to severe criticism of the British command, for it caused a serious delay in the progress of operations. The peninsula was joined to the mainland by a narrow causeway. The Americans held the landward end and could not have been driven off without great loss. Consequently, it was decided to re-embark and move eastward to Pell's Point, near New Rochelle. According to Clinton, the Hessians landed a little later with perfect safety at a place called Mill's Creek, which had originally been suggested to Sir William Howe but which had been rejected by the Admiral because the ships could not lie there.[30] The British misinformation that occasioned this delay excited wonder at the time and it is difficult to believe that someone was not seriously at fault.[31]

But this error has probably provoked more attention than it deserves. It was important only if the resulting delay prevented the cutting off of Washington's retreat. There is no evidence that Howe ever intended, or actually had a chance, to intercept Washington. Although the British need only have

[29] Clinton's *Historical Detail*, p. 65.
[30] Stedman, *American War*, Clinton's copy, vol. 1, p. 212, Clinton's notes.
[31] Johnston, *Campaign of 1776*, footnote to p. 265, letter of Wm. Duer.

marched a dozen miles to block the American retirement, the Americans could escape the net by a much shorter march. So apparent was this advantage that Howe seems not to have had the slightest expectation of capturing his opponent.

In that light we cannot attach much importance to Howe's much criticized wait of five days for bringing up provisions and reorganizing his troops.[32] His hope for victory lay in the possibility of bringing Washington to action during a campaign of manoeuvre whose limits of time and space could not be accurately foreseen. To make such a plan possible the army had to be carefully provisioned and prepared, else lack of supplies might bring the campaign to a halt when in sight of success. No more was expected of the move to New Rochelle than the dislodging of Washington from his entrenched camp. Howe did not expect to catch his opponent in a trap, but merely to deprive him of the advantage of his fortifications and force him to carry on the contest in the open field where British superiority in organization and discipline might possibly offer an opportunity for decisive victory.

The details of the British advance through Westchester do not require more than a glance at their general character. The only action of consequence was a sharp skirmish at Pell's Point in which a small American force maintained itself for several hours against odds. William Abbatt, who has made a thorough study of this contest, believes that the American resistance so impressed Howe that he waited for reinforcements before making a further advance.[33] Howe

<hr/>

[32] Clinton, in his *Historical Detail*, p. 66, mentions the lack of supplies that prevented an advance, as if there was no question about the adequacy of the excuse for delay.

[33] Wm. Abbatt, *The Battle of Pell's Point, Pelham*, p. 21.

attributed his delay in part to bad weather.[34] But
the daily chronicle of army movements and the record
of general orders indicate more clearly than anything
else the reason for the British deliberation. Emphasis
was constantly placed on adequate and systematic supply.[35] There was no indication of a definite strategic
move, according to the Napoleonic style, that must
be completed, within a certain period of time and for
the execution of which sacrifices must be made. There
was no bending of the general situation to the commander's will. Howe manoeuvred like any typical
eighteenth-century general, looking for his opportunity in small alterations of the situation from day to
day, especially in any mistake his opponent might
make. His aim was not so much to create his opportunity, as a Napoleon would have done, but to be
prepared to seize any that fortune might drop at his
feet. With a plan like his he must obviously have
his army and its supplies well in hand at all times.
Delay for that purpose was no sin, but a virtue. It
is not suggested that this plan was the best possible,
but in fairness to Sir William Howe it must be recognized that he manoeuvred pretty much as nine out of
ten eighteenth-century generals would have manoeuvred and that his deliberation was perfectly consistent with his plans.

The most hotly disputed point of the Westchester
campaign concerns its climax at White Plains. Washington, as soon as the British movements were known,
had seen the necessity of immediate retreat. He left
Manhattan Island with his entire army, except for two
thousand men left to garrison Fort Washington.
Washington chose a position near White Plains to

---

[34] C.O.5/93, pp. 589-604. Howe-Germain, 30 November 1776.
[35] *Kemble Papers*, vol. 1, pp. 392-399.

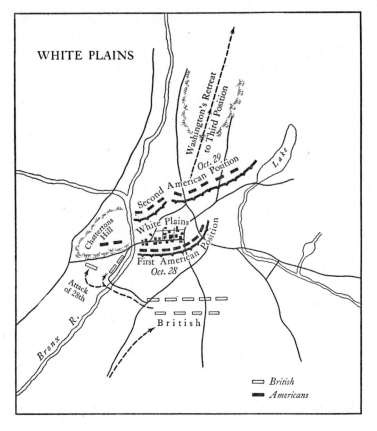

meet the attack of Howe, who possessed a slight advantage in numbers. The British commander was
ready on the 28th of October to begin his assault.
The American position was strong, on a hill, covered
on its right by a stream and on its left by what is described variously as a lake or a marsh. As a preliminary to the main attack, Howe sent the Hessians to
carry an American advanced position on the west of
the Bronx River and thus on the British left. They
succeeded, but only after overcoming an opposition so
obstinate that the first attempt was repulsed. Howe

was apparently so impressed by the strength of the
American position that he postponed further operations for two days until he could bring up reinforcements from New York. As Washington was already
in position, and made his situation a little stronger
by a short withdrawal the night after the affair of the
28th, little was to be gained by attempting to *brusquer
l'affaire*.

Now follows the mystery. The attack, for which
every preparation had been made, was first postponed
and then abandoned. Critics have charged Howe
with inexcusable neglect of a brilliant opportunity to
strike a decisive blow, with a refusal to seize the very
chance his campaign was designed to discover. It is
one of the points most frequently referred to by those
who picture Howe either as grossly incompetent or
lacking in real desire to win.

What is the explanation of his course? We must
first inquire what was to be gained by an assault on
the American position. It was not the key to the
whole district; it did not stand in the way of any move
imperatively necessary for the British to make. It
had, indeed, no great significance aside from the fact
that the American army happened to be at that point.
Was it not the case, however, that a successful assault
would have done irreparable damage to the Americans
because of the impossibility of easy retreat? Stedman
thought that a British attack on the American centre
would have been disastrous to the defenders of the
position. Closer examination of his criticism, however, shows that he did not suggest that the whole
American army would have been destroyed, but only
that the right wing would have been cut off.[36]   Clinton

[36] Stedman, *American War,* vol. 1, p. 213.

doubted even this, contending that there were fords by which it could have got away.[37]

Howe argued that an assault offered no prospect of inflicting decisive damage on the enemy.

> If, however, the assault had been made and the lines carried, the enemy would have got off without much loss, and no way had we, that I could ever learn, of cutting off their retreat by the Croton Bridge. . . The ground in their rear was such as they could wish for securing their retreat, which indeed seemed to be their principal object. . . If I could, by a manoeuvre, remove an enemy from a very advantageous position, without hazarding the consequences of an attack, where the point to be carried was not adequate to the loss of men to be expected from the enterprise, I should certainly adopt that more cautionary conduct, in the hopes of meeting my adversary on more equal terms.[38]

Howe's belief that the Americans intended to retreat in the face of any serious threat receives some support from the fact that, after the first action on October 28, they did withdraw their lines somewhat, and three days later withdrew completely to the north of the Bronx River.

Clinton gives an account of the decisions of the British command that tends, on the whole, to corroborate Howe's explanation.[39] He thought an immediate attack on the American position, before it had been reconnoitred, unwise. He was sent, with part of the army, to make a reconnaissance on the 27th. As a result of his observations he advised against a direct attack and felt considerably surprised when Howe finally decided to ignore his advice and

[37] Ibid., p. 213, Clinton's note in Clinton's copy.
[38] *Howe's Narrative*, p. 7.
[39] Clinton's *Historical Detail*, pp. 67-9.

make a frontal assault. Howe sent for Clinton at two in the morning of the day the attack was scheduled to take place, to ask about the prospects, in view of the fact that it was beginning to rain. Clinton said the rain made no difference, but he reminded his chief that he felt opposed to the attack on principle. The preparations, nevertheless, went ahead ; but the enemy had retreated.

Of what followed Clinton said :

It being now impossible to turn either the enemy's left or right, or to attack them in front with any effect, and ignorant as we were of the progress of the northern army ; it was deemed proper to avail ourselves of the direct communication we had thus opened with the North River, and approximate to New York Island. For though we might possibly have determined the enemy's retreat to New England by placing the King's army on the right of the Brunx, where it made a bend around their right, difficulties in getting up provisions and other supplies (as I am told) rendered a longer stay inexpedient.[40]

It appears from all this that Howe's original intention to attack was based upon his estimate of the strength of the position held by the Americans on the 28th. But before the plan could be put into operation his opponents had withdrawn about half a mile to a stronger position, much better protected on the flanks. It is not quite certain which position Clinton refers to, but it seems likely that he meant that of the 29th rather than that of November 1, for his mention of the bend of the river round the American right best fits the situation on that day. If this view is correct, the attack, for which the preparations went ahead in spite of Clinton's advice, must have been the assault planned upon the original positions of the Americans,

40 Clinton's *Historical Detail,* p. 69.

which they abandoned the night of the 28th. It is not clear whether rain threatened to postpone this attack, as it did the later one, even had Washington not withdrawn his lines, or whether Clinton, writing some time after the event, confused the attack planned for the 29th on the original American position with that planned for the 31st on the second position, which we know to have been halted by rain. As we are concerned more with the motives for British action than with its detail, the exact meaning of Clinton's reference is not vital. The main point is that his account supports *Howe's Narrative* in claiming that by the time the British were in position to attack nothing decisive could have been achieved.

Yet, even after admitting that the alteration in the situation had seriously diminished prospects of decisive success, it is not easy to accept the reasons advanced by Howe and Clinton as an entirely adequate explanation of the abandonment of the advance. Sir William, in his *Narrative,* seemed to feel that the decision demanded a lot of explaining. The Parliamentary Inquiry threw a new and mysterious light on the affair. Cornwallis testified that there were political reasons for the failure to order a general assault at White Plains.[41] The oft-criticized excuse of the rain, he said, was only an excuse for not attacking the rear guard that had been left after the main American army had retired to Northcastle. But Cornwallis refused to divulge the nature of these political reasons, although certain members tried to discover if they concerned failure on the part of the Hessian troops. Howe also mentioned the political reasons and displayed the same reluctance to explain their nature.[42]

41 Dom. State Papers, Geo. III, 18, the Howe Inquiry.
42 *Howe's Narrative*, p. 7.

For a long time this mysterious mention of political reasons puzzled historians. But information came to light in 1872 that seems to explain the matter in a way conformable to the familiar facts.[43] Alexander Graydon, a captain stationed at Fort Washington, had written in his memoirs that the British, when they captured the place, must have had perfect knowledge of the ground and fortifications.[44] The general information about the ground they might have acquired from local residents, but the more particular information about the works was probably secured from an officer in Magaw's battalion who deserted to the enemy about a week before the assault. The information that came to light in 1872 was to the effect that this officer was William Demont, Magaw's adjutant. Demont, years afterward, when in straitened circumstances, wrote a letter to an Anglican divine asking his intercession with the British government. In that letter he wrote:

On the 2d of November, 1776, I sacrificed all I was worth in the world to the service of my King and Country and joined the then Lord Percy, brought in with me the plans of Fort Washington, by which plans that fortress was taken by His Majesty's troops on the 16th instant, . . At the same time, I may with justice affirm, from my knowledge of the works, I saved the lives of many of His Majesty's subjects.[45]

Most historians, since the appearance of this letter, have identified it with the political reasons alleged by Howe and Cornwallis for the abandonment of the attack at White Plains. It showed that an easy victory awaited the British in another quarter. The refusal to specify the political reasons has been attributed to

[43] Winsor, *Narrative and Critical History*, vol. 6, p. 287.
[44] De Lancey, *The Capture of Mt. Washington the Result of Treason*, p. 19.
[45] Ibid., p. 20.

a desire to protect Demont, since the full extent of his treachery was not known.[46]

J. C. Schwab has, however, objected to this view:

Such an explanation assumed that Demont deserted, communicated with Lord Percy, reached the British army at White Plains, and that the latter broke camp and started for Dobbs Ferry — all in two days. It also overlooks the important fact that five days before Demont's desertion, General Knyphausen had been ordered by General Howe to march from New Rochelle to King's Bridge, and that he reached that place with his Hessians on the day Demont communicated with the English.[47]

The second objection may be disposed of quickly. As Howe had shifted his line of communications from New Rochelle to the Hudson, the Hessians would no longer be needed there. The other objection is more serious, but much of its force disappears upon closer examination.

It is first of all obvious that the cloak of political reasons is just the sort of screen that would have been used to cover a transaction such as that with Demont. Secondly, there is nothing impossible in the theory that Howe received the information and acted upon it in two days time. Demont's desertion took place the night of the first of November. Presumably Percy received the information he brought early on the morning of the second. As the distance to White Plains is not great, it is even possible that Howe received news of it late on the same day. It is quite improbable that it would have reached him later than the third. But even if it had been delayed until the morning of the fourth, it would not have come too late to figure in the final decision to retreat. The difficulty about sup-

[46] Ibid., p. 19, and Winsor, vol. 6, p. 287.
[47] J. C. Schwab, *The Revolutionary History of Fort Number Eight on Morris Heights, New York City*, p. 32.

posing that such news would occasion an instantaneous change of plan disappears when we recollect that Howe had already lost hope of real success and was persisting in his plan of attack only from a feeling that military good form required it. With the decision to retire half made already, Demont's information was very probably just what was needed to make the resolution final.

Howe had come into Westchester County hoping that fortune would, out of the unpredictable intricacies of manoeuvre, provide him an opportunity for an important victory. No such luck had been his lot and the situation facing him at White Plains was a strategical stalemate. Since every possibility of strategical advantage had escaped him, he was inclined to feel that he ought to do something to end the campaign with at least a tactical success. That was the spirit behind the projected attack. He thought that perhaps he ought to attempt it, since there was nothing else to do. But suddenly something else did offer, the prospect of an easy and crushing victory at Fort Washington. We cannot be certain that Howe had not decided upon retreat even before this. But if he had not, the news from Percy relieved him of any feeling that he ought to go ahead with an attack in which he felt little confidence. Demont's information, coming exactly when it did, at least reinforced Howe's decision to return to New York and led him to carry it out instantly.

The retirement from White Plains ended the Westchester campaign. Howe attacked Fort Washington on November 16 and carried it in short order. Of that action nothing need be said except that it was, by general agreement, a thoroughly competent performance. If Howe was really eager to secure the appearance of victory without doing the Americans serious damage, as his critics charge, he chose a curious way to go about it when he launched an irresistible attack against a position from which retreat was impossible. Nor did any recollection of Bunker Hill deprive him of the courage needed to attack entrenchments. Of course, a really decisive victory over Washington's army would have been preferable, but Howe could see little prospect of securing it at White Plains. 'All these actions,' he wrote to Germain, 'plainly indicating the enemy's design to avoid coming to action, I did not think the driving of their rear guard further back an object of the least consequence.'[48] If the prospect at White Plains was so uninviting, and both Clinton and Cornwallis agreed that it was, the substitution of the attack on Fort Washington certainly formed a highly satisfactory alternative.

Among general features of this campaign was an ominous increase of marauding, particularly on the part of the Hessians. Aborn, the Muster Master General, wrote to Germain that the Hessians 'were unfortunately led to believe, before they left the province of Hesse-Cassel, that they were to come to America to establish their private fortunes, and hitherto they have certainly acted upon that principle.'[49] Kemble noted in his journal how Loyalists as well as Revolutionaries felt the results of their rapacity and that the evil example thus set was too generally followed by the British troops.[50] There was, however, no suspicion that Howe was responsible for the laxity.[51] On the

---

[48] C.O.5/93, pp. 589-604. Howe-Germain, 30 November 1776.
[49] Ibid., pp. 1003-1006. Aborn-Germain, 28 October 1776.
[50] Kemble Papers, vol. 1, p. 91, Journal entry of October 3.
[51] Ibid., vol. 1, p. 99, Journal entry of November 9.

contrary, he did everything possible to prevent it. But the marauding certainly hampered his efforts to win public support for the British government.

The results of the campaign round New York had been disappointing to the British. Although the Americans had lost one position after another and had seen their early hopes crumble, they had escaped destruction. Yet it seemed to many on the British side that even this small comfort ought to have been denied them, that Howe's campaign ought to have put a final end to Washington's army. But in every case where it can be maintained that Howe had the enemy in his grasp, it is apparent that the action he took was supported by reasons well founded in the military ideas of the day. Had he been a man of genius he might have seen that final victory in the 1776 campaign was so important as to justify great risks. Although occasionally he seems to have had a momentary inkling that perhaps boldness would be the best policy, in general he acted upon the assumption that caution was necessary and that the invincibility of British arms would be more certainly demonstrated by steady progress which avoided any check than by brilliant feats which might be punctuated with occasional disasters. American opinion had proved less easy to convince than he had hoped, but he did not therefore conclude that it had been a mistake to avoid risks. Rather the conviction grew upon him that the entire country must be reconquered piecemeal, that British resources must be used with the parsimony necessary where a long and arduous struggle is in prospect.

CHAPTER XI

THE NEW JERSEY CAMPAIGN

THE capture of Fort Washington on November 16 was a major disaster for the Americans. It entailed the loss of a large garrison, with all its precious stores and equipment, and dealt a serious blow to the already shaken American morale. Most important of all, it gave the British a new freedom of action. So long as Fort Washington remained in American hands, the defense of New York City required a powerful garrison. This deduction from the field army greatly limited the scope of possible British action in New Jersey. With this threat to the security of his base out of the way, Sir William Howe could consider plans that before would have been unsafe.

He took prompt advantage of this new liberty of action. Cornwallis crossed the Hudson at Yonkers and marched upon Fort Lee, situated upon the west bank of the Hudson opposite Fort Washington. Determined not to fall into the same trap twice, the Americans abandoned Fort Lee precipitately. It was only just in time. Clinton wrote that the Americans would have been caught had Cornwallis struck at their line of retreat at New Bridge, on the Hackensack, instead of advancing directly upon Fort Lee.[1] Greene, who directed this retirement, was soon joined by Washington, who had come down from the north after crossing the Hudson. After a brief stand to protect

[1] Stedman, *American War*, Clinton's copy, vol. 1, p. 219, Clinton's note.

199

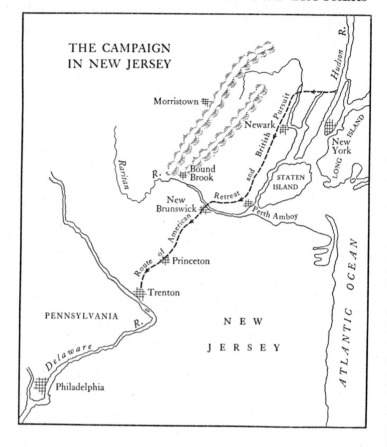

THE CAMPAIGN
IN NEW JERSEY

certain detachments seeking to join the main body,
they continued on to Newark, and from thence toward
New Brunswick.

Cornwallis followed in close pursuit as far as New
Brunswick, where the British halted for six days before resuming their advance. As a result of the British failure, or inability, to pursue more rapidly, the
Americans got safely across the Delaware. Their
escape brought severe criticism upon the British command. It was alleged that the Americans were prac-

tically cornered when orders from Howe to Cornwallis stopped the pursuit at New Brunswick.[2] Kemble, who served in the British army, described in his journal certain things that he thought ought to have been done.

After Fort Washington was taken, why not send a detachment of the army to Brunswick to cut off Mr. Washington's retreat, while Lord Cornwallis was pursuing him to Newark, etc? General Clinton's troops would have answered that purpose effectually. Why not pursue Washington from Brunswick with more spirit? — his cannon and baggage must have fallen into our hands. Provisions might have been sent to Brunswick for all these services by water, and no delay in the proceedings of the troops.[3]

Clinton records that he suggested to Howe a move similar to that recommended by Kemble.[4] The case for the critics seems strong.

But there is another side to the question. First of all, there is clear evidence that, until New Brunswick was reached, the British advance went forward as rapidly as possible. One British officer who took part in it wrote that the pursuit was pushed with the barest minimum of rest against an enemy who thought of nothing but flight.[5] By this time so many of the men had worn out their shoes, and fatigue was so general that a halt for recuperation was necessary. As the British were but a short distance behind their quarry when they reached New Brunswick, the explanation of the failure to capture Washington must be sought in what happened later.

Cornwallis, who commanded the advance, testified very fully before the Parliamentary Inquiry about the

2 *Observations upon a Pamphlet, etc.,* p. 64.
3 *Kemble Papers,* vol. 1, pp. 104-105.
4 Clinton's *Historical Detail,* p. 72.
5 Wilkin, *Some British Soliers in America,* pp. 217-22. Letter from Lieutenant W. Hale, 19 December 1776.

reasons for the halt at New Brunswick. He was asked if it would have been prudent to push the pursuit beyond New Brunswick immediately. He answered:

I could not have pursued the enemy from Brunswick with any prospect of material advantage, or without greatly distressing the troops under my command.[6]

When pressed for an elucidation of this last point he said:

We arrived at Brunswick the night of the first of December. We had marched that day twenty miles, through exceedingly bad roads. We subsisted only on the flour we found in the country; and as the troops had been constantly marching ever since their first entry into the Jerseys, they had no time to bake their flour; the artillery horses and the baggage horses of the army were quite tired; that sufficiently proves that we were not in a good condition to undertake a long march. The bridge over the Raritan was broken, which caused a necessary delay of one day. If the enemy could not have passed at Trenton, they might have marched down the east side of the Delaware. What I have said, I believe, is sufficient to prove that we could not reap any considerable advantage from such a pursuit.[7]

He admitted that the troops would have been ready to move before the 6th, when the advance was resumed, but reiterated that there was then no object in haste. It might even have proved dangerous.

We wanted reinforcement, in order to leave troops for the communication between Brunswick and Amboy. It was likewise necessary to pay some attention to a considerable body of troops then passing the North River under General Lee.[8]

[6] *Observations upon a Pamphlet, etc.*, p. 65.
[7] Ibid.
[8] Ibid.

Cornwallis also maintained that he had too few troops with him for a headlong advance.

I remember Col. Griffin, an Adjutant General of the Rebel Army, met me on the march, and I was unwilling he should see the troops, as they were so few.[9]

It seems clear that the British troops were considerably fatigued by the speed of the advance and that its immediate resumption would have occasioned at least some loss of good order and efficiency. It must also be remembered that the pursuit was a straight stern chase, and that another day or two, or even more, would not necessarily have brought it to an end. If Washington were pressed too closely to find time for crossing the Delaware, he might easily, with his small force, have turned up or down the east bank of the river and so have prolonged the chase. The Americans were retiring into their own country; the British were moving farther and farther away from their base of supplies. It is at least an open question whether a relentless pursuit by Cornwallis would have offered sufficiently bright prospects of success to justify its undeniable cost.

Yet the difficulties of Cornwallis do not entirely explain the course of events. It was rumoured that definite orders from Sir William Howe stopped the British at New Brunswick. Cornwallis was questioned upon the point. He answered:

I understood it to be the General's directions, that I should halt at Brunswick, but had I seen that I could have struck a material stroke, by moving forward, I certainly should have taken it upon me to have done it.[10]

Howe wrote to Germain that only the breaking of the bridge over the Raritan prevented the destruction

[9] Dom. State Papers, Geo. III, 18. The Howe Inquiry.
[10] *Observations upon a Pamphlet, etc.*, p. 66.

of the American army.[11]   But the following paragraph throws a somewhat different light on the matter.

> My first design extending no further than to get and keep possession of East Jersey, Lord Cornwallis had orders not to advance beyond Brunswick, which occasioned him to discontinue his pursuit, but finding the advantages that might be gained by pushing on to the Delaware, and the possibility of getting to Philadelphia, the communication leading to Brunswick was reinforced.[12]

Cornwallis evidently understood his orders correctly. Howe admitted that he had only a limited objective in mind when he gave his orders for the advance into New Jersey.[13]   The exciting chase to which it gave rise resulted from the unexpected discovery, by Cornwallis, that he had a chance of forcing the enemy to a decisive engagement.   When his prey escaped he returned to his original orders and stopped at New Brunswick until Howe reconsidered his first plan and decided to push on into west Jersey.

It may be urged against this view that Howe was only seeking to excuse his failure.   But the idea of stopping at New Brunswick conformed so closely to Howe's general plan of operations that there is little reason to question the accuracy of his account.   He had long before given up hope of securing decisive success in 1776.   As early as August 10 he wrote Germain that no expedition southward was intended for the winter, as he expected full employment in maintaining winter cantonments, in which he hoped to include a large part of Jersey.[14]   Nothing that happened afterward seemed to change his intention. The move into New Jersey was originally planned with

---

[11] C.O.5/94, pp. 31-6. Howe-Germain, 20 December 1776.
[12] Ibid.
[13] C.O.5/93, pp. 609-15. Howe-Germain, 30 November 1776.
[14] *H.M.C. Mss. of Mrs. Stopford-Sackville,* vol. 2, p. 37.

an eye to securing a better position for the winter and for the opening of the next campaign, rather than for the purpose of doing immediate damage to Washington's army.

With that in mind we can understand Cornwallis' halt. We can appreciate why no force was sent to Perth Amboy by water. Even had that force been sent, General Robertson was of the opinion it would have done no more than deprive Washington of a retreat towards Trenton and drive him to the mountains instead.[15] We must also remember, to understand the British caution, that Howe and Cornwallis knew that Lee was to the north of them with a considerable body of troops. Lee then enjoyed a reputation for ability and his presence on the flank of the British advance could not be ignored.

When, after the renewal of the pursuit, Cornwallis reached Trenton he discovered the Americans had already crossed the river. As they had collected all the boats for many miles above and below the town, an immediate crossing was out of the question. Consequently, any intention of pushing on to Philadelphia was abandoned and the British army prepared to go into winter quarters. Although Howe had originally intended that the area of occupation should reach only as far as New Brunswick, Cornwallis's last advance led to a change of plan that made Trenton the British outpost and sent the Hessians under Col. Rhall to hold it. The story of the disastrous results of that arrangement, of the subsequent battle of Princeton and the withdrawal of the British from western Jersey, is too well known to require retelling. We have only to ask why these things happened and how far the

[15] Dom. State Papers, Geo. III, 18. The Howe Inquiry, evidence of General Robertson.

action of Sir William Howe contributed to the result.

Cornwallis acknowledged on the witness stand that it was he who first suggested extending the British cantonments as far as Trenton.[16] Howe agreed, but with obvious reluctance. In his letter to Germain of December 20 he admitted that the chain of cantonments was rather too extensive, although he hoped that the general submission of the country and the strength of the corps at Trenton would ensure security.[17] Clinton advised against the extension on the ground that the Americans showed peculiar skill in surprising isolated posts and Howe admitted to Clinton that the step he had been prevailed upon to take presented risks.[18]

Sir William described, after his return to England, the reasons which led him to follow the advice of others.

My reason for extending to Trenton was, that a considerable number of the inhabitants came in with their arms, in obedience to a proclamation of the commissioners on the 30th of November. . . The possession of Trenton was extremely desirable; could we have preserved it we should have covered the greatest part of the country to the eastward of Princetown, including the whole county of Monmouth, where I had reason to think were many loyal inhabitants. We should also have been so near to Philadelphia that we might possibly have taken possession of it in the course of the winter; though I confess I had several reasons for doubting the expediency of that measure at that time.[19]

This explanation was confirmed by the reasons Cornwallis advanced for advising the step.[20] He thought

---

[16] *Observations upon a Pamphlet, etc.*, p. 68.
[17] C.O.5/94, pp. 59-61. Howe-Germain, 29 December 1776.
[18] Clinton's *Historical Detail*, p. 73.
[19] *Howe's Narrative*, pp. 8-9.
[20] *Observations upon a Pamphlet, etc.*, p. 68.

it worth while to protect a region where so many inhabitants were coming in to take the oath of allegiance, where so much forage and provision could be obtained, and where, in his judgement, little danger was to be apprehended.

How dangerous was it? Cornwallis said:

> I apprehended no danger, but the chance of having our quarters beat up in the winter; and the object in my opinion, towards the finishing of the war, was of greater consequence than two or three victories.[21]

This was not an unreasonable view. Trenton was separated from the Americans by a broad river, especially difficult to cross at that season of the year. The American army had been weakened by successive disasters. The troops at Trenton could protect themselves by works capable of withstanding attack long enough to make it possible to bring up assistance. It scarcely seems that the risk was out of proportion to the advantage to be secured.

Howe was condemned for placing the Hessians at Trenton since, as events demonstrated, they were the troops least suitable for the post. A purely routine reason dictated the arrangement. The position of the Hessians in the line of the army was on the left and, had it been changed at this time, it would have been considered a disgrace. The Hessians had done nothing up to that point to merit lack of confidence. In the command of a mixed force it was important to avoid the creation of ill feeling between the two elements.[22] Although Howe had some doubts, the British officers in general thought well of the Hessians.[23] The risk from their presence at Trenton scarcely

21 Ibid.
22 *Howe's Narrative*, p. 8.
23 *Observations upon a Pamphlet, etc.*, p. 68.

seemed to justify arousing friction within the army by displacing them.

All the evidence points to the conclusion that it was not the general arrangement, but the failure of certain individuals, that brought disaster at Trenton. Cornwallis laid the blame entirely at the door of the commanding officer.[24] Howe contended that both Rhall, at Trenton, and Donop, his superior, had information of the intended attack, but that Rhall failed to obey the orders sent by Howe directing him to construct redoubts.[25] Donop also said:

> If Col. Rhall had executed the orders he had delivered to him from Sir William Howe, which were to erect redoubts at the post of Trenton, that his opinion was, it would have been impossible to have forced Col. Rhall's brigade before he could have come to his assistance from Bordentown.[26]

Clinton placed the blame higher up, attributing a part of it to Grant, who commanded in that part of New Jersey. He thought Grant ought to have visited the post and seen personally that Howe's orders were executed.[27] There is thus a great deal of support for Howe's claim that this disaster at Trenton was due far more to the failure of Rhall than to any fundamental error in placing the Hessians in that exposed position.

When everything has been considered, it appears that the New Jersey campaign has been somewhat misunderstood. The British command has been criticized upon the assumption that it was the original intention to pursue and capture Washington's army and

24 *Ibid.*, p. 68.
25 *Howe's Narrative*, p. 8.
26 *Observations upon a Pamphlet, etc.*, p. 69.
27 Stedman, *American War*, Clinton's copy, vol. 1, p. 225. Clinton's note.

that the neglect of any measure that could contribute to that end constituted grave negligence. But Sir William Howe had no such intention or expectation. He expected to capture Fort Lee and to extend the area of British occupation as far as New Brunswick. The hot chase in which Cornwallis became involved resulted from the unexpected appearance of an opportunity which Cornwallis felt able to grasp at the same time that he complied with the orders from Howe. But, as he said, he could not feel justified in pushing ahead at all costs beyond New Brunswick unless he saw immediate prospect of cornering his adversary.

The failure, if such it was, to give maximum effectiveness to the pursuit was the result of a failure to anticipate the opportunity that presented itself. As Howe's orders were designed to secure the occupation of territory rather than the headlong pursuit of the opposing army, it is not surprising that the unexpected transformation of his plan resulted in hesitations that made the pursuit less persistent than it might otherwise have been.

Trenton, although a major disaster, was an occasion where, four times out of five, the fortunes of the day would have been different. Howe knew he was taking a risk in extending his posts that far and in placing the Hessians at the point of greatest danger. But the arguments in favour of both measures seemed then, by any reasonable criterion, to outweigh the hazard. According to orthodox ideas and calculations, Howe did the correct thing.

Although Trenton was for Howe a misfortune where the improbable came true, few events in the American Revolution had a more decisive influence on colonial opinion. Before that reverse the British had good reason to hope that their opponents had been so shaken by successive defeats, and particularly by their inglorious flight across New Jersey, that it would be impossible for them again to take the field with anything like the strength they had possessed in 1776.[28] It was thought that the Americans had been taught the certainty of ultimate defeat and that therefore all, except perhaps a small group of irreconcilables, would anticipate the inevitable and make an early submission.

Just how legitimate this hope was can never be known, for the defeat at Trenton destroyed its foundation. The puncturing of the bubble of British invincibility, followed as it was by the withdrawal of the British lines and the advance of the American army to Morristown, where it was potentially on the offensive, made a vast difference in public opinion on both sides. The Americans had expected a winter of constant alarm for Philadelphia. Instead, the British were to live in perpetual dread of what Washington might do to their outposts. Many witnesses testified to the change brought about in public opinion by the *éclat* of the American victory and the alteration in the relative positions that ensued. Cresswell wrote in his journal:

The news [of Trenton and Princeton] is confirmed. The minds of the people are much altered. A few days ago they had given up their cause for lost. Their late successes have turned the scale and now they are all liberty mad again. Their recruiting parties could not get a man, except he bought him from his master, no longer since than last week, and now men are coming in by companies. . . They have recovered their panic and it will not be an easy matter to throw them into that confusion again.[29]

28 *Cresswell's Journal*, p. 176. Entry for 14 December 1776.
29 Ibid., pp. 179-80. Entry of 5 January 1777.

Major Hutcheson wrote to Haldimand:

Our affairs have not so promising an aspect since the defeat of Rall's brigade at Trentown, had not that happened we should by this time have pretty near finished the war, which I believe will now cost us another campaign. I often rejoice that you are not concerned in this troublesome business.[30]

Nor did the evil effect of the disaster confine itself to buoying up the spirit of the Americans and stimulating their recruiting. It gave rise to grumbling and complaint in the British army, as evidenced by a letter from New York at that time:

This loss has given great scope to growlers of which we have many among our officers, who I think despair sooner than any class of men. The British cause in America certainly does not depend on the conduct of a Hessian colonel and the behaviour of one thousand Hessians: It is plain that there was no foul play. that might have been alarming. . . I confess I wish that a necessary point of honour in the army (I must suppose it was necessary because it was done) had not placed the Hessians on the frontier as their luggage (not to mention their unmerciful plundering and destroying) is against all sort of intelligence. Having however behaved well everywhere as fighting men (in no other sense of the word) they certainly were entitled to proper attentions: They have had those attentions, we have paid for them.[31]

The effect upon Sir William Howe, so far as can be discovered, was not so great as upon those about him. Long before Trenton he had become convinced of the inevitability of another campaign and only for a moment did he permit the pursuit across New Jersey to arouse hopes of decisive success. His letters to Ger-

[30] B.M.Add.Mss. 21,680, ff. 171-2. Major Hutcheson-Haldimand, 20 January 1777.
[31] B.M.Add.Mss. 34,413, ff. 152-5. Unsigned letter from New York, 3 January 1777.

main after Trenton show less emotion over the incident than those of anyone else.[32]   Perhaps he wished to minimize his chagrin, but it seems more likely that his relative unconcern was sincere. He had never entertained the sanguine expectations of his subordinates, and he seemed to see in Trenton little more than a forced modification of his winter cantonments. Indeed, Howe seems to have been rather blind to the psychological effect of the British defeat. He consented to occupy Trenton because of a sense of duty toward the loyal inhabitants in that district and because Cornwallis urged so strongly the advantages of doing so. He regarded its loss with something of the feeling of, 'I told you so,' and accepted it as evidence that his own belief in the need of waging the war prudently and systematically was correct.

[32] *H.M.C., Mss. of Mrs. Stopford-Sackville,* vol. 2, pp. 53-5. See also Howe-Germain (private) 20 January 1777, C.O.5/94, pp. 201-04.

CHAPTER XII

IN approaching a discussion of the British plans for 1777, we confront a topic that has produced endless controversy. The miscarriage of these plans during that year was probably the decisive event of the war. It meant the failure of the most formidable effort the British were ever able to make and, most decisive of all, it was the prelude to French intervention.

The manner in which the British plans were prepared has also served to focus attention upon this campaign. The Howes in America prepared the course of their own operations: the ministry in England mapped out the actions of Burgoyne. Although the Howes secured official approval of their plans, there were, in fact, two distinct sources of initiative behind the British schemes. This fact has occasioned very perplexing historical problems: how far were the two plans intended to co-operate? were adequate measures undertaken to ensure that co-operation? exactly what was to be accomplished? Although the preparation of measures for 1777 went on simultaneously on both sides of the Atlantic, it will present a clearer picture and be more in accord with the true nature of the facts if we treat them separately. This chapter will deal with the Howes' plans for their own campaign. The planning of the Burgoyne expedition will be dealt with later.

We have seen that when Washington was in flight across New Jersey Howe had momentary visions of advancing to Philadelphia. As the leading city of America and the capital of the revolutionary government it presented a natural objective. The government in England also desired its capture for Germain, who had received a report that Howe intended to take the city before the end of the campaign, had written Sir William in October approving his intention.[1] But events prevented the early fulfilment of that wish.

The first definite word sent by Sir William Howe to Germain on the subject of the 1777 campaign was written on 30 November 1776.[2] Howe first observed that word had come to him that the northern army under Carleton, which had been endeavouring to pass the lakes, had been unable to do so and had retired to Canada. Upon that news Sir William based an assumption fundamental to his plans for the following year: he assumed that the advance of the northern army, when renewed in the spring, would be so slow, because of the difficulties to be overcome, that it could not reach Albany before September at the earliest. In view of Carleton's experience, that seemed a thoroughly reasonable assumption.

Upon this basis Howe proposed a plan which he felt might finish the war during the course of the year.[3] To begin with, an army of ten thousand, based upon Rhode Island, was to conduct an offensive campaign in the direction of Boston and, if possible, capture the city. A small force would be left in Rhode Island which, with the help of the navy, would make raids on the Connecticut coast and thus embarrass the American defence of New England.

---

[1] *H.M.C., Stopford-Sackville Mss.,* vol. 2, p. 43. Germain-Howe, 18 October 1776.
[2] C.O.5/93, pp. 609-15. Howe-Germain, 30 November 1776.
[3] Ibid.

A second offensive army, of similar size, was to move up the Hudson to Albany and thus secure the line of the river in anticipation of the arrival of the northern army. The junction of the two armies would sever New England from the other colonies. Five thousand men would have to be left at New York for the protection of the city and its surrounding posts.

The third feature of the plan called for an army of eight thousand men to act in New Jersey. Howe intended that this army should keep Washington in check by making him fear for the safety of Philadelphia. Then, in the autumn, if the other expeditions had met with the expected success, a general advance was to be made on Philadelphia. Operations were to follow in Virginia during the early winter; South Carolina and Georgia were to be the objectives for the later months of the winter.

It is difficult to see how the Americans could have prevented the various armies reaching their destinations, although it may be open to question whether the mere completion of the moves would have ended the war. Yet it cannot be denied that the irresistible advance of such formidable armies would have made opposition to the British appear so futile that the revolutionary morale would have been taxed as never before. Absolutely necessary to Howe's plan, however, was a reinforcement of fifteen thousand men, which he hoped might be secured from Russia or Germany. He apparently had no hope that the men could be raised within Great Britain itself.[4] This reinforcement he calculated would raise his total force to thirty-five thousand effectives, with which to face the fifty thousand which the American Congress had voted for the coming campaign.

4 Ibid.

This letter of November 30, particularly the closing part, throws a good deal of light on Howe's strategical ideas. After stating that the only thing that now buoyed up the American spirits was hope of assistance from France, he prophesied that, if the danger of such assistance were counteracted, 'and the force I have mentioned sent out, it would strike such terror through the country that little resistance would be made to the progress of H. M. arms in the provinces of New England, New York, the Jersies, and Pennsylvania after the junction of the northern and southern armies.' Psychology, rather than hard fighting, was to reduce the rebellion. Washington's army figured in the plans only to the extent that it was to be kept from interfering with the main expeditions. The chief thing was to move with impressive force through the chief areas of disaffection, to interrupt communication between the main centres of rebellion, and to demonstrate to the population the hopelessness of continuing the contest. Of course, everything possible would be done to embarrass American operations, routes of supply would be cut, recruiting areas occupied, civilians driven to flight or submission, and Loyalists given an opportunity to assert themselves. But the fundamental thing was the magnitude of the demonstration, which it was thought would so discourage the Americans as to enable the Loyalists to recapture control of American affairs.

Howe's letter caused a flurry in Germain's department when it arrived on December 31. Germain replied on January 14:

When I first read your requisition of a reinforcement of 15,000 rank and file, I must own to you that I was really alarmed, because I could not see the least chance of my being able to supply you with the Hanoverians, or even with the Russians in time.[5]

But Germain soon managed to comfort himself with the calculation that by sending four thousand more Germans and a little over three thousand recruits of various sorts, Howe would still have substantially the thirty-five thousand he needed for his plan. The difference in calculation appears to have been due to the fact that Germain made almost no allowance for loss in effectives owing to sickness, wounds, and the attrition of the winter, whereas Howe allowed perhaps too much.

We may sympathize with the alarm Germain felt when he received a request asking for fifteen thousand extra troops in America by spring. It was especially startling to a minister who had hoped that the effort of the year just closed would finish the war or carry it so near to completion that the final touches could be administered easily in the spring. It is, however, always risky to assume in war that things can be calculated to such a nicety. In normal conflicts a government must expect to replace at least a third of its force annually. Germain had received adequate warning from Howe that another campaign would be required; and if he calculated that it could be prosecuted successfully with less than the usual reinforcement, it was his own estimate and he must assume responsibility for it.

Attention should be called to a fundamental difference between the theories of Howe and those of Germain. Howe's plans for subduing the revolution required a constant expansion of British military effort until it extended throughout all the colonies. The nearer he approached the goal of success, the more

[5] C.O.5/94, pp. 1-12. Germain-Howe, 14 January 1777.

troops he would require to hold what he had won and to support the effort needed to win the remainder.[6] Germain seems not to have allowed for the task of maintaining the ground already won, or to have assumed that the decisiveness of the British victory would frighten the colonists out of any thought of further resistance. Thus large reinforcements seemed unnecessary to him, for he thought the great majority of the troops would be embodied in the field army and that seemed already large enough for the task. In this difference of view lay the basis for a misunderstanding between the two men that exerted a strong and perhaps decisive influence upon the course of events.

This difference in ideas implied different standards of military conduct. If the British commander was to have a force large enough to garrison every conquered district, caution in the field was the best policy so long as enough was done to expand steadily the area of British occupation. But if rebellion, even in remote districts, was to be paralysed by the psychological effect of brilliant British victories, unassisted by systematic occupation, then everything must be risked to make success in the field as complete and convincing as possible. The difference between the two ideas was vital.

Even before Sir William Howe's letter reached England he had reshaped his ideas. The advance across New Jersey had just ended and its fruits had not yet been sacrificed by the defeat at Trenton. Howe wrote:

The opinions of the people being much changed in Pennsylvania, and their minds in general, from the late progress of the army, disposed to peace, in which sentiment they would be confirmed by our getting possession

6 *Howe's Narrative*, pp. 12-14.

of Philadelphia, I am from this consideration fully persuaded the principal army should act offensively on that side where the enemy's chief strength will certainly be collected.[7]

This change involved other alterations in the original plan. The offensive toward Boston must be deferred until reinforcements arrived, 'that there may be a corps to act defensively upon the lower part of Hudson's River to cover Jersey on that side, as well as to facilitate in some degree the approach of the army from Canada.'[8] The details of the plan called for two thousand to be left at Rhode Island, which had been taken during the winter, four thousand for the defence of New York, three thousand for action on the Hudson, and ten thousand for the offensive against Philadelphia, a total of nineteen thousand.

How can we explain so radical a change of plan? The new proposal required little more than half the number of troops called for in the first. Did word come to Howe that he could not hope for the reinforcements required by his original plan? Or did the favourable prospects just before Trenton tempt him to believe that the war might be ended more easily than he had supposed a short time before? It is difficult to discover the answer except in so far as it is to be found in the letter of December 20.

But as these operations . . . may depend upon the exigencies of the moment, I request your Lordship to point out any general plans that may be thought most advisable, both with respect to the present strength of the army, and in the event of reinforcements, remarking the periods of time in which these troops may be expected.

He added that the northern army must not be expected at Albany until the middle of September and that its

---

[7] C.O.5/94, pp. 41-50. Howe-Germain, 20 December 1776.
[8] Ibid.

future actions would depend upon the state of things at the time.

The first plan probably represented Howe's ideal. Uncertain, however, about the amount of support he could expect from the government and encouraged by reports of a friendly disposition among the population around Philadelphia, he felt ready to suggest a second plan that would not require the heavy reinforcements needed for the first.[9] The final decision he apparently wished to put on the shoulders of Germain. That Howe was willing to leave to Germain the decision between two quite different plans, based on very different assumptions, indicates great uncertainty in his own mind as to the best way to proceed. Such uncertainty tended to prevent the consistent and vigorous prosecution of any scheme.

When, on January 14, Germain replied to Howe's proposal of November 30, he refused either to approve or disapprove. But when the plan of December 20 arrived, with its much more modest demand on the resources of the government, Germain approved it at once.[10] He modified it only by suggesting that the two brothers should consider seriously the possibility of a diversion on the coast of New England, which the King evidently had much at heart. But the letter also brought the bad news that the government could not even provide the reinforcement mentioned in the earlier letter, that it would not now be possible to send more than 2500 fresh troops. The authorities in London comforted themselves with the thought that this would not prove as much of a hardship as might at first sight appear, since Howe had not included in his estimates the provincial troops, which ought to be

[9] *Howe's Narrative,* pp. 11-12.
[10] C.O.5/94, pp. 1-12. Germain-Howe, 14 January 1777.

quite numerous by spring.[11] But before this letter reached America other ideas were at work in the minds of the British commanders.

During the New Jersey campaign of the preceding autumn the American general Charles Lee had been captured by the British. They regarded this as a great stroke of luck because at the time Lee enjoyed the reputation of being the real genius of the American resistance, since he was one of the few persons serving with the American army who had had much formal military experience. Lee appears to have been greatly worried by his predicament, since his former membership in the British army put his participation in the revolution in an unusually bad light. He therefore sought some means for ingratiating himself with his captors. The compulsory hospitality which was the lot of captives of high rank in the eighteenth century made it possible for him to get on terms of considerable intimacy with Howe. This friendship, and his desire to do the British government some favour that would lessen his danger of being brought to trial for treason, led Lee to suggest a plan of operations for 1777 which has been thoroughly discussed in George H. Moore's *Treason of Charles Lee.*

Lee's plan, dated 29 March 1777, assumed that the British would dispose of a field army of twenty thousand men and that they intended to clear the Americans out of New Jersey and seize Philadelphia. This seizure Lee characterized as of no particular use, since Congress and the people expected it and would not be unduly disheartened by the event. The real problem was to unhinge the organization of the American resistance. Although a good deal must depend upon the utilization of unpredictable circumstance, the dis-

11 Ibid., pp. 215-21. Germain-Howe, 3 March 1777.

position of the middle colonies of Maryland, Virginia, and Pennsylvania would be of great importance.   The American army in Pennsylvania depended so much upon material support from the south that, if Maryland could be occupied and Virginia kept from sending aid, Washington's position would be undermined. The transfer of operations to that quarter would almost certainly reduce the American numbers, for the difficulty of communications across the North River and the fear of invasion from Canada would prevent the sending of supplies or reinforcements from New England.   Offensive operations against New England Lee thought useless.   He then suggested that fourteen thousand men be sent to clear the Jerseys and take Philadelphia at the same time that four thousand were sent by water to the Chesapeake, where, upon arrival, half of them would go up the Potomac to Alexandria, and the other half up the bay to Annapolis.   Such a movement, Lee predicted, would present no difficulties, for the communication by sea was perfectly safe, the two forces could support each other, and the inhabitants of the region would probably make a general submission.[12]

Moore believes that this offer was an unsolicited attempt on the part of Lee to ingratiate himself with the British authorities, and that it considerably influenced the British plans.   But we have no real knowledge about the circumstances of its submission : in fact, our principal evidence that it was submitted at all is to be found in the change of plan that the Howes made early in April.

This change was described in a letter to Germain dated the 2nd of April.   Howe acknowledged the receipt of Germain's letter of January 14, which arrived

---

[12] Moore, *Treason of Charles Lee,* p. 93 and after.

the 9th of March, and said that he must relinquish any idea of an offensive from Rhode Island. He enclosed a new distribution: 11,000 for the invasion of Pennsylvania, 4,700 for the defence of New York and its vicinity, 2,400 for Rhode Island, and 3,000 provincials to act around New York.[13] The chief apparent difference between this distribution and that of December 20 was the omission of any provision for offensive operations on the Hudson. The troops round New York would apparently act on the defensive.

This change in distribution, however, was not the most important alteration in plan. The later paragraphs of the letter of April 2 described an entirely new method of carrying out the proposed advance.

From the difficulties and delay that would attend the passage of the River Delaware by a march through Jersey, I propose to invade Pennsylvania by sea, and from this arrangement must probably abandon the Jersies which by the former plan would not have been the case.[14]

This decision to go to Pennsylvania by sea meant that the British army, instead of remaining constantly in touch with New York and the Hudson during its advance, would be entirely without contact until Philadelphia had been taken. This change was highly significant.

The world has never known, and will never know certainly, just why the Howes made this decision. Cornwallis said there were very real obstacles in the way of an advance across the Delaware. A large stream had to be crossed and a line of communications nearly a hundred miles in length maintained. Howe was at the time complaining of the strain placed on his resources by the necessity of protecting territory,

[13] C.O.5/253, p. 299. List of troop dispositions suggested by Howe for 1777. Also, C.O.5/94, p. 295. Enclosure of April 2.
[14] C.O.5/94, pp. 287-94. Howe-Germain, 2 April 1777.

posts, and communications as his army advanced. The overland route to Pennsylvania would have required a larger force for protecting communications than had been found necessary in any previous British advance. This drain upon the army could be largely avoided by use of the water route. The distance the army must march from any probable landing place was far less than the distance from New York to Philadelphia, and once the latter city was taken, the matter of communications could be left entirely to the navy.

Howe showed in his letter of April 2 that he felt much restricted in his action by the need of maintaining a great many posts.

In the former campaign the force was suitable to the operation, whereas in the ensuing one, from the several posts necessary to be preserved, the offensive army will be too weak for rapid success. . .

From these considerations, and the delays which may attend the evacuation of the Jersies, from the vicinity of the enemy's principal force, it is probable the campaign will not commence so soon as your Lordship may expect, even though we should not undertake anything offensive in that quarter, which I mean to avoid, unless some very advantageous opening should offer.[15]

This passage, revealing as it does Howe's anxiety to avoid frittering away his forces in garrisons, creates a supposition that the avoidance of this danger was uppermost in his mind when he and his brother decided to move to Pennsylvania by sea.

In this change of plan what influence can be attributed to the ideas of Lee? Probably not a great deal. It is not necessary to suppose that some outside influence was needed to induce Howe to adopt such

[15] C.O.5/94, pp. 287-94. Howe-Germain, 2 April 1777.

a plan, for the advance by water was a logical answer to his desire to economize troops. Furthermore, the plan adopted resembled Lee's only superficially. Lee deplored the taking of Philadelphia for its own sake, but that seems to have been the main purpose of Howe's scheme. The crucial feature of Lee's suggestion was the establishment of posts in Maryland and Virginia, but this recommendation was ignored. The Howes went to the Chesapeake only as a means of reaching Philadelphia.

Thus the only part of the Howes' plans that exactly resembled Lee's was the use of water transport to support an effort in the Chesapeake region. It should be noted, furthermore, that Lee did not contemplate taking the main army by sea. He intended the navy to be used merely to establish and support the posts in Maryland and Virginia. At best, Lee did no more than suggest, without so intending, the idea of transporting the army to Pennsylvania by sea.

But there are reasons for doubting whether he had even that much influence. Lee's plan was dated March 29; the plan of the Howes had taken definite shape not later than April 2. Moore concluded that the proximity of the two dates proved Lee's influence. But the probabilities of the case seem to point in the opposite direction. Is it likely that within four days Lee's plan was read, considered, adopted, and put in final form in a letter to Germain? It does not seem like the Howes. Nowhere else did they show such haste in arriving at decisions, and there was no particular reason why they should abandon their usual deliberation at this time.

There are other ways of explaining the close sequence of Lee's suggestion and Sir William Howe's

letter to Germain. It may have been merely a coincidence that Lee's proposal and the letter to Germain describing the Howes' change of plan, which
had perhaps been under consideration for weeks, came
so close together. Or it is possible that Lee, through
his social contact with the Howes, may have discovered that they intended an expedition by sea to the
southward and have thought a suggestion from him as
to the proper objectives would be appreciated. He
may have heard no more than that plans for the season
were under consideration and have decided, in order
to ingratiate himself, to advance his own ideas. This
last suggestion seems the most probable, for the Howes
were such taciturn men that it is difficult to believe
they would have admitted Lee to their confidence,
although they might have remarked that they were engaged in making plans. Whatever the exact explanation, it seems likely that Lee's ideas had little if any
influence on the British strategy for 1777 and that the
scheme finally adopted was chosen because it was the
logical result of the general view of the situation held
by the Howes at the time.

A further quotation from the letter of April 2 will
throw additional light on the ideas in the mind of Sir
William Howe.

I have reason to expect in the case of success in Pennsylvania, there will be found a considerable part of the
inhabitants who may be embodied as militia, and some
as provincial troops, for the interior defence of the
province.

And again :

Restricted as I am, from entering upon more extensive
operations by the want of force, my hopes of terminating
the war this year are vanished.

But he expected to hold New York, New Jersey, and Pennsylvania by the end of the campaign.

Here Howe returned once more, with perhaps a sigh of resignation, to his fundamental concept, that of a methodical and safe occupation of as much territory as his numbers would permit. Revolution was to be choked by having military force available for use in every district where opposition might show its head. The British army was to be a police force on a glorified scale.

The letter of April 2 crossed one written by Germain on March 3 expressing approval of Howe's second plan of December 20.[16] As Howe remarked, his December 20 communication reached England before Burgoyne left; so the approval of March 3 came in time for Burgoyne to be informed of it. The second and third plans were alike in that they called for offensive action toward Philadelphia and only a defensive on the Hudson. So Howe's final scheme did not deprive Burgoyne of any co-operation which he might have expected from the plan which was received before he left America.

The April 2 letter reached Whitehall the 8th of May and was answered on the 18th.[17] Germain wrote that the King approved of any alteration in plan Howe might think wise, 'trusting, however, that whatever you may meditate, it will be executed in time for you to co-operate with the army ordered to proceed from Canada.'[18] The Secretary then expressed his concern at the discovery that Howe did not consider the force under his command as adequate to the task ahead as

---

[16] *Howe's Narrative*, pp. 12-13. The letter is in C.O.5/94, pp. 215-21.
[17] C.O.5/7, pp. 359-62. Précis of plans for 1777.
[18] C.O.5/94, pp. 339-44. Germain-Howe, 18 May 1777.

it had been the previous year. But he professed his anxiety greatly diminished by news that the Americans were having great difficulty in raising the troops voted by Congress.

> If we may credit the accounts which arrive from all quarters relative to the good inclinations of the inhabitants, there is every reason to expect that your success in Pennsylvania will enable you to raise from among them such a force as may be sufficient for the interior defence of the province, and leave the army at liberty to proceed to offensive operations. . . the information which I have received of the disposition of the people, and the high opinion which I entertain of your abilities, inspire me with no small degree of hope that this campaign will put an end to the unhappy contest.[19]

Germain was certainly an optimist to have, or claim to have, such hopes after the pessimistic accounts he had received from Howe. It indicates how far the attitudes of the two men toward the conduct of the war had drifted apart. Howe saw every reduction in the reinforcements promised him as compelling a postponement of the conclusion of the contest, an opinion which was logical enough in view of the strategy he thought ought to be pursued. Germain maintained that the British force, even if not so large as originally hoped, was still powerful enough to end the war by one more campaign. He thought that if the British could strike shattering blows at the American army and interfere with the maintenance of the revolutionary military system, the framework of the revolution would collapse from the vibrations set up. He intended to bring the rebellion down with a resounding crash by attacking its underpinning. Howe, believing such an effort doomed to failure, thought the structure must be removed brick by brick, beginning at the top.

19 Ibid.

As we look back over the letters exchanged between the two men since the beginning of the war, we can see these ideas cropping out, although neither perhaps understood the full implication of his views. The plans for 1777 saw a more precise development of each view and a further divergence between the two.

CHAPTER XIII

THE WINTER AND SPRING OF 1777

THE dramatic nature of a campaign in the field, with its rapid manoeuvres and hard fought battles, sometimes blinds the public to the fact that developments may take place between periods of crisis that affect very radically the capacity of an army to meet the tasks assigned it. Some inconspicuous influence that undermines the morale of the troops may mean the difference between victory and defeat. Among such influences is the manner of life of an army while in winter quarters. Adequate comfort will mean that the troops will take the field in the spring in good health and spirits. A winter of privation will bring into the field an army reduced in numbers and wearied in body and mind.

For these reasons we must devote some attention to the life of the British in New York during the winter of 1776-77 in order to discover if their experience during those months exercised any appreciable influence upon the next campaign or upon the war in general. The British authorities were keenly aware of the possible damage of the winter and sought to guard themselves against it. The strongest statement of the need for caution is found in a letter by Germain to Sir William Howe :

The troops had been so much harrased in the course of the last campaign, that I could not but wish that no manoeuvre of the enemy might hinder them from enjoy-

ing that repose, in their winter quarters, which their late
fatigues rendered necessary, and their services entitled
them to expect. I was, therefore, extremely sorry to find
. . . that their quiet and comfort had been in any degree
interrupted, and it gives me additional concern to think
there is a prospect of their experiencing but little inter-
mission of toil and danger before the opening of the next
campaign.[1]

Germain clearly regarded the winter as a season designed for giving the troops the utmost possible rest in
order that the army might be fully prepared for the next
campaign. If Howe merited any criticism, from this
point of view, it was for being too vigorous and exposing his troops to needless exertions. But there is
no real reason for believing that the annoyances they
suffered had any ill effect.

There were, of course, a few difficulties. Housing
presented a problem at first, since a large section of
the city of New York was laid waste soon after the
beginning of the British occupation by a fire supposed
at the time to have been of incendiary origin. The
severity with which the suspected incendiaries were
treated bore witness to the threat to British safety
which the blaze entailed. The crowding that resulted
from the destruction of houses led to an increase of
illness. The number of prisoners to be cared for
aggravated the difficulty.[2] Yet little permanent ill
effect appears to have resulted. Before long the army
managed to make itself quite comfortable and nothing
happened within the city itself to alter the situation.

Sir William Howe soon discovered that the occupation of a city in the course of a civil war required di-
plomacy quite as much as skilful military management.

[1] C.O.5/94, pp. 269-78. Germain-Howe, 19 April 1777.
[2] B.M.Add. Mss. 34,413, ff. 152-5. Letter from New York, 3 January 1777.

The kindness towards the Americans demanded by his plans for conciliation often conflicted with the consideration the supporters of the government thought their loyalty merited. One Loyalist declared, 'Nobody would complain at all, were it not apparent that every mild, coaxing method is used toward the rebels, and no care taken to protect the Loyalists,' who were plundered first by the Americans, then by the Hessians, and then by the Americans again.[3] Indeed, it was alleged :

The Friends of Government have been worse used by these troops (British and especially Hessians) than by the rebels. Plundering, and destroying property, without distinction, have been practiced ; insomuch that many people have joined Washington, because they found most protection from him, though otherwise well affected to the King.[4]

The writer was particularly critical of the Hessians, whose aggressive greed deterred the inhabitants from ever coming near their quarters.

But the Hessians themselves complained of the mild manner in which the inhabitants were treated and contrasted it unfavourably with their experience in former wars. One of them wrote :

There is likewise nothing more vexatious than the fact that by an express order of the King the soldiers are obliged to treat this people, who are in reality all rebels, with the greatest courtesy — so much so, that not a grain of salt may be taken from them without compensation.[5]

Too many of the Hessians acted in the spirit of this letter rather than in that of the King's instructions. It was, for example, reported that De Heister at-

[3] *Historical Anecdotes relative to the American Rebellion.* Letter from New York, 9 February 1777, pp. 1-4.
[4] Ibid., pp. 4-8. Letter from New York, 16 February 1777.
[5] Stone, *Letters of Brunswick and Hessian Officers during the American Revolution,* pp. 203-11. Letter from New York, 24 June 1777.

tempted to sell the house in which he was quartered, although it was owned by a Loyalist.[6]

Thus Sir William Howe's policy appeared faulty to every group — too lenient to rebels from the point of view of the Loyalists, too easy on civilians from the military point of view, and too lax in affording protection from the military in civilian eyes. This universality of criticism is probably the best possible proof that the Howes were endeavouring to be just to all.

It may be urged, as several critics have suggested, that whatever the abstract justice of the case, the Howes would have contributed more directly to the success of the British cause had they shown full favour to the Loyalists. But those embittered people would have used this assistance to revenge themselves upon their opponents, a course incompatible with the plans of the Howes for subduing the revolution. The British commanders wished to pursue a policy of magisterial compromise, to offer hope of pardon at the same time that they demonstrated to the recalcitrant the impossibility of escaping defeat. To embitter still further the civil war would have destroyed all hope of success by these means.

The same spirit animated the activity of the navy under Lord Howe. On 23 December 1776 he gave Hotham instructions for interrupting the commerce along the coasts of the southern colonies and for preventing the introduction of military supplies into the country. The first was required by act of Parliament, the second by military common sense. But Lord Howe qualified the instructions in significant fashion.

You are nevertheless at liberty in respect to these instructions to grant, and it is advisable to allow, the inhabitants dwelling upon the coasts adjacent to the stations of

6 *Fugitive Pieces,* p. 102.

the ships under your orders, use of their ordinary fishing craft, or other means of providing for their daily subsistence and support, where the same does not seem liable to any material abuse. And in your signification thereof to the several captains, you are to recommend them to encourage and cultivate all amicable correspondence with the said inhabitants, to gain their good will and confidence, whilst they demean themselves in a peaceable and orderly manner; and to grant them every other indulgence which the necessary restrictions on their trade will admit, in order to conciliate their friendly dispositions and to detach them from the prejudices they have imbibed.[7]

A secret letter from Lord Howe to Hotham on the same day directed the latter to gather information about the best means for distressing the inhabitants, as by raids or seizures of cattle, should such measures become necessary.[8]   But the knowledge was to be got without great stir and without partial attempts leading to temporary advantages, in order that the inhabitants might not be taught by experience the proper measures for defeating the program.   Very possibly similar ideas restrained Sir William Howe from the indiscriminate activity urged upon him by certain people who thought his operations lacked vigour.

Lord Howe's idea of the proper use of the navy seems substantially similar to his brother's plans for the army.   He intended to hinder as much as possible the military support of the revolution.   He assumed, however, that the people living on the coast held such equivocal opinions about the contest that, if left unmolested in their own immediate affairs, they could be kept from assisting the revolution by an imposing demonstration of the power of the British arms.

[7] Adm. 1/487, pp. 343-5. Lord Howe-Commodore Hotham, 23 December 1776.
[8] Ibid., pp. 347-53. Lord Howe-Hotham, secret, 23 December 1776.

Hence, when he heard that some inhabitants who had fired upon a flag of truce had been subjected to severe reprisals, he expressed great concern that civilians, who presumably did not understand the gravity of their offense, should have been so roughly treated. He thought some milder measure ought first to have been used to show them their fault.[9]

In the case of both the army and the navy this plan of operations would, if successful, have possessed the inestimable advantage of finishing the war with a minimum of bitterness. But it would probably have taken longer and have required larger forces than a more relentless policy. To a government impatient for victory and short of resources the prospect of a postponement of success and indefinite further demands for support could not fail to bring disappointment and irritation.

The manœuvres of the army during the winter were not such as to require detailed examination, but their general character and result merit some attention. Trenton and Princeton had served notice upon the British that the plan for holding all of New Jersey must be abandoned. Howe withdrew his outposts to New Brunswick, while Washington made Morristown his headquarters. Cornwallis felt confident that lack of subsistence would prevent Washington remaining at Morristown during the winter and that in the retreat that must ensue the severity of the weather would destroy his army.[10] Cornwallis was, however, doomed to disappointment. Washington not only remained but information soon reached the British that he was receiving reinforcements. Because of this news the

---

[9] Ibid., pp. 331-9. Lord Howe-Sir Peter Parker, 22 December 1776.
[10] *H.M.C. Mss. of Mrs. Stopford-Sackville,* vol. 2, p. 55. Cornwallis-Germain, 18 January 1777.

British posts were contracted so that the enemy's actions might be watched without subjecting the troops to long marches in the bitter weather.[11]

Washington intended to prevent this repose and, by keeping the British troops assembled where there was insufficient cover, to force them to abandon the Jersies. To accomplish this purpose he sent out numerous small parties that appeared suddenly and disappeared as quickly. That these efforts annoyed the British seriously is shown by a letter from New York in the middle of February:

> For these two months, or nearly, have we been boxed about in Jersey, as if we had no feelings. Our cantonments have been beaten up; our foraging parties attacked, sometimes defeated, and the forage carried off from us; all travelling between the posts hazardous; and, in short, the troops harassed beyond measure by continual duty.[12]

There is no evidence, however, that this war of attrition reduced the British numbers appreciably nor did it compel them to abandon their posts. But it did have some moral effect. The return to an offensive pose raised the spirits of the American troops. The British, on the contrary, grew less confident as they saw themselves compelled, in spite of their numerical superiority, to suffer annoyance when and where their opponents might choose. It also seems probable that the American revival and the embarrassment it occasioned the British contributed to the growing pessimism of Sir William Howe. Small annoyances, for which no solution can be found, often cause more discouragement than major dangers.

Critics have argued that Howe should have at-

[11] B.M.Add. Mss., 21,680, ff. 171-2. Maj. Hutcheson-Haldimand, 20 January 1777.
[12] *Historical Anecdotes*, pp. 4-8.

tacked Washington at Morristown and either stormed his camp or forced him to abandon it. Although it is undeniable that the success of such an advance would have placed the Americans in serious straits, an attack upon Morristown was not to be undertaken lightly. Washington's position was, according to British information, strong and difficult of access.[13] Yet it was not so much the tactical obstacle as the cost of a campaign during the inclement weather that deterred the British. An advance upon Morristown might have required several weeks in the open for the greater part of the army. The losses inflicted by the severity of the American winter might have damaged the British army so seriously as to destroy the value of any military success secured. Furthermore, as Cornwallis told the Inquiry, the British loss could not be repaired in that campaign, whereas the American could.[14] It would have been contrary to contemporary military doctrine and also to the wishes of the government to undertake a winter campaign unless decisive results could be counted upon as almost a certainty.

Possibly, in the light of our knowledge of the difficulties that were shortly to gather round the British cause, we may feel that the risk ought to have been taken. But, before he could undertake such a plan, Sir William Howe must have been prepared to stake everything on it. If it were attempted, and failed with serious loss, the careful plans for a systematic occupation and reduction of the colonies would have to be abandoned for lack of adequate force. Had Sir William Howe known that he was to be required to carry on operations without the increase of numbers which he expected and thought necessary to his plans,

13 Dom. State Papers, Geo. III, 18. The Howe Inquiry.
14 Ibid.

he might have seen matters in a different light. But that disappointment had not yet overtaken him and he viewed the winter's work in the light of his plans for the coming spring and summer. It had not yet become apparent that victory could be had only by taking greater risks than he had hitherto been willing to accept.

The situation in New Jersey remained substantially unaltered until nearly the end of May, when Washington abandoned his position at Morristown and moved south to Middlebrook in order to be nearer the line of a possible British advance upon Philadelphia. Although Washington's move was deprived of most of its significance by the fact that Howe had no intention of moving upon Philadelphia by land, the British commander endeavoured to manœuvre Washington out of his new position. He first moved across the Raritan, as if to advance upon Philadelphia, but the gesture brought no corresponding move from Washington and was soon abandoned. It could not have been pushed very far without exposing the British communications.

The British retreat was planned to give the Americans the impression that the British were evacuating New Jersey hurriedly and amid some confusion, in order to tempt them to strike a blow at the rearguard. To heighten this impression the pontoon bridge, which had been prepared for crossing the Delaware, was placed in position between the mainland and Staten Island and certain excesses took place calculated to irritate the Americans into a hasty advance.[15]

Washington struck at the bait and moved after the British. Then Howe turned and advanced once more to the westward. At the same time he sent Corn-

[15] *"The Boston History,"* vol. 2, p. 494.

wallis on a circuit to the right in order to cut off Washington's retreat to the mountains. Stirling, on the American left, had been the most precipitate in his advance and ran into Cornwallis, who gave him a sound beating. But that misfortune apprised Washington of his danger. The American right had not advanced so far as to compromise itself and the whole army succeeded in retreating to the strong position at Middlebrook. Howe then abandoned his attempts to draw Washington into a general action and moved his army to Staten Island, preparatory to embarking it for the trip to the southward.

Howe's conduct in this campaign was much criticized on the ground that he neglected the obvious measure of bringing Washington to action by an assault upon the American position at Middlebrook. A number of British officers reported in New York that natives familiar with the locality had offered to act as guides and conduct the British by a road which would make possible a successful assault upon the American lines, but that Howe took no notice of the offers.[16] The person who recorded this rumour said he was not sure of its accuracy, but it is not improbable that it was correct. Persons in responsible position never lack offers of assistance from self-appointed experts who later ascribe any misfortune that may ensue to the rejection of their proposals.

Howe's caution excited praise as well as criticism. Cornwallis testified that Sir William took great pains to inform himself of the situation of the American camp at Middlebrook and that 'the intelligence he received was by no means encouraging.'[17] General Grey expressed the opinion that attack at Middle-

---

[16] *Kemble's Journal*, p. 124. Entry of 4 July 1777.
[17] Dom. State Papers, Geo. III, 18, The Howe Inquiry.

brook was 'utterly impracticable with any prospect of advantage.'[18] It is thus extremely difficult to tell whether an attack at Middlebrook would have offered a fair prospect of success.

But that perhaps is not the real question. Howe had already decided to make an attack upon Phila- delphia by sea, his main effort of the year. His ma- nœuvres in New Jersey were to be pushed only as far as compatible with that larger purpose. He had no intention of staking everything upon some risky procedure during this subordinate phase of his op- erations. The same point of view provides the answer to those critics who argued that Howe ought to have compelled Washington to decamp by threatening his communications. That object might have been achieved, but it would have done little to advance the British cause. As Washington had no fixed point in New Jersey that he must defend, he might have shifted his base as often as the British threatened it. Only a serious slip on his part could have given Howe an opportunity for a general action upon favourable terms. In view of his other plans, he could not spend the summer in New Jersey waiting for the error that might not occur. In the operations that have been described, Howe attempted to lead Washington into error. Having failed, although by a narrow margin, he felt he could not spare the time necessary for fur- ther efforts of a similar nature.

Howe was also severely blamed for his delay in open- ing the campaign. His critics argued that this delay postponed the capture of Philadelphia so far into the autumn that it prevented the sending of assistance to Burgoyne. Sir William expected some delay when he wrote to Germain on April 2 that the failure of the

18 *A View of the Evidence*, p. 4.

reinforcements to measure up to expectations and the delays incidental to evacuating New Jersey in the face of the main army of the enemy would lead to a later opening of the campaign than he had originally intended.[19] But that does not explain why the manœuvres in New Jersey were not begun until almost the end of May and then only by Washington's move to Middlebrook.

Cornwallis and Grey agreed in their explanation of this delay. They testified before the Inquiry that the campaign could not have been begun earlier because until that time the ground was not sufficiently covered with verdure to provide green forage for the animals of the army.[20] Cornwallis even stated that the campaign began earlier than he remembered taking the field in Germany. His evidence about exact conditions in America in the spring of 1777 was, however, second hand, for he did not arrive from England until the 5th of June. In addition to the problem created by the backwardness of the vegetation, the new camp equipage expected from England had not yet arrived, nor had the year's reinforcements. The former arrived on May 24, but it was the 7th of June before all the new troops put in an appearance.[21] Thus the British army was not complete until about the time that Howe began his moves in New Jersey.

Nevertheless, in spite of the opinion of Cornwallis, it is difficult to believe that Howe's reasons for inaction were entirely adequate. It scarcely seems that the obstacles to early action were insuperable had he been thoroughly determined upon such a course. Sir

[19] C.O.5/94, pp. 287-94. Howe-Germain, 2 April 1777.
[20] Dom. State Papers, Geo. III, 18. The Howe Inquiry. Also *A View of the Evidence*, p. 18.
[21] *A View of the Evidence*, p. 18 and C.O.5/253, p. 507, Précis of the arrival of reinforcements for Howe in 1777.

William appears to have sacrificed prompt action to a routine trend of thought. Doubtless it was desirable to be completely equipped before taking the field, but the value of such perfection does not seem to justify so long a wait.

Whether greater haste would have brought decisive results is not easy to determine. Howe's critics argued that he could have completed his Philadelphia campaign in time to assist Burgoyne. But, had he not finished it more decisively than was actually the case, he could scarcely have spared enough troops for any very formidable expedition up the Hudson. He had not then received directions which showed that the government expected him to co-operate with Burgoyne before the end of the campaign, nor did he even have at hand a copy of Burgoyne's instructions. Thus the full significance of his delay was not apparent at the time.

Howe's lack of exact knowledge of the government's plans is not, however, a completely adequate excuse. He knew in a general way that another expedition from Canada was probable, that Carleton's retreat of the previous autumn was only a postponement. He could scarcely have been ignorant of the fact that the completion of a chain of posts along the Hudson would require some assistance from his army. He probably ought to have realized that the advantages of beginning the year's campaign promptly were sufficient to justify operations in New Jersey before conditions were entirely suitable.

On the other hand it may be pointed out that, since Howe's plans called for a rapid embarkation of his army if the manoeuvres in New Jersey proved fruitless, it was logical to postpone the beginning of those manoeuvres until the army was entirely ready for the

southern expedition. It was a situation where plausible arguments can be advanced on both sides, where
the authority of routine procedure was perhaps on
the side of Howe, but where one cannot but feel that
routine might have been modified without serious risk
and to the distinct advantage of the British cause.

These delays and other shortcomings in the conduct of British operations have often been attributed
to the private habits of Sir William Howe. His in-
ertness and inability to grasp decisive success were said
to be the result of his debauchery and his example,
so it was claimed, had an evil influence upon the army
as a whole.

The general influence of Howe's private life upon
British fortunes will be more thoroughly examined
in a later chapter. The influence of his personal shortcomings upon the decisions that have just been described has certainly been exaggerated by his critics.
The decisions usually criticized as products of Sir
William's indulgence were practically all taken in consultation with his brother, who would scarcely have
permitted such foibles to stand in the way of vigorous
action. In the field, where Lord Richard's influence
could not be felt directly, Sir William's actions have
been much less criticized and those that have been
attacked were of the sort that could scarcely be attributed to indulgence. This is not to say that his
personal habits did not occasionally diminish his effectiveness. But to make them the key to all his failures, or even one of the two or three main reasons for
failure, seems a serious exaggeration.

When we attempt to sum up the influence of the
winter and spring of 1777 upon British fortunes in
America, our verdict must be that the period was in
no way decisive. Although the army suffered fre-

quent annoyances, although things did not go as well or as comfortably at New York as might have been hoped, they did not go so badly as to cause any appreciable diminution in British strength. If certain chances for action may have been missed during the brief spring campaign, little was originally expected from this campaign. Nor is it certain that the British had any real opportunities. The worst that can be said is that several months went by without the accomplishment of anything definite toward subduing the revolution and that the fruitless passage of so much time served to lower the morale of the troops, and more especially that of their commander, who grew increasingly pessimistic about the outlook. But the delays and apparent inadequacies of the British command during the season need not be attributed to personal vice, to rank incompetence, nor to a desire to let the Americans off easily. They were perfectly consistent with the routine ideas of an eighteenth-century soldier, and with the strategical plans of the Howes, which called for a safe, methodical advance from one district to another in order to overawe the colonists by the majesty of that progress. Such ideas required the husbanding of British strength, rather than the risking of heavy loss in an attempt to run Washington ragged. This is not to say that British leadership was the ablest possible during the winter of 1777. But it is fair to say that its character requires no melodramatic explanation and did not, in itself, influence the outcome of the war decisively by anything that was done or left undone at that time.

CHAPTER XIV

THE BURGOYNE AFFAIR

No PHASE of the command of the Howe brothers in America gave rise to more adverse criticism than their attitude towards the expedition of General Burgoyne. The utter failure of that attempt and the disastrous results that followed focused attention upon every detail in the conduct of the Howes which might in any way have contributed to the disaster. The fact that the advance from Canada was, in some fashion, to be co-ordinated with British military activity to the southward aroused suspicion that the British commanders at New York must have been responsible, at least in part, for the final result.

Historians have assumed too readily that the idea of sending the expedition from Canada originated with Burgoyne and Germain. It was really a familiar scheme. As has been mentioned before, a letter written by Dartmouth to Gage in April 1775 expressed the idea as unmistakably as anything Burgoyne ever wrote.[1] It stated specifically that the purpose of such an expedition would be to isolate the New England colonies. Nor was Dartmouth the only one to entertain such ideas. Sir William Howe's earliest plans for subduing the revolution, communicated in the summer of 1775, mentioned the same scheme and assigned to it an identical purpose. The abortive Carleton expedition of 1776 was attempting to put the plan

---

[1] C.O.5/92, pp. 197-221. Dartmouth-Gage, 15 April 1775.

into execution when the arrival of winter forced a retreat.

Nor was Burgoyne even the first one to suggest this operation for inclusion in the government's plans for 1777. Carleton, who commanded the unsuccessful expedition the year before, took it for granted that another attempt would be made in 1777. When Burgoyne returned to England for the winter he took with him a memorandum on the subject prepared by Carleton for consideration by the government.[2] Carleton urged a reinforcement of four thousand beyond the number needed to complete the army then in Canada. He suggested that with these means a large detachment could be spared to operate down the Mohawk Valley and that another might possibly penetrate to the Connecticut River. He appears to have assumed that this expedition would be able to stand on its own feet; that however much it might co-operate with Sir William Howe, it would not have to rely upon him for safety.

Thus it is obvious that many others had thought or were thinking of plans similar to those suggested by Burgoyne. Burgoyne's own ideas were submitted to Germain in a paper dated 28 February 1777, entitled, *Thoughts for Conducting the War on the Side of Canada*.[3] He first discussed the difficulties in the way of executing the movement and expressed the belief that they could be overcome without great trouble. Burgoyne then turned to the fundamental strategy of the move.

These ideas are formed upon the supposition that it be the sole purpose of the Canada army to effect a junction

[2] C.O.42/36, pp. 7-8. Carleton's memorandum relative to the next campaign communicated to Burogyne to be laid before the government.
[3] Ibid., pp. 37-49. The copy of the memorandum is contained among the Canadian papers of the Colonial Office.

with General Howe, or after cooperating so far as to get possession of Albany, and open the communication to New York, to remain upon the Hudson River and thereby enable that general to act with his whole force to the southward.

There was no suggestion here that the safety of his army would depend upon his being joined at Albany by Howe.   Rather, there was a clear implication that he could get through unaided and maintain himself successfully upon the Hudson while Howe campaigned to the southward.   It is not even certain that Burgoyne expected Howe to take upon himself the work of clearing the lower Hudson, for he appears to speak, not of Howe's co-operation with him, but of his with Howe.   The whole suggestion by Burgoyne seems to indicate that he knew Howe intended to direct his main offensive effort to the southward.   Burgoyne might have secured that knowledge from Germain, since Howe's second plan had arrived in England by the time he submitted his memorandum.   Whether this was the case, or whether he surmised a movement to the southward as probable under the circumstances, Burgoyne certainly expected it when he drafted his plan.

Burgoyne's confidence was, in fact, greater than the passage just quoted would indicate.   In a later paragraph of his memorandum he wrote:

But should the strength of the main American army be such as to admit of the corps of troops now at Rhode Island remaining there during the winter, and acting separately in the spring, it may be highly worthy consideration whether the most important purpose to which the Canada army could be employed, supposing it in possession of Ticonderoga, would not be to gain the Connecticut River.

Burgoyne could not have expressed himself in that fashion had he felt his safety would depend upon powerful assistance from Howe.

Some writers have assumed that the purpose of the expedition from Canada was primarily to bring a reinforcement to Howe and that the conduct of the participants should be judged by the degree to which their actions facilitated this junction. Burgoyne had such a possibility in mind, for in his memorandum he considered a contingency in which his force would be inadequate for the pursuit of any independent objective and would be limited to a mere junction with Howe. In that case, however, he recommended that his army be moved to New York by sea. Hence it is abundantly clear that in planning his advance overland he expected to be able to accomplish a great deal independently of Howe. The junction was to be merely the final act, a celebration of victory already won, not a hairbreadth escape from disaster.

It is also significant that in his memorandum Burgoyne specifically assumed that a considerable force would oppose his advance and would take every advantage of the favourable ground for defence. His confidence that he could act independently was not based on a belief that the only difficulty ahead would be one of transport and supply. This anticipation of vigorous resistance was reaffirmed after his arrival in America, when he possessed more recent intelligence of the conditions awaiting him.[4] But he showed undiminished confidence in his ability to overcome all opposition.

It is, of course, not safe to assume that Burgoyne's understanding of his rôle represented the exact inten-

[4] C.O.42/36, pp. 299-302. Burgoyne to Germain, Montreal, 19 May 1777.

tions of the government until we have examined what Germain said on the subject. The most important document is his letter to Carleton 26 of March 1777, which gave the general instructions for the year.[5] It opened with a lament over the failure of the attempt to pass the lakes during the preceding year and then proceeded to plans for the future.

Upon these accounts, and with a view to quelling the rebellion as soon as possible, it is become highly necessary that the most speedy junction of the two armies should be effected.

The letter then told Carleton that he was to remain in Canada and that Burgoyne, who was to command the field army, 'is to force his way to Albany.'
The orders to be given Burgoyne were then explained.

You are to give him orders to pass Lake Champlain and from thence, by the most vigorous exertion of the force under his command, to proceed with all expedition to Albany, and put himself under the command of Sir William Howe. . . I shall write to Sir William Howe by the first packet, but you will nevertheless endeavour to give him the earliest intelligence of this measure ; and also direct Lieutenant-General Burgoyne and Lieutenant-Colonel St. Leger to neglect no opportunity of doing the same, that they may receive instructions from Sir William Howe.

Until then they were authorized to act as exigencies dictated, 'but that in so doing they must never lose view of their intended junction with Sir William Howe as their principal objects.'
There is a certain ambiguity in these instructions.

---

[5] Ibid., pp. 107-13. Germain-Carleton, 26 March 1777. Also in *Mss. of Mrs. Stopford-Sackville*, vol. 2, p. 60.

They seemed to point to Burgoyne's junction with Howe as the sole matter of importance. But they must not be read too narrowly. It is not necessary to suppose that the phrase 'speedy junction of the two armies' meant that Burgoyne was to make a dash to get under the sheltering wing of the army at New York. Burgoyne was expected to 'force his way to Albany.' The passage that authorized Burgoyne and St. Leger to act as exigencies dictated until they should 'receive instructions from Sir William Howe' is significant. It is unlikely that commanders whose sole mission was to assure the safety of their armies by a speedy junction would receive such latitude, and even more unlikely that their earliest direct connection with Howe should be thought of in terms of receiving instructions. This indicates that Howe was, the moment the junction was effected, to command the whole, but it also seems to envisage a period of action under general directions from Howe, but without actual physical contact with his army. Such an idea could not have been entertained had Germain thought that Burgoyne might be in need of rescue.

It must be admitted that the evidence so far adduced does not afford an absolutely conclusive index to Germain's intentions. Were it our only source of information our conclusions would have to be extremely guarded. Fortunately there is more evidence available, especially a précis prepared by his own department about the reasons for the Canadian expedition.[6] This document explains the nature of the plan and makes it clear that its origin must be sought in the very early days of the war. One passage in it merits quotation.

---

[6] C.O.5/253, pp. 331-7. Précis about the reasons for the Canadian expedition.

It was expected that not only Canada would be recovered, but a communication opened with the King's forces on the side of the Atlantic, and by that means place the rebel army between two fires. That by harassing the western frontier of the rebel provinces, the inhabitants, who now supplied their troops with provisions, would be forced to fly to them for protection, and instead of relieving, increase their difficulties of finding subsistence, and, by thus bringing on a general distress, create a general disposition to submission.

These ideas applied to conditions at the very outbreak of the struggle.

The précis also pointed out the advantage that Howe would reap from the diversion of the American forces and declared that the practicability of the enterprise was never for a moment doubted. It is obvious that this early concept of the function of the Canadian expedition called for an army perfectly capable of working out its own salvation. It could afford no diversion if it needed to be rescued. Fonblanque, in his life of Burgoyne, accepts this view.

The political object of the plan of operations was the disseverance of the New England states from the other insurgent colonies by the introduction of two strong military bodies converging upon their center, and the establishment of a chain of posts extending from the Canadian frontier to New York.[7]

Such an object would not have been assigned to an army believed to be incapable of maintaining itself without assistance.

But the best evidence comes from Germain himself. In a speech in the House of Commons on 18 November 1777, he said:

With regard to the Canada expedition, the honourable gentleman was under a mistake when he imagined that

[7] Fonblanque, *Burgoyne*, pp. 238-9.

General Burgoyne had orders to fight his way to New York.
there to join Sir William Howe; that his orders were to
clear the country of rebels as far as Albany, which town
was prescribed to him as the boundary of his expedition,
unless circumstances might make it necessary to cooperate
with General Howe, in which case he was to assist him to
the utmost of his power.[8]

The meaning is unmistakable. Burgoyne was expected to get to Albany and hold the ground won without assistance. He was then to co-operate with Howe,
if necessary. The necessity that Germain had in mind
appears to have been the possible discovery of some
obstacle to Howe's completion of his section of the
chain between New York City and Albany. He evidently thought it far more likely that Burgoyne would
have to rescue Howe than that the opposite would be
the case. In spite of some apparent ambiguity in the
instructions of the government, of which Burgoyne
later took full advantage in defending his actions, it
seems clear that the real intention of the plan was to
have Burgoyne perform his part of the task and maintain his conquest without assistance.

Sometimes, however, the instructions of a government are mistaken by its agents. It is important to
know if Burgoyne understood his instructions in the
sense in which they have been interpreted above. Fortunately, Burgoyne's fondness for writing lengthy letters provides us the necessary evidence. His letter to
Germain just before the capture of Ticonderoga fairly
bulged with confidence.[9] Soon afterwards he wrote to
Howe that he wished he had been left more latitude in
his instructions, in order that a diversion might have
been made towards Connecticut; but that his 'orders

---

8 *Parliamentary History*, vol. 19, p. 434.
9 C.O.5/94, p. 575. Burgoyne-Germain, 2 July 1777.

being precise to force the junction,' he would, of course, carry them out.[10] He showed even greater assurance in a letter to Germain :

> Your Lordship will pardon me if I a little lament that my orders do not give me the latitude I ventured to propose in my original project of the campaign, to make a real effort instead of a feint upon New England. As things have turned out, were I at liberty to march in force immediately by my left instead of my right, I should have little doubt of subduing before winter, the Provinces where the rebellion originated. If my late letters reach General Howe I still hope this plan may be adopted from Albany.[11]

In a private letter to Germain on the same day Burgoyne mentioned again his Connecticut ambition.

> But finding the enemy are preparing to strengthen themselves by all possible means upon the Hudson's River, I shall employ their terrors that way and after arriving at Albany it may not be too late to renew the alarm toward Connecticut.[12]

Burgoyne clearly thought he possessed a large margin of force over that necessary to open the road to Albany and that once that city was reached, he could devote himself to other objects. He could never have held this view had he thought his safety would depend upon assistance from Howe or that his mission was merely to join his army to Howe's. The junction that Burgoyne expected was not a merging of the armies, but the completion of the barrier between New England and the other colonies. That done, he planned to use his army in other expeditions, subject only to the general orders of Sir William Howe. He felt no worry

---

[10] Fonblanque, *Burgoyne*, p. 233.
[11] Ibid., p. 256. Burgoyne-Germain, 11 July 1777.
[12] C.O.42/36, pp. 719-28. Burgoyne-Germain (private), Skenesborough, 11 July 1777.

over the fact, which he communicated to Germain on July 30, that he had heard nothing from Howe nor had any information about that general's intentions or situation.[13]   In a letter to Howe a week later he showed the same high confidence.[14]   He remarked that he did not expect to reach Albany before the 22nd and that he had heard Arnold intended to give battle near the city.   Clinton, through whose hands this letter passed, wrote of it:

> This letter shewed him to be in the highest spirits and did not contain an expression that indicated either an expectation of desire of cooperation from the southern army.[15]

It seems absolutely certain that, both at the beginning and during the early part of his march, Burgoyne felt not the slightest doubt of his capacity to reach Albany and maintain himself there without assistance.

The reactions in government circles in England to the progress of the campaign indicated similar expectations.   Germain wrote on August 23 that, since Washington had sent only three thousand men towards Albany, Burgoyne would have no trouble.[16]   The same letter mentioned that Howe had gone up the Delaware; so it is obvious that Germain only feared for Burgoyne if, as he said in so many words, Washington had taken all his forces northward without being diverted by Howe.   A letter of Lord North on October 7 is also suggestive of what the government expected from the campaign.

It seems to me that if Sir Henry Clinton and General Burgoyne make themselves masters of the North River,

[13] C.O.42/36, pp. 771-5. Burgoyne-Germain (private), 30 July 1777.
[14] C.O.5/94, pp. 707-12. Burgoyne-Howe, 6 August 1777.
[15] Clinton's *Historical Detail*, p. 85.
[16] *H.M.C., Mss. of Mrs. Stopford-Sackville*, vol. 1, pp. 138-9. Germain-Gen. Irwin, 23 August 1777.

and Sir William Howe cuts off Washington from the southern provinces, Washington must, after a little time, be reduced to fight or disband his army.[17]

If this idea was to be carried out it was not only justifiable but necessary that Howe should make his expedition to the southward while Burgoyne advanced to the Hudson.

A great deal has been made of the supposed failure of Germain to see that Howe received instructions to co-operate with Burgoyne. Shelburne, in a paper re-printed in Fitzmaurice's *Life of Shelburne,* held that Germain's haste and slackness led to the instructions missing the packet and that weather delayed the vessel by which they were sent later.

Among many singularities he had a particular aversion to being put out of his way on any occasion ; he had fixed to go into Kent or Northamptonshire at a particular hour, and to call on his way at his office to sign the dispatches, all of which had been settled, to both these Generals. By some mistake those to General Howe were not fair copied, and upon his growing impatient at it, the office, which was a very idle one, promised to send it to the country after him, while they dispatched the others to General Bur-goyne, expecting that the others could be expedited before the packet sailed with the first, which, however, by some mistake, sailed without them, and the wind detained the vessel which was ordered to carry the rest. . . It might appear incredible if his own Secretary and the most re-spectable persons in office had not assured me of the fact.[18]

When the Knox manuscripts appeared in the reports of the Historical Manuscript Commission, Professor Egerton, in an article in the *English Historical Review,* called attention to Knox's version of the manner in

[17] *H.M.C. Various Collections,* vol. 6, *Mss. of Miss Eyre Matcham,* p. 139. North-Wm. Knox, 7 October 1777.
[18] Fitzmaurice, *Life of Shelburne,* vol. 1, pp. 358-9.

which the instructions were sent.[19]   Knox stated that
he was himself responsible for bringing to Germain's
attention the lack of any instructions to Howe about
the Canadian expedition.   D'Oyley promised to prepare some in order that Germain, who was about to
leave for the country, would not have to delay his
departure.   But D'Oyley neither showed the letter he
prepared to Knox nor kept a copy, and, wrote Knox,
'If Howe had not acknowledged the receipt of it, with
the copy of the instructions to Burgoyne, we could
not have proved that he ever saw them.'[20]   Thus it
would appear that Howe, by his own acknowledgement, was properly informed of the part he was to play.

But the truth of the case was somewhat different.
The communication which Howe acknowledged early
in July was a copy of the instructions to Burgoyne.
It contained no orders to Howe about what he was
to do, if anything, towards co-operating with Burgoyne.[21]   There was good reason for the lack of any
record of D'Oyley's letter, for none was ever written.
D'Oyley apparently thought it sufficient to send word
of what was expected of Burgoyne.   The letter to
which Knox said that Howe sent an acknowledgment
must have been merely a note from D'Oyley explaining
that the instructions enclosed were those given to
Burgoyne.   Hence there was no more information for
Howe in the communication than could be gleaned
from those instructions.

The more specific letter of Germain, written May
18, urging that Howe complete what he had under
way in time to facilitate the junction with Burgoyne,
was not received until August 16, after the army had

---

[19] *English Historical Review*, vol. XXV, p. 315.
[20] Ibid.
[21] *Howe's Narrative*, p. 15.

sailed and was already committed to the southern expedition.[22]   But the whole question of the instructions
has been much exaggerated in importance by the supposition that the instructions, if sent, or if received and
obeyed, would have directed Howe to move up the
Hudson and rescue Burgoyne.   There is not the
slightest reason for believing that such would have
been the case.   The Government certainly contemplated that Howe would, before the end of the season,
stretch out his posts to meet Burgoyne, but not that he
need intervene to save the northern army from destruction.   Hence the question of whether Howe received more definite instructions than the copy of
Burgoyne's orders becomes insignificant.

Lack of specific orders is not, however, an adequate
excuse for failure, if an intelligent appreciation of the
situation would have indicated the proper course of
action.   We must endeavour to discover Howe's view
of his own relationship to the Burgoyne venture and
to ascertain whether that view was correct and whether
he acted consistently with it.   The first specific mention of the matter is in Howe's letter of April 5 to
Carleton, in which he said he would not have strength
enough to detach a separate corps at the beginning of
the campaign to act upon the Hudson, and that consequently Burgoyne would have to make his own way
as far as Albany.[23]   Burgoyne would therefore have to
act as he thought best, but Howe felt confident that
Loyalists would be found around Albany in sufficient
numbers to make it possible to reduce the more rebellious parts of the province.   He would himself
endeavour to see that communication was opened
through the Highlands for the shipping.

---

[22] Fonblanque, *Burgoyne,* p. 380-81.
[23] C.O.5/94, pp. 299-303.   Howe-Carleton, 5 April 1777 (confidential).

But Howe realized that Burgoyne might find himself in peril should Washington move against him. In that case, so he wrote Burgoyne on July 17, he would follow hard on Washington's heels to the relief of the Canadian army, although such a move by the Americans was contrary to his expectations.[24] He explained his attitude more fully to Germain on July 16.[25] If, as he expected, Washington followed him to Pennsylvania, Burgoyne would 'meet with little interruption otherwise than the difficulties he must encounter in transporting stores and provisions for the supply of his army.' But the prospect of having to aid Burgoyne, in case Washington did move against him, had led him to decide to go up the Delaware, instead of up the Chesapeake as originally intended, in order to be nearer New York.[26]

Clinton recorded a conversation he had with Howe on July 13 on the subject of Burgoyne's position.

I told him I thought Washington had before this detached a great force to meet Burgoyne. he said he hoped he would go with his whole Army, for that he could never come back, and could not live there. . . Said I did not know whether he could come back, but was sure Burgoyne could not come forward, upon which depended the whole campaign. he said he hoped to see Burgoyne no further than Albany, and he wrote him word he could not co-operate with him early.[27]

In a letter to Germain on October 22 Howe expressed his surprise that Burgoyne had declared he expected a co-operating army at Albany.

[24] Burgoyne, *State of the Expedition from Canada,* Appendix, p. xlix. Howe-Burgoyne, 17 July 1777.
[25] *H.M.C. Mss. of Mrs. Stopford-Sackville,* vol. 2, p. 72. Howe-Germain, 16 July, 1777.
[26] Ibid.
[27] Clinton Papers, Memorandum of conversation with General Howe, 13 July 1777.

In my last letter to Sir Guy Carleton, a copy of which was transmitted to your lordship in my despatch of April 2nd, 1777, no. 47, and of which His Majesty was pleased to approve, I positively mentioned that no direct assistance could be given to the northern army. This letter I am assured was received by Sir Guy Carleton and carried by him to Montreal before General Burgoyne's departure from thence.[28]

Under the belief that Burgoyne had retreated, he ordered the demolition of the forts in the Highlands, since they could not be maintained during the winter.

Sir William Howe appears to have believed throughout that Burgoyne's expedition was capable of standing upon its own feet, except in the unlikely contingency that Washington should decide to march northward instead of moving to protect Philadelphia. In that case, and in that case alone, Sir William was ready to move energetically to Burgoyne's assistance. From what has already been said about the real intentions of the Government, it seems fair to conclude that it was not expected that Howe need do more for the safety of the northern army.

Yet it must be confessed that there was something a little inadequate about Howe's attitude, technically correct though it may have been. There was a noticeable aloofness and lack of enthusiasm in his letters to Burgoyne. His letter of July 17 is an instance of it.

After your arrival at Albany, the movements of the enemy will guide yours; but my wishes are that the enemy be drove out of this province before any operation takes place in Connecticut.[29]

Sir William wrote a little like a man with an unwelcome servant forced upon him, whom he was obliged

---

[28] C.O.5/94, pp. 729-34. Howe-Germain, 22 October 1777.
[29] Burgoyne, *State of the Expedition from Canada*, Appendix, p. xlix. Howe-Burgoyne, 17 July 1777.

to keep busy but for whose services he felt no enthusiasm. Such subtle points are incapable of proof,
but one cannot escape the suspicion that Howe felt that
the northern expedition was Burgoyne's private show;
that, in order to support it, the Government had curtailed the reinforcements to the army at New York
and hence diminished the prospects of its commander.
Consequently Howe may have been more ready than
he might otherwise have been to ignore Burgoyne and
postpone the junction with him until after the completion of his own plans. It would have required
remarkable unselfishness had he been eager to subordinate the entire activity of his much larger army
to the glorification of Burgoyne. But it must be kept
clearly in mind that in doing no more than was technically required of him, Howe at no time thought he
was endangering the safety of the northern army. He
certainly expected no more than a delayed completion
of its mission and a diminution of the éclat that would
have attended Burgoyne's success had his junction with
Howe been treated as the immediate and paramount
object of the entire campaign.

It will be interesting to examine briefly the steps by
which Burgoyne, as difficulties gathered about him,
altered his opinion of the proper function and destiny
of his expedition. The reader will recall that on
August 6 Burgoyne had written to Howe in most
optimistic vein, without even a hint that he might need
assistance. But by the 20th he had become aware that
he must face greater opposition than at first expected.
He began to grow a little worried. His letter of that
date to Germain complained that no co-operation had
yet appeared to the southward.

Had I latitude in my orders, I should think it my duty
to wait in this position or perhaps as far back as Fort Ed-

ward . . . till some event happened to assist my movement forward; but my orders being positive to "force a junction with Sir William Howe" . . . etc.[30]

This letter marks the transition from his confident expectation of being able to brush aside all opposition to a belief that he must run a great risk, if need be, to complete the junction. As the month of September went by and the danger ahead increased, Burgoyne grew more and more anxious and began bombarding Clinton, who he knew commanded at New York in Howe's absence, with appeals for assistance.[31] He also besought Clinton to instruct him whether he should attack or retreat to the lakes, and said he would not have given up his communications with Ticonderoga had he not expected a co-operating army at Albany.[32] Clinton replied:

That not having received any instructions from the Commander-in-Chief relative to the northern army, and unacquainted even with his intentions concerning the operations of that army, except his wishes that they should get to Albany, Sir H. Clinton cannot presume to give any orders to General Burgoyne.[33]

Nor could he promise any measures of assistance with the force at his command, except very limited diversions. But as late as September 27 there were traces of the original concept in Burgoyne's mind when he wrote:

General Burgoyne thinks he could force his way to Albany, but unless assured that communication between

[30] Burgoyne, *State of the Expedition from Canada*, Appendix, p. xlvii. Burgoyne-Germain, Saratoga, 20 August 1777.
[31] C.O.5/94, p. 715. Burgoyne-Clinton, 23 September 1777.
[32] Ibid., pp. 717-18. Burgoyne-Clinton, 28 September 1777.
[33] Ibid., pp. 718-19. Clinton-Burgoyne. Sent by Capt. Campbell, who brought Burgoyne's message of September 18. Clinton mentions (C.O.5/94, p. 717) that Campbell arrived October 5. He must have begun his return journey within a day or two.

that place and New York was kept open, he could not subsist his army during the winter.[34]

Even at this late date he professed to fear, not destruction, but an inability to maintain his portion of the Hudson River line without assistance. This incapacity he attributed to lack of supplies rather than to the fighting powers of his adversary.

After Saratoga Burgoyne developed another view of the purpose of his ill-fated expedition. He wrote to Germain:

> I reasoned thus; the expedition I commanded was evidently meant at first to be hazarded; circumstances might require it should be devoted. A critical juncture of Mr. Gates' force with Mr. Washington might possibly decide the fate of the war; the failure of my junction with Sir Henry Clinton, or the loss of the retreat to Canada, could only be a partial misfortune.[35]

He wrote in similar vein to Howe on the 20th of October, and again on the 25th, picturing his expedition as one that was to be hazarded 'for the great purpose of forcing a junction, or at least of making a powerful diversion in your favour, by employing the forces that otherwise would join General Washington.'[36] Burgoyne himself thus contradicts those who hold that Howe was supposed to march up the Hudson with his principal army; for, if such had been the intention, what use would have been a diversion to draw troops away from Washington? Of course, no such diversion was really intended, but the concoction of such a theory by Burgoyne indicates that he understood Howe's main effort during the summer was to be directed to the southward. It is a most significant admission.

---

[34] C.O.5/94, p. 725. Burgoyne-Clinton, 9 October 1777.
[35] C.O.42/37, pp. 567-79. Burgoyne-Germain, Albany, 20 October 1777.
[36] *H.M.C. American Mss. in the Royal Institution*, vol. 9, No. 181, Burgoyne-Howe, 20 October 1777, and also No. 187, Burgoyne-Howe, 25 October 1777.

During the controversy provoked in England by the surrender of Burgoyne and by the inquiry into the conduct of the Howes, a great deal of attention was devoted to the feasibility and advisability of a movement up the Hudson to assist Burgoyne. Most of this discussion, however, assumed that Howe's main army would have been used for the purpose. As neither Howe nor the government ever intended this should be done, or at least, not until late in the season and after the completion of the Pennsylvania campaign, the debate was rather pointless.

There were, however, many in America as well as in England who believed that Howe ought to have gone up the Hudson and who thought the expedition to the southward fraught with peril for the British cause. One observer, who remained at New York after the sailing of the expedition, reported that criticism was rife, some of it very facetious:

> One said on the coffee house bridge last night, that the army was gone to Bermuda, as a place of greater safety than any on the continent: Another was certain they had sailed for New Providence, to eat Turtle in perfection; upon a supposition that those which are brought hither from thence are emaciated and lose their flavour in the passage.[37]

Clinton wrote, at a later date:

> I owe it to truth to say there was not, I believe, hardly a man in the army, except Lord Cornwallis and General Grant, who did not reprobate the move to the Southward, and see the necessity of a cooperation with General Burgoyne.[38]

At the time he expressed himself much more vigorously:

[37] *Historical Anecdotes*, pp. 17-20.
[38] Stedman, *American War*, Clinton's copy, vol. 1, p. 295. Clinton's note.

By God these people cannot mean what they give out they must intend to go up Hudson's river and deceive us all. . .[39]

Clinton's opinion was not, however, the sudden outburst of amazed objection that it would at first sight appear. Months earlier, while in England for the winter, he had advised against the campaign to the southward and urged the superior advantages of the Hudson. He continued his protests after his return to America.

I lost no time therefore when asked in delivering to Sir Wm. Howe my opinions upon the intended southern move with the same freedom I had done in England to the minister. . . And I took the liberty at the same time to say that it was highly probable the instant the fleet was decidedly gone to sea Mr. Washington would move with everything he could collect either against General Burgoyne or me, and crush the one or the other; as neither would be capable of withstanding such superior force unless timely intelligence should fortunately bring the fleet to our relief. My arguments were at first but little attended to, tho' from a conviction of the solid grounds upon which they were founded repeated perhaps oftener than was agreeable. By degrees, however, I thought I was listened to; and the momentary suspense which seemed to have been occasioned by what I said, soon yielded to the predilection Sir Wm. Howe had for his own plan, which he told me could not now with propriety be laid aside on account of its having been approved at home.[40]

For a page more Clinton continued to particularize about the critical state of his own position occasioned by the inadequacy of the forces left him by Howe.

Among Clinton's papers are memoranda of repeated discussions with Sir William Howe on this topic. On

[39] Clinton Papers, Clinton-Duncan Drummond, 6 July 1777.
[40] Clinton's *Historical Detail*, pp. 76-7.

July 8 he recorded in the somewhat incoherent fashion
typical of his memoranda :

I told him with regard to his present plan I saw it a
good one upon the principle of raising friends etc. but I
thought the time of year bad, and that the better move
would be to act upon the Hudson's R. form if possible
the Junction and then the four provinces were (crushed ?) .
As that seemed to be the present plan of the war he agreed
he had once thought so but now differed from an idea of
the good of raising friends which I ever (approved) that
I dreaded the time of year and thought it better to close
the campaign by that than begin it. . . I lamented that he
was obliged to act on the defensive in two plans to enable
him to act offensively in a third. . . he agreed, but said
he had sent home his plan, it was approved and he would
abide by it. . . I told him freely my opinion of this war ;
and his was that another campaign would do it even with
the present army ; I confess I doubted, and said no rebellion could be quelled by armies on the defensive. he
seemed to be struck.[41]

A few days later Clinton wrote to General Harvey :

The only thing therefore in my opinion left for us now
in the middle of July, is to cooperate in force with the
northern army, not by a junction with it (for that I can
never advise) but that sort of communication which will
give us possession of Hudson's River ; As it is, I almost
doubt whether the northern army will penetrate as far
as Albany.[42]

He protested to Howe again on July 13, but without
result except to secure Howe's admission that he expected Burgoyne to get no farther than Albany.[43]
Clinton held that even after the departure of Howe's
army he could not bring himself to believe it was really

[41] Clinton Papers, Clinton's minute of a conversation with Sir W. H.,
8 July 1777.
[42] Ibid., Clinton-Gen. Edw. Harvey, 11 July 1777.
[43] Ibid., Memorandum of a conversation with Gen. Howe, 13 July 1777.

intended for Pennsylvania, but thought that the first move must be a feint, to be followed by a quick return and a move up the Hudson.[44]

Clinton's barrage of objections to the southern expedition appears to have been prompted in considerable part by an excessive fear for his own position. He imagined that Washington would pounce upon him the moment the fleet disappeared. Added to this was Clinton's morbid sensitivity which took the shape of conviction that Howe had wronged and neglected him. A perusal of his papers compels one to conclude that Clinton was almost mentally unbalanced on this one topic. It coloured all his thinking. Hence, what he said about Howe at this time must be read with great caution. Clinton also admitted that some measure of his disgruntlement was due to the fact that Burgoyne, instead of himself, secured the Canadian command.[45]

In addition to the allowance that must be made for Clinton's extreme personal animus, there are several important admissions in his papers. It has usually been urged by critics of Howe that he ignored the true intentions of the government when he went to Pennsylvania instead of marching north to join Burgoyne. Clinton's account of his protests against the southern expedition while in England during the winter effectively refutes that supposition.[46] He would not have needed to protest had the government not intended that Howe should act in the fashion that aroused his criticism. His protests show clearly that Howe was not disregarding the aims of the government.

Clinton also admitted, both at the time and later, that he never expected a junction of Burgoyne's and

[44] Clinton's *Historical Detail*, p. 79.
[45] Clinton Papers, Clinton-Howe, private, 2 December 1777.
[46] Clinton's *Historical Detail*, p. 76.

Howe's armies.[47]   All he expected was a co-operation that would open up communications between the two and lead to the control of the line of the Hudson.   He feared for the safety of the northern army only if Washington should move against it with his main body, which of course never happened.   The nature of the disaster that overtook Burgoyne was quite as foreign to Clinton's calculations as to those of Howe and the government.

Thus it would appear that Clinton's criticism of Howe, when examined carefully, does not impugn the loyalty with which Howe followed the wishes of the government, but tends rather to show that he acted in a fashion that was expected and approved by the authorities in England.   Even Clinton's objections, which he aimed at the government as well as at Howe, did not envisage disaster for Burgoyne at the hands of Gates's army, but only a failure to secure the entire line of the Hudson.

So far we have listened mostly to evidence for the prosecution.   We must hear Sir William Howe in his own defence.   In a speech in the House of Commons he took up the charge that his first move in 1777 should have been an advance up the Hudson :

What would have been the consequences of such an expedition?   Before the object of it could have been at-tained, the forts in the Highlands must have been carried, which would probably have cost a considerable number of men, defended, as they would have been, by Washington's whole force.   But those forts being carried, how would the enemy have acted?   In one of these two ways; He would either have put himself between me and New York, or between me and the northern army.   In either case I am of opinion, that the success of our efforts upon Hud-

[47] Clinton Papers, Clinton-Gen. Edw. Harvey, 11 July 1777, and Sted-man, *American War*, Clinton's copy, vol. 1, p. 289, Clinton's note.

son's River, could not, from the many difficulties in penetrating so strong a country, have been accomplished in time to have taken possession of Philadelphia that campaign. But admitting I had at length reached Albany, what would I have gained, after having expended a campaign upon that object alone, that I had not a right to expect by drawing off General Washington, with the principal American army, from my operations on that side?

Had I adopted the plan of going up Hudson's River, it would have been alleged that I had wasted the campaign . . . merely to ensure the progress of the northern army, which could have taken care of itself, provided I had made a diversion in its favor by drawing off to the southward the main army under General Washington. Would not my enemies have gone farther, and insinuated, that, alarmed at the rapid success which the honourable General had a right to expect when Ticonderoga fell, I had enviously grasped a share of that merit. . . Would not ministers have told you, as they truly might, that I had acted without any orders or instructions from them; that General Burgoyne was instructed to force his own way to Albany, and that they had put under his command troops sufficient for the march. Would they not have referred you to the original and settled plan of that expedition . . . to prove that no assistance from me was suggested? And would they not have readily impressed this house with the conclusion, that, if any doubt could have arisen in their minds of the success of such a well digested plan, they should, from the beginning, have made me a party to it, and have given me explicit instructions to act accordingly? [48]

Sir William then went on to say that his decision to go southward had been taken only after frequent consultation with his brother, with Cornwallis, and with other general officers.

We must now attempt an evaluation of the evidence. One point at least admits of no doubt. The northern

[48] *Howe's Narrative*, p. 20.

expedition was never intended, as Burgoyne maintained after his capture, to be 'hazarded.' While the
scheme was being devised it never occurred to anyone
that a desperate diversion was needed to assist Howe's
army, nor was it in fact needed. A diversion that
would have required, in order to save the diverter, the
abandonment of the movement which the diversion
was designed to facilitate would have been of unsurpassed folly. Such a plan would have labelled both
Burgoyne and Germain as simpletons, which they were
not.

The expedition was intended to accomplish exactly
what Carleton had failed to do, exactly what Dartmouth had suggested even earlier, to sever the New
England colonies from the others by establishing close
military control of the line of the Hudson. There
were advantages in beginning the work from both ends.
It might be completed earlier, and meanwhile Canada
would be protected by the advance of the northern
army. It was not supposed that the advance of this
army would be unresisted, but the force under Burgoyne was thought fully adequate to crush any opposition. Therefore, if the northern army arrived at
Albany before the southern, it could wait safely, like
the completed half of the span of a bridge, until the
other half had been built out to meet it.

The co-operation expected from Howe was an extension of British control up the Hudson until it should
meet that established by Burgoyne. Burgoyne himself
certainly contemplated nothing more when he set out.
In fact, he appears to have regarded his junction with
Howe, not as an avenue to safety, but as an annoying,
although perhaps necessary, limitation upon his freedom of action. The man who itched to cross over
into the Connecticut valley and march down into

southern New England could have felt no doubt of his ability to accomplish the much lighter task of marching to Albany. Nor did anyone suppose that an army as powerful as Burgoyne's would so exhaust itself by the task of reaching Albany that it would require immediate support. Howe, when he felt himself unable to co-operate, merely assumed that Burgoyne would either winter in Albany or retreat, as he saw best.

Certainly Howe never expected, nor did the government expect him, to rescue Burgoyne. Criticism of Howe on the ground that he did not make that the first feature of his plans for 1777 is without warrant. He is, however, open to criticism when we seek to discover what he did to carry out his part of the plan for securing possession of the Hudson. It is true that his definite instructions to complete the work in Pennsylvania in time to co-operate with Burgoyne did not arrive until after he was on his way southward; but Howe had, before he left New York, a copy of Burgoyne's orders. He knew what the government intended. Clinton pointed out that his instruction from Howe directing that something be done to assist Burgoyne preceded the arrival of Germain's letter of May 18.[49] Clinton, who thought this request outrageous, in view of the smallness of the force left at New York, attributed it to a fear that Burgoyne might lack supplies and to a wish to have it on record that something had been done to help him. It does indicate, however, that Howe understood he was expected to make an effort to open the lower reaches of the Hudson.

In spite of that knowledge, he made no very adequate preparations for clearing the Hudson as far as Albany. He contented himself with rather vague directions to Clinton which, in view of the state of

[49] Clinton's *Historical Detail*, p. 81.

mind of that officer, were unlikely to produce definite results. Nothing of importance was done until Clinton discovered Burgoyne was in great danger and in need of immediate rescue. Had Burgoyne run into no more serious difficulty than the stoppage of further advance, there can be little assurance that anything would have been done until at least very late in the season. Howe certainly seemed somewhat indifferent to the need of reaching out from New York to join hands with Burgoyne, or at least determined to subordinate it entirely to his other plans.

The obvious answer to such criticism is that Howe felt his forces inadequate for both the southern expedition and a simultaneous move to secure the Hudson. Since the government had approved the former and Burgoyne was expected to be able to stand on his own feet, it was the southern move that ought to receive first and, if for the moment necessary, exclusive attention. Such an interpretation was probably justified by the letter of his instructions, but such a defence is not entirely satisfying. Howe was warned by some of his officers that the Pennsylvania expedition would endanger the Hudson project, although the danger they contemplated was not the loss of Burgoyne's army but the failure to complete the British chain along the Hudson. They feared another year of futility in the field unless vigorous measures were initiated at New York. Howe knew that the government regarded the seizure of the Hudson as a vital part of the campaign; and, if he saw the success of the effort imperiled, ought he not to have modified his own plans, even if they had received government approval at the time when it was confidently expected that both tasks could be carried through to completion?

There is merit in such a criticism. Howe undoubtedly hoped to join hands with Burgoyne after the completion of the Pennsylvania campaign, but he seems to have accepted the possibility that the junction might have to be postponed until the following year. Probably the best defence that can be advanced for him is that he deliberately accepted such a possibility in the belief that it would be less of a misfortune than a failure to use the summer to secure Pennsylvania. He was certainly correct in believing that the government would have blamed him for inaction had he marched up the Hudson with his main army and spent the summer in meeting Burgoyne and establishing posts to hold the river. It would have taken unusual moral courage for Howe to abandon his own plans and run the gauntlet of government criticism in order to save the government from its own miscalculations, especially when those miscalculations seemed to threaten, not disaster, but merely postponed fulfilment and when, had Howe rushed to the rescue, it would never have been possible to prove that the government had miscalculated.

Thus, when all is said, the key to the Howe-Burgoyne affair does not lie in any single despatch, nor in any letter that was ordered but never written. Howe knew what the expedition was intended to accomplish. He was entirely justified in supposing that Burgoyne's safety was not expected to depend upon assistance from New York. But in his failure to take steps to join hands with Burgoyne after the latter had reached Albany he either overestimated the capacity of Burgoyne's force, or, what is more likely, deliberately accepted a postponement of the completion of the Hudson chain in order to ensure success in Pennsylvania. Although it would be entirely mistaken to assume that Howe sacrificed Burgoyne either through intention, indifference, or stupidity, there was, nevertheless, in his correspondence about the northern expedition a lack of enthusiasm for it that leaves the impression that the failure of the government to send Howe reinforcements as numerous as he wished had put him in a mood prejudicial to a sympathetic handling of the problem presented by Burgoyne's advance.   He did all that was specifically required of him and asked no more of the northern army than Burgoyne had originally expected to be able to provide.   He did not betray Burgoyne or knowingly expose that general to disaster.   But he did show a willingness to postpone the accomplishment of the Hudson River plan which, in view of the unexpected turn of events, may have contributed to the overthrow of Burgoyne.   It must be remembered, however, that a modification of Howe's original plan sufficiently extensive to have saved Burgoyne would have been in itself a severe criticism of the government and have brought Howe no thanks.   Since it was not obviously necessary, it is not surprising that he refused to make it.

CHAPTER XV

THE PENNSYLVANIA CAMPAIGN

AFTER Washington had escaped the trap set for him during the brief June campaign in New Jersey, the British devoted themselves exclusively to the task of embarking the troops for the southern expedition. The destination of the fleet was kept as secret as possible in the hope that Washington's doubt about its destination might delay his arrival in Pennsylvania until too late to contest the landing.

But the embarkation progressed slowly, so that over two weeks elapsed between the retreat to Staten Island and its completion. Another period of delay ensued and it was July 23 before the fleet sailed. This delay, which aroused much criticism, was explained later by Sir William Howe. He waited, so he said, first, for the arrival of Clinton from Europe, and secondly, for despatches from Burgoyne.[1] He felt unwilling to leave New York until the officer who was to command there in his absence was actually on the spot. Word from Burgoyne on July 15 that his army was progressing favourably and that Ticonderoga would be garrisoned from Canada, leaving his army free to advance upon Albany, reassured Howe on the second point. Howe wrote to Clinton on the 18th that he had just received reliable intelligence that Washington was awaiting the move of the British, without any intention of crossing the North River unless his opponents moved

[1] *Howe's Narrative*, p. 21.

THE
PHILADELPHIA
CAMPAIGN

-------- *British Advance*
+ + + + + + + *American Retreat*

up it.[2] It is not to be supposed, however, that Howe was waiting to secure this last piece of information. Nor does his excuse of waiting for news from Burgoyne sound entirely convincing, since it is reasonably clear that Howe never intended to do anything for the northern army until after the conclusion of the Pennsylvania campaign. It is possible, however, that in response to objections from some of his officers, he did delay until the receipt of some favourable news from Burgoyne.

It must also be remembered that the embarkation of an army cannot be accomplished in a day. Much

2 The Clinton Papers, Howe-Clinton, On board the *Eagle* 18 July 1777.

of the time before sailing was needed for practical preparation. The defence of New York also needed attention.[3] Cornwallis thought that the embarkation at Staten Island could not have taken place earlier than it did.[4] Very possibly, measured by routine practice, the delay before sailing was not excessive. But one cannot avoid the feeling that a determination to proceed rapidly would have overcome such obstacles as existed. The British command showed a subservience to difficulties rather than a bold determination to surmount them. Other persons besides the Howes, however, did not consider the delay excessive. Germain wrote to Knox that he thought Howe ought to postpone beginning operations until the arrival of the *Isis* with the camp equipage.[5] This was exactly what Howe did. Germain, the sponsor of the Burgoyne expedition, by holding this opinion while back in England and unplagued by the immediate difficulties of the commander in the field, makes Howe's deliberation appear much less extraordinary.

The delay appears more excusable when we remember that Howe had given up any intention of cooperating with Burgoyne on a large scale until well into the autumn and that he had no definite orders to march to his assistance. The mildly urgent letter written by Germain on May 18 did not arrive until the middle of August. In Howe's mind the conquest of Pennsylvania was the only task of the summer for his army and there would be time enough for that without abandoning routine deliberation. Burgoyne could be looked after when, and if, time was available

---

[3] *Journal of Capt. Montressor, New York Historical Society Proceedings,* 1881, p. 427.
[4] Dom. State Papers, Geo. III, 18. The Howe Inquiry.
[5] *H.M.C. Various Collections, vol. 6, Mss. of Miss Eyre Matcham,* p. 131. Germain-Wm. Knox, 24 June 1777.

in the autumn. It must be confessed, however, that a curious paradox had appeared in Howe's thinking. He seems to have decided he could do nothing for Burgoyne because it would have left him insufficient time for his own plans, and at the same time to have decided that his own operations required no great haste because the chance of doing anything substantial for Burgoyne had disappeared. Possibly his growing pessimism prompted him to this manner of thinking. By midsummer, perhaps, it was an accurate view of the situation, for it was too late to carry out two important operations during the season and yet time enough was left to make it unnecessary to hurry about one.

The final departure of the fleet was delayed several days either because the wind was unfavourable or failed to blow at all.[6] Not until the 23rd of July did the fleet move out of New York Harbour. Its progress down the coast proved very slow. Delaware Bay was not reached until the 29th, and the Virginia Capes only on the 14th of August. But between those two dates a perplexing feature of the campaign took place. The fleet nosed into Delaware Bay, with every apparent intention of landing the army on the banks of the Delaware River somewhere near Philadelphia. After proceeding some distance, however, it turned round and sailed out again. Thanks to light and unfavourable winds, three weeks elapsed before it was brought to anchor at the Head of Elk.

What is the explanation of this change of intention, which has sometimes been cited as another example of the incompetence of the Howes? There can be no doubt that the British commanders originally intended

---

[6] *Journal of Capt. Montressor, New York Historical Society Proceedings*, 1881, p. 427. Also, Lord Howe to the Admiralty, 28 August 1777, Adm. 1/487, pp. 959-63.

to proceed to the Chesapeake, not the Delaware. In a letter to Germain on July 16 Sir William spoke of 'the course of Chesapeake Bay which I once intended and preferred to that of the Delawar provided the enemy had discovered a disposition to defend Pennsylvania.'[7] On July 23 he wrote to Clinton that, as the wind was fair for running down the coast, he thought he would go to the Chesapeake, but, as circumstances might change, expresses should call at the Delaware until further orders.[8] The British knew, months before the expedition sailed, that the Americans were preparing for the defence of Philadelphia by placing obstacles and fortifications along the Delaware below the city. As early as 23 December 1776, Lord Howe commented upon these activities in giving instructions for observing the river.[9] By February 20 he knew more detail, that there were floating batteries and obstructions sunk in the river.[10] Nor was the British information based only on the reports of spies. Early in May, Hammond, who commanded the squadron observing the Delaware, took a trip up the river to reconnoitre and was attacked by several row galleys and fire ships, which he beat off only after a protracted engagement.[11] There was thus abundant evidence to make the Howes prefer the Chesapeake to the Delaware.

There seems also to have been a broader strategical reason for the preference. Sir William Howe wrote to Clinton on July 30, while still on board ship in the Delaware :

[7] C.O.5/94, pp. 583-5. Howe-Germain, private, 16 July 1777.
[8] Clinton Papers, Howe-Clinton, *Eagle* outside Sandy Hook, 23 July 1777.
[9] Adm. 1/487, pp. 347-53. Lord Howe-Hotham, secret, 23 December 1776.
[10] Enclosures in letter of Lord Howe to the Admiralty of 20 February 1777. Adm. 1/487, p. 587.
[11] Ibid.

Had our passage been more successful we might possibly have landed in the Delaware in time to have got between the Susquehanna and Mr. Washington's army, which there would not now be the slightest prospect of.[12]

This statement, supplemented by that in which Howe expressed his preference for the Chesapeake in case Washington showed a disposition to defend Pennsylvania, is susceptible of two interpretations. It may mean that Howe hoped to interpose between Washington and the Susquehanna in order to drive a wedge between the southern and the middle colonies. But it may merely indicate that he wished to keep Washington in front of him so that he could, by the same move, advance on Philadelphia, face the enemy, and protect his communications against flank attack from the west. In either case, keeping Washington east of the Susquehanna offered the best chance of bringing him to action. If he retired beyond the river he could not easily be followed, yet he might strike eastward at will. Whatever Sir William's exact reasoning, it is clear that he originally preferred the Chesapeake as a landing place.

What was it then, that led the British to look into Delaware Bay with an eye to a possible landing? Sir William Howe explained it in a letter in which he discussed what he would do for Burgoyne in case Washington showed signs of moving northward with his main army.

Under these circumstances I propose going up the Delaware, in order to be nearer this place than I should be by taking the course of Chesapeak Bay, which I once intended and preferred to that of the Delaware, provided

---

[12] Clinton Papers, Howe-Clinton, *Eagle* off mouth of Delaware, 30 July 1777. Also in Dom. State Papers, Geo. III, 18, the Howe Inquiry.

the enemy had discovered a disposition to defend Pensil-vania.[13]

In view of his indubitable original preference for the other route and his certain knowledge that the Americans had been preparing defences in the Delaware below Philadelphia, there is little reason to doubt that this statement represents accurately the motives behind the British move. Although at first sight the mouth of the Delaware is not much nearer New York than the head of the Chesapeake, the difference, from a military point of view, was great. If the British army were landed on the Delaware and then it suddenly became necessary to hurry north to the assistance of Burgoyne, the presence of the fleet in the river would make it easy to transfer the army to the eastern bank, from which point it might march without serious impediment to New York. If confronted by a similar emergency while on the Chesapeake, the army would have to pass Philadelphia and cross the Delaware without assistance from the fleet. Difficulty and delay would almost certainly result.

It is less easy to explain why the Howes, after having sailed into Delaware Bay, turned round and sailed out again at the sacrifice of what later appeared to be valuable time. A great dispute raged over this decision, to the accompaniment of elaborate evidence about the strength of the American naval armament at Philadelphia, the nature of the obstacles in the river and along its banks, and the ease or difficulty of landing an army at various places below Philadelphia. From a detailed examination of the evidence the following conclusions seem warranted. The Howes knew in at least some detail about the seriousness of the obstacles

---

[13] *H.M.C. Mss. of Mrs. Stopford-Sackville*, vol. 2, p. 72. Howe-Germain, New York, 16 July 1777.

facing them before they turned into the Delaware.[14] These obstacles were sufficiently formidable to make their overthrow a task of some magnitude.[15]   From the point of view of the Philadelphia campaign alone the only advantage offered by landing on the Delaware was an earlier establishment of communication between Philadelphia and the sea.   Nevertheless, in spite of difficulties that might have led to loss and delay, the army could have been landed and, in all probability, the city have been captured earlier than was possible by going to the Chesapeake, even had the latter move not been attended by unexpected delay.[16]

All these conclusions are, however, of less consequence than the debate that raged over the topic would indicate.   The important thing is that, as soon as the British fleet put into Delaware Bay, it was discovered that there was no longer any reason for preferring the Delaware to the Chesapeake.   The British naval forces on the spot brought word that Washington and his army had crossed the Delaware and were moving on Wilmington.[17]   This meant that the British landing would probably have to face active opposition and also that Washington could not be cut off from retreat beyond the Susquehanna, should he choose that course. Furthermore, and most important of all, Washington's presence made a landing on the Delaware unnecessary, for he was obviously not on his way to attack Burgoyne. Howe's belief that Washington would defend Philadelphia had proved correct and the American army would certainly stay in the neighbourhood of the city so long as it was threatened.   There was, therefore, no

---

[14] Dom. State Papers, Geo. III, 18.   The Howe Inquiry.
[15] *Observations upon a Pamphlet*, pp. 71-94.   The evidence of Andrew Snape Hammond.
[16] Dom. State Papers, Geo. III, 18.   The Howe Inquiry.
[17] Ibid.

further need of haste lest Washington have designs upon Burgoyne. The advance upon Philadelphia could now be pursued with an eye to getting the greatest advantage out of the local situation. From that point of view the Chesapeake was still the most suitable landing spot, and to that place the fleet was now directed.

Not until three weeks later did the fleet appear off the Head of Elk, a delay that seemed to many contemporaries a tragic waste of good summer weather. The Howes had not expected, however, to be so slow in rounding the Virginia Capes. Unfavourable or inadequate winds retarded the voyage. Such weather conditions were, however, so common along the coast in the summer that the possibility of delay must, or at least ought to, have entered the calculations of the British commanders. From the facts mentioned in the previous paragraph, the danger of delay seems not to have been considered a very telling argument against going to the Chesapeake.

The trip up the bay was not without difficulties. The water proved so very shallow that the British concluded the Americans had not expected a landing in that region.[18] Although the ships frequently scraped along the bottom, the yielding mud permitted them to escape. The use of pilot ships to mark the channel and skilful navigation finally enabled the fleet to arrive safely at its destination.[19] Lord Howe and General Howe reconnoitered the shore on the 23rd of August and fixed upon the mouth of the Elk for the landing, which was planned for the 25th. The landing was unopposed, for the disappearance of the fleet after its

[18] *Journal of Capt. Montressor, New York Historical Society Proceedings*, 1881, p. 442.
[19] Adm. 1/487, pp. 959-63. Lord Howe-Admiralty, 28 August 1777.

THE BATTLE OF
BRANDYWINE

being sighted in the Delaware had left the Americans
entirely in the dark about British intentions. Some
thought they had gone to the Carolinas, others that they
were returning to co-operate with Burgoyne. Washington first inclined to the latter view but, as time
passed, concluded that Charleston must be the destination of his adversary.[20]

Before describing the Brandywine campaign, a further word is needed about the ideas guiding the British
commanders during the contest round Philadelphia.
It is extraordinarily difficult to disentangle the truth
from the mass of controversy that the campaign pro-

---

[20] Ford, Washington-John Augustus Washington, Germantown, 5 August 1777, vol. VI, p. 13, and Washington-Gates, Bucks City, 20 August
1777, vol. VI, p. 45.

voked. The testimony of the Howes themselves often appears contradictory, for they were endeavouring to refute points made by their critics and frequently the refutation of one point was best achieved by a line of argument not entirely consistent with the answer made to another point. Two passages from Howe's *Narrative* will illustrate this difficulty. After discussing the inadvisability of operating on the Hudson, Howe said :

> In Pennsylvania the prospect was very different. The increase of force which the country could afford Washington was small in comparison to the other, and the defence of Philadelphia was an object which I justly concluded would engage the whole of his attention. It was incumbent upon him to risk a battle to preserve that capital. And as my opinion has always been, that the defeat of the rebel regular army is the surest road to peace, I invariably pursued the most probable means of forcing its commander to action under circumstances the least hazardous to the royal army; for even a victory, attended by heavy loss of men on our part, would have given a fatal check to the progress of the war, and might have proved irreparable.[21]

But a little later in the same document he mentioned that he expected to capture three provinces by the end of the year, Pennsylvania, New York, and New Jersey.

Here is apparently a triple contradiction in Howe's strategical ideas. First he professed himself eager for battle, convinced that the proper way to destroy the revolution was to defeat the principal American army. But almost in the same breath he declared that he could seek battle only under favourable circumstances, for even a victory, if purchased at a great price, would be disastrous. Finally, he declared the object of the campaign to be the reconquest of three provinces.

Must we conclude from this that Howe's plans lacked

[21] *Howe's Narrative*, p. 19.

any consistent idea? A superficial reading of the evidence would lead to an affirmative answer, but more careful study justifies a somewhat different reply. Howe's principal idea was apparently a slow, methodical reoccupation of the colonies, an overawing of the refractory by the physical presence of British troops. The defeat of Washington he does not appear to have regarded as alone sufficient for the purpose. It would only facilitate the occupation which he planned. A successful battle would have removed organized military resistance to British control but would not, of itself, have dissolved the pervading general resistance. Even if Washington were annihilated, the British Army must still be large enough to effect a general occupation of the country, which it might not be if the victory were too dearly purchased.

The sort of battle that Howe desired need not, in fact must not, be secured by hectic manœuvring and deliberate risk. Rather, Washington must be forced into a position where he must either defeat the British or witness the disintegration of his army. Howe believed that an attack on Philadelphia would create such a situation and Washington's response to his moves shows that he was correct. The nature of his efforts seems to have been understood in England, to judge from a letter of Lord North.

If Sir Henry Clinton and General Burgoyne make themselves masters of the North River, and Sir William Howe cuts off Washington from the Southern Provinces, Washington must, after a little time, be reduced to fight or disband his army.[22]

This letter, incidentally, strongly reinforces the conclusion reached in a previous chapter that the government

[22] *H.M.C. Mss. of Miss Eyre Matcham, Various Collections*, vol. 6, p. 139. Lord North-Wm. Knox, 7 October 1777.

fully understood that Howe was not going to march to the assistance of Burgoyne but was planning to devote his attention to the middle colonies.

Thus, amid the apparent confusion of ideas mentioned above, there was a certain thread of consistency. It must be confessed, however, that Sir William Howe did not always escape the inconsistency with which his enemies charged him. His plan required a nice balance of caution and vigour and an unusual capacity to measure immediate needs in terms of ultimate purpose. Howe seems, from time to time, to have been unable to maintain so exacting a balance. Especially did his growing pessimism, as matters developed less favourably than he had hoped, render him less capable of the exact mixture of daring and prudence which his original concept required.

The Brandywine campaign, which followed the British landing, needs no detailed description, for it would be the retelling of a familiar story. But certain features of it that provoked controversy require examination. The first of them is the delay in the British advance after the landing at the Head of Elk. That delay was, however, not great. The troops went ashore on August 25; Brandywine was fought on September 10. Immediately after debarkation, and before the tents could be unloaded, a period of rainy weather came on that drenched the troops to the skin.[23] The confusion that usually attends the landing of an army was evident and seems to have been increased by changes of intention concerning the amount of equipment to be put ashore.[24] There is no indication, however, that these delays led to the sacrifice of any

---

[23] Wilkin, *Some British Soldiers in America*, pp. 236-47. Letter of W. Hale, 23 March 1778.
[24] *Kemble Papers*, vol. 1, pp. 478-80.

opportunity. After the long voyage both men and animals were in need of recuperation and it took time to bring order out of the inevitable confusion of the landing. A serious campaign lay ahead which demanded that every care be taken to assure the efficiency of the army. A precipitate advance offered nothing to compensate for the loss of efficiency it would have entailed.

Brandywine was almost the counterpart of the battle of Long Island, except that the British encircling movement went by the left instead of the right. A deficiency in the intelligence work of the Americans permitted Cornwallis, who commanded the flank march, to get far ahead with it before any measures were taken to oppose him. When opposition did finally appear he defeated it decisively. Washington's army might well have been cut to pieces had not Greene appeared in the nick of time to stop the advance of the British wing. He in turn was driven back, but not until so late in the evening that the British decided it was too dark for a further advance.

The British command was severely criticized for halting the attack. The critics claimed that the destruction of the American army would have been the certain result of its continuance. The accuracy of the charge can never be surely determined. With darkness approaching and both armies in considerable confusion, who can say with any confidence what would have happened? Howe justified himself on the ground that his outflanking force had marched seventeen miles that day, fought a stubbornly contested action, and come up against fresh troops over whom a superiority was not established until after dark.[25] Without doubt an endeavour to push the attack under

[25] C.O.5/94, pp. 639-58. Howe-Germain, 10 October 1777.

such circumstances would have entailed considerable risk and might possibly have led to losses so serious as to counterbalance the results of the victory. Opinions may differ as to whether the prize was worth the risk, but it was certainly in accord with the strategical ideas of Sir William Howe to be content with the very considerable defeat he had inflicted upon Washington. His plan required the conservation of his army at all costs. If a safe opportunity to shatter Washington's army in battle did not appear, he felt he could cause its disintegration by the steady pressure of the campaign. Hence it was unnecessary to assume unusual risks in battle and, by contemporary standards, a continuation of the action at Brandywine after dark was certainly an unusual risk.

After the battle the Americans hastened toward Philadelphia and from there retreated up the north bank of the Schuylkill to Germantown. Cornwallis followed them a short distance and then turned to rejoin the main body of the army not far from the scene of the recent battle. The British advanced so deliberately that Washington had time to double back over the Schuylkill and confront them once more before they had moved many miles. Howe has been blamed for not pursuing Washington to the limit after Brandywine, but the idea never seems to have occurred to him seriously. It is questionable whether such a chase, in which the Americans would have possessed the advantage of lighter equipment and the British the disadvantage of a rapidly lengthening line of communication, would have yielded any important result. It certainly would have fatigued the pursuers and confused their organization. When Washington pulled his head out of the noose at Brandywine, Howe appears to have concluded that any chance of doing him more serious harm had for the moment disappeared.[26]

The return of Washington to his front led Howe to attempt to force a battle. One promising opportunity was ruined by rain that wet the powder of both sides, and further attempts were prevented by the retirement of the Americans once more across the Schuylkill. The defeat of Wayne's rearguard at Paoli was the only important British success during this interval. When it became clear that Washington was not to be trapped, Howe turned and marched his army into Philadelphia. The campaign had won him the city and had inflicted upon Washington a severe, although not decisive, defeat. The British victory had been secured without great risk or serious loss, and to that extent had been according to plan. Towards opportunities for success that demanded great risks Howe's attitude was that it was too bad, but that nothing could be done about it, for it was contrary to general policy to take such chances.

We have reached the practical end of the campaign except for two phases, only one of them of great strategical importance. Before Philadelphia could be occupied comfortably, communication had to be opened with the sea via the Delaware. This required the capture of the American fortifications along the river below the city. The first attempt was on Fort Mercer at Red Bank by the Hessians under Donop. It failed with heavy loss, but the responsibility was entirely that of Donop. Howe instructed him that, if he discovered the fort could be carried easily, he was to 'brusquer l'affaire,' but that he was not to sacrifice troops if the attempt appeared desperate.[27] In the latter case he would be supplied with the necessary

26 C.O.5/94, pp. 639-58. Howe-Germain, 10 October 1777.
27 *A View of the Evidence*, p. 15.

artillery and equipment for a methodical siege. Cornwallis, who carried the Commander-in-Chief's orders to Donop, testified before the Parliamentary Inquiry as to the discretionary nature of the instructions.[28] Donop, although gallant, showed no intelligence in the execution of his orders, tried to storm a position much too strong for such methods, and was himself among the victims of his stupidity. After this setback larger forces with adequate siege equipment were assigned to the task and the reduction of the fort was carried through methodically, without further incident of more than routine importance. There was some criticism of the slowness of the operation, but there were days of heavy rain, and low ground to be traversed, so that the task was accomplished with as much despatch as could have been expected in the circumstances.

The other incident was the battle of Germantown, in which the Americans suddenly appeared before the British lines, nearly captured the British quarters, and might have done so but for the fog which complicated the manœuvre which Washington had planned. Howe was blamed for not having taken more precautions and for letting himself be surprised. He admitted that Washington's advance to a pitched battle so soon after Brandywine had surprised him, for he had not thought his adversary sufficiently recovered for so bold an attempt. This belief had guided his dispositions.

In this idea I did not direct any redoubts to be raised for the security of the camp or outposts, nor did I ever encourage the construction of them at the head of the line when in force, because works of that kind are apt to induce an opinion of inferiority, and my wish was, to support by every means the acknowledged superiority of the King's

[28] Dom. State Papers, Geo. III, 18. The Howe Inquiry.

troops over the enemy, which I considered more peculiarly essential, where strength was not to be estimated by numbers, since the enemy in that respect, by calling in the force of the country upon any emergency, must have been superior.[29]

In this show of boldness he only followed routine military practice, for it was the accepted principle that entrenchments, unless absolutely necessary, tended to rob troops of the offensive spirit. It was also in accord with Howe's essential plan of campaign, to impress the colonies with the superiority of the British troops and with the inability of the Americans to do anything against them. In view of the supposedly shaken condition of Washington's army, it seemed reasonable to believe that this impression could be created without serious risk. Unfortunately for Howe, he misjudged the condition and the determination of his opponent. As a consequence, his action had just the opposite effect from that he intended. The British lost more prestige than they stood to gain. It was, however, a mischance that might have befallen the best of generals, although Howe perhaps ought to have remembered from the previous year that Washington had a tendency to such riposts.

In summarizing the immediate results of the campaign, those features that concern the attitude of the inhabitants of Pennsylvania toward the British occupation will be reserved for the next chapter. In a purely military way the campaign was both victorious and unsatisfactory. Washington was beaten, but not destroyed. Philadelphia was taken, but in such fashion that great vigilance was needed to retain it. For those who thought everything should be sacrificed in an attempt to destroy Washington's army in open

[29] *Howe's Narrative,* p. 27.

battle, the campaign could not be otherwise than disappointing. For those who, like Sir William Howe,
believed the proper plan was to proceed carefully, to
establish a manifest superiority without undue hazard,
the campaign could afford some measure of satisfaction. Washington's army had been hard pressed,
Philadelphia taken, the prestige of the revolutionary
movement seriously shaken, and the American forces in
the field placed in a position that made their survival
through the winter very uncertain. These were
favourable results of real importance, although their
psychological value was appreciably diminished by the
near-defeat of the British at Germantown.

There is a close parallel between the campaign of
1777 around Philadelphia and that of 1776 in New
York. In both cases, the planned advance of the
British was carried out successfully, and the Americans
proved utterly unable to prevent it, or even to delay
it appreciably. But in each case, when the limit of the
advance had been reached and dispositions were made
for holding what had been gained, a certain calculated
venturesomeness proved, under the circumstances, a
little too bold and led to defeat or near-defeat that
robbed the previous accomplishment of a good deal of
its impressiveness. In both cases the unlucky daring
had been part of Howe's plan to impress the colonies
with the invincible power of the British arms. It was
the irony of fate that the disasters he feared might
result from imprudence in battle actually occurred during the supposedly safer process of methodically occupying a region vacated by a beaten enemy.

Had Trenton and Germantown never taken place,
who can say but that the majestic spectacle of the apparently irresistible advance of the King's troops might
not have had the effect desired, that the American

morale might not have slumped disastrously? The British desire to make the impression as effective as possible gave Washington his opportunity, and he showed his greatest genius in the riposts of Trenton and Germantown. It was to his great nerve and discernment at these junctures, rather than to any serious inadequacy in the British command, that the result must be attributed.

CHAPTER XVI

THE OCCUPATION OF PHILADELPHIA

FOR the third winter in succession the British army settled down to life in a city, with the enemy uncomfortably situated some distance outside the city limits. In all three cases it was assumed without question that the army would go into winter quarters and attempt nothing of importance until the return of warm weather. At Philadelphia, as at New York, the management of the campaign had been guided in considerable part by a belief that the inhabitants of the district would, when given a chance to do so safely, show themselves friendly to the British government. This friendliness would, it was hoped, make it possible to place the local government under Loyalist control.

Assurances of a favourable attitude on the part of the inhabitants of Pennsylvania had come months before the advance on Philadelphia and had appeared thoroughly authentic.[1] Consequently, before the army landed at the Head of Elk, great precautions were taken and special orders issued to prevent, if possible, the plundering that had characterized the previous campaign.[2] Howe was anxious not to sacrifice the friendliness of the inhabitants to the marauding propensities of the Hessians.

But, to his great disappointment, the warm welcome which Howe planned so carefully to encourage failed

[1] *A View of the Evidence,* pp. 66-7.
[2] *Kemble Papers,* vol. 1, p. 473.

to appear.   By August 30, five days after the debarkation, he reported to Germain :

> My progress . . . must be greatly impeded by the prevailing disposition of the inhabitants, who, I am sorry to observe, seem to be, excepting a few individuals, strongly in enmity against us, many having taken up arms and by far the greater number deserted their dwellings, driving off at the same time their stock of cattle and horses.[3]

It seems likely, however, that much of this shyness is to be attributed, not to opposition to the Crown, but to fear engendered by stories of the plundering that took place during the previous campaign.

Further disillusionment awaited Howe at Philadelphia.   He found only forty-five hundred males of military age in the city at the time of its capture.

> By degrees they came in, some to get possession of their houses and effects, some to do us all the mischief they could by sending out intelligence to the enemy, inveigling the troops to desert, and smuggling such supplies for Washington's army as could not be purchased in the country.   That the people of the country brought in fresh provisions to us, and refused such supplies, as much as they dared, to the rebel general is certain ; but I do not admit that this conduct proceeded from the motives ascribed to it by the author.[4]   The people of the country had no opinion of the value of Congress paper money, and the rebel general compelled them to take it in payment for the supplies he collected.   But they knew they should receive instantly hard money for everything they should bring us ; and they had also the opportunity of

---

[3] C.O.5/94, pp. 625-8.   Howe-Germain, 30 August 1777.

[4] Howe here referred to Joseph Galloway, author of the pamphlet upon which he was making observations.   Galloway was originally an opponent of the policy of the British government in America and a member of the Continental Congress.   He was, however, opposed to actual revolution.   When the quarrel reached the point of declaring independence from the British Crown Galloway could no longer keep company with his former associates.   He became one of the leading Loyalists of Philadelphia and was later one of the sharpest critics of the Howes.

carrying back with them, for use of their families, a variety
of necessary articles, that could only be had by the British
army and navy.[5]

Howe suspected that Washington connived in this col-
laboration with the British because he could not prevent it, and also because it brought money into circulation, would not benefit the British, who could secure
supplies from their ships if necessary, and saved the
inhabitants from much real hardship that might have
made them hostile to the Revolution.

The best available evidence points to the conclusion
that the populace of Philadelphia and the surrounding
country endeavoured, during the early weeks of the
British occupation, to remain as neutral and aloof as
possible. They sought to protect their own property
and persons and postponed committing themselves
to either side until they could see which party could
offer them the most protection. If possible, they
wished to know who would win. Perhaps Galloway
was right, that their private preference was for the
British cause. Their enthusiasm for it did not, however, tempt them to display their partisanship until
they could be sure it was safe to do so.

Howe admitted that a marked change took place
before the end of the winter, after a period of 'equivocal neutrality.'

Our successes and apparent ability to retain our advantages, induced the inhabitants at last to be less reserved.
Secret intelligence, which, until that period, had been
extremely difficult to procure, was then so good, and so
readily obtained, that I could not but attribute it to the
possession of Philadelphia, which convinced the country
of the superiority and persuaded them of the established
power of His Majesty's arms. The difficulties of the Congress, in raising supplies, and in recruiting Mr. Wash-

[5] *Observations upon a Pamphlet, etc.,* pp. 42-3.

ington's army, then indeed became real, and had the appearance of being unsurmountable.[6]

Whether or not one accepts Howe's compliment to his own plan of operations, the attitude of the populace toward the British did grow more cordial. But in this gradual substitution of a calculating friendship for a cautious neutrality, there is little evidence of the suppressed enthusiasm for the government which Loyalists such as Galloway professed to see. It seems unlikely that such a populace would have risen *en masse* in response to the friendly gestures that Galloway thought Howe ought to have made. Even a brilliant British victory in the field would have scarcely aroused them, unless they could have seen in it a guarantee of permanent and effective occupation.

The Loyalist's complaints that the British officials were inattentive to the friends of government were increased by the fact that the British command, of necessity, could not always treat the inhabitants just as they wished to be treated. Some people, who suffered interruptions of business as the result of military restrictions, felt themselves unjustly used and suspected certain favourites of the General were usurping the trade denied to them.[7] Other annoyances were inevitable. Stedman reported :

During the winter a very unfortunate inattention was shown to the feelings of the inhabitants of Philadelphia. . . They experienced many of the horrors of civil war. The soldiers insulted and plundered them : and their houses were occupied as barracks, without any compensation being made to them. Some of the first families were compelled to receive into their habitations individual officers, who were even indecent enough to introduce their

6 *Howe's Narrative,* pp. 32-3.
7 C.O.5/155, p. 84. Extract of a letter from McLean and Kilseck, 19 August 1778, at New York.

mistresses into the mansions of their hospitable entertainers. This soured the minds of the inhabitants, many of whom were Quakers.[8]

There was, of course, no calculated unkindness to the population, but it requires unusual excellence of discipline to make the presence of even a friendly army comfortable to the inhabitants of a city. When a considerable part of the army is composed of troops who make no distinction between friend and foe, and when, in fact, that distinction is often difficult to make, frequent friction is inevitable. Galloway, Howe's severest critic, admitted that Howe's 'inhumanity' was not personal, but lay in his failure to protect the people from the troops.[9] The most that can be said is that Howe, disappointed perhaps by the aloof and calculating attitude of the inhabitants towards the British cause, did not make as strenuous an effort to protect them from the annoyances of war as he might have made had he been more hopeful of favourable results from such care.

At a later date there was much discussion about Howe's failure to bring Washington to action during the British occupation of Philadelphia. During the winter months Washington was very uncomfortably situated, so far as living conditions were concerned, at Valley Forge; whereas the British enjoyed excellent quarters in the city. Before going into winter quarters Washington had issued what appeared to be a challenge to action by taking post at Whitemarsh, a few miles north of Germantown. Howe thought this might indicate a willingness to give battle on even terms and so marched out toward Whitemarsh in the early days of December. After various manœuvres,

[8] Stedman, *American War*, vol. 1, pp. 308-09.
[9] *A Reply to the Observations, etc.*, p. 17.

however, it developed that if the British were to have a battle they must get it by assaulting the American camp. This Howe refused to do.

The enemy's camp being as strong on their center and left as upon the right, their seeming determination to hold this position, and unwilling to expose the troops longer to the weather in this inclement season, without tents or baggage of any kind, . . . I returned on the 8th.[10]

Washington moved soon afterward to Valley Forge and both armies settled down for the winter.

Howe made a few gestures toward attacking the American camp, but never pushed them to the point of assault. His failure to do so aroused severe criticism. Galloway said that, in considerable parts at least, the lines did not present serious obstacles, and Stedman agreed with him.[11] There was, however, some disagreement with this verdict. General Grey believed the position at Valley Forge, as well as that at Whitemarsh, was so strong as to make attack inadvisable.[12] Perhaps the fairest idea of the situation may be secured from a letter which described Washington as being 'too strongly intrenched to admit of our forcing his lines under the loss of 2000 men, much too great a price at this advanced season.'[13]

Howe's own explanation of his refusal to attack Washington is significant.

The intrenched situation of the enemy at the Valley Forge, twenty-two miles from Philadelphia, did not occasion any difficulties so pressing as to justify an attack upon that strong post during the severe weather, and though everything was prepared with that intention, I

---

[10] C.O.5/95, pp. 127-8. Howe-Germain, 16 January 1778.
[11] *A Reply to the Observations, etc.*, pp. 110-12. Also Stedman, *American War*, vol. 1, p. 310.
[12] Dom. State Papers, Geo. III, 18. The Howe Inquiry.
[13] Wilkin, Letter of W. Hale, 20 January 1778, pp. 233-5.

judged it imprudent, until the season should afford a prospect of reaping the advantages that ought to have resulted from success in that measure; but having good information in the spring that the enemy had strengthened the camp by additional works, and being certain of moving him from thence when the campaign should open, I dropped all thoughts of an attack.[14]

Little more need be said to explain the British failure to attack. Minute calculations about the vulnerability of the American works, or the exact losses that would have been suffered in carrying them, are scarcely relevant. Granted Sir William Howe's point of view, only an opportunity for easy victory, and a certainty that it could be followed up so as to yield the full fruits of success, would have justified exposing the troops to shot and shell and the weather. Only a very serious mistake by Washington could have presented such an opportunity. The weaknesses of the American camp at Valley Forge were not sufficiently marked to provide it.

This decision was supported by military orthodoxy. As was mentioned in a previous chapter, contemporary teaching thought it utterly foolhardy to attempt serious operations in the dead of winter, and Germain had specifically warned Howe against it the previous year. At the same time, this policy fitted in with Howe's plan of campaign. The comfortable life of the British in Philadelphia, especially when contrasted with the grinding hardship endured by their opponents, would, it was hoped, convince the populace of British invincibility. This cautious policy would likewise prevent the moral and physical loss that might result from hard marching in the depth of winter, a loss that might not be compensated by decisive success.[15] Thus the British

---

[14] *Howe's Narrative*, p. 30.
[15] C.O.5/95, pp. 17-18. Howe-Germain, 19 April 1778.

would resume operations in the spring with strength undiminished, whereas the Americans must be seriously reduced both in numbers and confidence by the long agony of the winter.

In so far as the maintenance of the British army in health, plenty, and comfort was an object of importance, there can be no doubt that it was accomplished.[16] The foraging parties sent out met with almost uniform success.[17] The efforts to make life as nearly normal as possible, especially the attempt to open the markets of Philadelphia and save the army from any want, brought excellent results and showed wise planning.[18] Some difficulties, of course, arose, but few armies have passed a more comfortable winter with the enemy only twenty miles away than did the British army in Philadelphia in 1777-78.

Perhaps the comfort was a little excessive. In the midst of such ease a great many persons in the army entertained themselves somewhat too freely, with consequent loss of morale. A letter written in March 1778 complained that the army was much worse officered than two years earlier because of the excessive gambling that went on at New York and New Brunswick, a rage so extravagant that many excellent officers would soon be obliged to sell out in order to pay their debts, to be replaced by men whose only merit was that their bets had been fortunate.[19] Much of the blame for this state of affairs was laid to the bad example of Sir William Howe. Especially was he charged with letting himself be surrounded by a 'pack

---

16 B.M.Add.Mss. 35,912, p. 244. Letter from New York, 21 March 1778.

17 C.O.5/95, pp. 451-4. Howe-Germain, 19 April 1778.

18 *Simcoe's Military Journal*, p. 37.

19 Wilkin, Letter of W. Hale, March 23, 1778, pp. 236-247. The phrase 'obliged to sell out' refers, of course, to an officer's sale of his commission in order to meet his debts, a familiar practice in the British army in the 18th century.

of self-interested puppies' who flattered him in order
to secure opportunities to advance their own fortunes.[20]   This criticism was aimed at 'some known adherents to the American cause,' by which Galloway was
meant.   Yet Galloway complained that Howe was indifferent to his advice and wishes.   Howe evidently
replaced his first affinity, Mrs. Loring, by another, and
undoubtedly indulged his love of the gaming table,
but much of the criticism levelled at him was of the
sort that is always aroused by a public man who creates
enemies because he will not grant this request or accept
that bit of advice.   In spite of the injustice of most of
these attacks, it does nevertheless seem probable that
Sir William Howe's growing discouragement and his
dissatisfaction over what he conceived to be inadequate support made him more addicted to pleasure
than would have been the case had he seen ultimate
victory in the offing.   But to attribute to Howe's
habits, or to those of his subordinates, a decisive influence on affairs at this juncture would be a gross exaggeration.

There is some reason for thinking that Howe had
intended, during the early stages of the Pennsylvania
campaign, to link up the British forces at Philadelphia
and New York and to take both under his control.
He wrote to Clinton from Germantown on October 9 :

As I shall probably be detained here this winter, I must
beg of you not to think me unreasonable when I request
you to continue in the command at New York.[21]

Possibly, in view of Clinton's querulous nature, Sir
William had felt unwilling to inform him earlier that
he was to be left to his own resources in New York,

[20] *Historical Anecdotes*, pp. 38-48. Letter from New York, Jan. 25,
1778.
[21] Clinton Papers, Howe-Clinton, 9 October 1777.

but it may indicate that the decision not to unite the command of the two posts was taken only after the outcome of the Pennsylvania campaign made it apparent it would be impractical to do so.

However that may be, Howe had decided by October, in spite of the news that Burgoyne was in serious difficulties, that he himself had his hands full at Philadelphia.[22] His suggestion to Clinton that he make a diversion in behalf of Burgoyne, if compatible with the safety of New York, carried with it no reinforcements for the task. Instead, so Clinton complained, Howe's demand that Clinton send reinforcements to Philadelphia compelled the abandonment of the posts captured in the Highlands.[23] Sir William's letter to Germain after receipt of the news of Burgoyne's surrender certainly showed no indication that he thought any fault of his own might have contributed to the disaster. He commented upon the rise in the spirits of his opponents occasioned by Saratoga, and then went on :

I do not apprehend a successful termination of the war from any advantage His Majesty's troops can gain while the enemy is able to avoid or unwilling to hazard a decisive action which might reduce the leaders in rebellion to make an overture for peace ; or that this is to be expected, unless a respectable addition to the army is sent from Europe to act early in the ensuing year. . . If this measure is judged to be inexpedient or cannot be carried into execution the event of the war will be very doubtful.[24]

Thus the principal lesson to be drawn from the experiences of the year was the need for more troops. Howe reiterated that idea in the closing paragraphs of

[22] C.O.5/94, pp. 671-4. Howe-Germain, 21 October 1777.
[23] Clinton's *Historical Detail*, pp. 95-6.
[24] C.O.5/95, pp. 27-9. Howe-Germain, 30 November 1777.

his letter, in which he discussed the possibility of remaining on the defensive for an entire year.

> This measure would undoubtedly expose the enemy to
> much distress for the support of their armies, from the
> difficulties of obtaining exterior supplies, as also from the
> continuance of a very heavy expense for their subsistence.
> It might on the other hand, by protracting the war, pro-
> duce events which it may not be prudent to risk. . . I
> candidly declare my opinion, that in the apparent temper
> of the Americans, a considerable addition to the present
> force will be requisite for affecting any essential change
> in their disposition, and the reestablishment of the King's
> authority, and that this army acting on the defensive will
> be fully employed to maintain its present possessions.[25]

It is apparent from this letter that Howe's strategical
ideas had not changed. He still believed in the necessity of an imposing and all-sufficient army, or perhaps
armies, of occupation that would crush all open opposition, as the area of occupation was enlarged, and
gradually discourage even the secret hopes of those
with rebellious proclivities. If we remember how
little faith he had in the adequacy of a single scheme,
such as the occupation of the Hudson, for stifling the
revolution, his lack of excitement over the Burgoyne
disaster becomes somewhat understandable.

Germain answered this letter by telling of the enthusiasm in England for the prosecution of the war
and urging a descent upon the New England coast during the months that must elapse before reinforcements
could arrive.[26] Howe, upon receipt of these instructions, replied that he had been misunderstood, that his
mention of a general defensive, upon which Germain
had based his assumption that the troops could be

---

[25] Ibid.
[26] Ibid., pp. 59-62. Germain-Howe, 18 February 1778.

spared for the New England raid, had been taken too literally, that he did not mean to deny the army the means to improve any opportunity that happened to present itself.[27]   He only meant to exclude any breaking of new ground, such as had occurred in the past two years.   If the army was to be in a position to take advantage of opportunities that might present themselves on the ground now held, it would be impossible to spare the troops needed for a successful raid on New England.

But this interchange of ideas led to nothing, for Sir William Howe's days as commander-in-chief were numbered.   Ever since he had learned that he could not expect the reinforcements he wished for 1777 he had begun to feel that the government was not supporting him adequately.   This feeling appears to have been accentuated by the fact that so appreciable a portion of the year's supply of troops was diverted to Burgoyne.   The failure of his own campaign to achieve as much as he had hoped added to it.   This pessimism and discontent led him to ask to be relieved of his command, a request that was received in England early in December, of 1777.[28]   It was February, however, before a letter was sent authorizing Howe to turn over his command to Clinton and return home.[29]   His brother, the admiral, remained a few months longer to gain distinction against the French, but as that falls outside the period of the joint command of the brothers, it will not be dealt with in this study.   After certain ceremonies, particularly the famous and, to modern eyes, ridiculous Mischianza, Sir William Howe turned over his command to Sir Henry Clinton and

27 Ibid., pp. 451-4. Howe-Germain, 19 April 1778.
28 Ibid., pp. 755-6. Germain-Howe, 11 December 1777.
29 Ibid., pp. 51-3, Germain-Howe, 4 February 1778.

sailed for England on the 25th of May, 1778. With his departure a new stage of the war began.

Not only did a new commander take charge of the British operations, but a new policy was put into effect. It was outlined in Germain's letter to Clinton 8 March 1778.[30] After discoursing upon the friendly disposition of the inhabitants which, with the assistance of the new peace commission about to be sent out, would probably end the war without further fighting, Germain went on to tell Clinton how to fight the next campaign. As only a few thousand of the year's reinforcements could be spared to Clinton, he was to abandon any idea of an offensive, unless an early opportunity for decisive battle with Washington appeared. Instead, he was directed to organize attacks on various parts of the coast and to make life as miserable as possible for those who dwelt on or near it. To facilitate this policy, he was authorized to evacuate Philadelphia. In the autumn the conquest of Georgia and South Carolina was to be undertaken, since reports had come of strong Loyalist sentiment in that region. With the reconquest of the southern colonies, the northern colonies were then to be left alone, except for a blockade. The hardships of the blockade, plus the political loneliness resulting from the return of the south to British allegiance, would, it was thought, undermine the stamina of the Revolution in the north.

Thus the government signalized not only its unwillingness to pay the price of the methodical occupation which the Howes had sought to carry out, but also its refusal to support a policy of bringing Washington to bay at any cost. If the decision to direct the main British efforts against other objects constituted in some measure an agreement with the contention of

[30] C.O.5/95, pp. 69-94. Germain-Clinton, most secret, 8 March 1778.

Sir William Howe that Washington could not be brought to earth except at too great a price, the plan to subdue the Revolution by harassing the colonies as widely as possible was a radical contradiction of the plans of the Howes. It was, perhaps, a confession of the accuracy of Sir William's complaint of inadequate support, in the sense that the government felt unable or unwilling to grant the measure of support needed for the scheme of operations he had devised. Since that was so, whatever the merits of Howe's plans, his usefulness as a commander had come to an end.

CHAPTER XVII

THE LOYALISTS AND OTHER MATTERS

THE frequency with which the Howes were criticized for not taking full advantage of the support which, it was alleged, they might have secured from the Loyalists, has made it seem best to reserve a separate chapter for the discussion of this problem. This will also serve as a convenient place to discuss certain other phases of the British command which influenced the entire course of operations but are most easily examined apart from the narrative.

The critics of the Howes argued that adequate encouragement to the Loyalists would have ensured the defeat of the Revolution. The shortage of troops, of which Sir William Howe complained, they thought might easily have been remedied by recruiting among the Loyalists. With proper support the friends of government might have overthrown the supporters of the Revolution in many districts and have spared the government the necessity of maintaining troops at those spots. Enough troops would have been freed, so it was claimed, to have ended the revolt in the districts where it was particularly strong. This brilliant avenue to success the Howes were accused of having neglected through failure to protect Loyalists from the marauding of the royal troops, through refusal to show them proper courtesy and attention, and through rejection of the assistance of the Loyalist troops which might, with little difficulty, have been recruited.

The Howes undoubtedly received abundant notice of the strength of Loyalist sentiment. While Sir William was still in Boston, Tryon wrote him from New York that the bulk of the people in the counties round the city felt favourably disposed to the British government, that the presence of five thousand regulars would ensure the restoration of British authority, and that two or three thousand provincial troops might be enlisted from among the Loyalists.[1] Although the force of this report was doubtless diminished by the fact that Tryon was at the time a refugee on board a man of war in the harbour, the contents of the despatches written by Sir William Howe during the campaign of 1776 show that he entertained strong hopes of at least some measure of the support which Tryon promised him.

Some support was, in fact, found at New York, but it fell far short of Howe's expectations. The Loyalist enthusiasts then described New Jersey as a region overflowing with loyal adherents of the Crown who only awaited a safe opportunity to declare themselves. To accommodate these potential supporters, Howe decided, rather against his better judgement, to extend his cantonments to Trenton. Their enthusiasm for the British cause did not survive the military disaster which the effort to encourage them brought about.

The following year, when the expedition to Pennsylvania was proposed, those who advised the move urged the advantage of cultivating the Loyalist sentiment in that colony. Germain hoped that the sentiment would prove so strong and widespread that a provincial force could be raised which would pro-

[1] C.O.5/93, pp. 79-80. Tryon-Howe, 3 December 1775.

tect the colony from further revolt from within and free the regular army for operations farther afield.[2]

The Howes' most severe critic, Joseph Galloway, was the most enthusiastic believer in Loyalist zeal and numbers. The experience of the war brought no change in his opinion, for as late as 1780 he wrote:

I pledge myself to you, to prove by the most satisfactory evidence, that a very great majority of the people of America are at this moment loyal to their sovereign and wish to be perfectly united in polity with the British government and to become perfect subjects of the British State.[3]

When, however, he was questioned carefully on this point during his testimony before the Parliamentary Inquiry on the Howes, his answers were much less emphatic.[4] A mass of evidence had been introduced to show that Howe in reality got very little response from the Loyalists. Galloway ascribed this diffidence to fear, since they were not armed or disciplined to protect themselves. This led to his being questioned about the exact amount of assistance that could be expected from the Loyalists.

Q. On the whole, will Mr. Galloway undertake to say from his own knowledge, while he remained with the army, that he saw any appearance or probability, either in the four lower counties, Pennsylvania, the Jersies, or provinces of New York, of a number of inhabitants sufficient to maintain themselves against the power and government of the Congress, though they had been armed?
A. He believed not, unless the army remained with them for some time: but the people of the Jersies, who had been deserted and left to the power of Congress, were

[2] C.O.5/94, pp. 339-44. Germain-Howe, 18 May 1777.
[3] Galloway, *Plain Truth*, pp. 31-2.
[4] *A View of the Evidence*, p. 68.

fearful of shewing themselves ever again friendly to Great Britain.

Q. Will the witness undertake to say that when the inhabitants were armed, disciplined, and protected by the Royal army, that they were able to defend themselves as soon as they lost the protection described, either in Pennsylvania, New York, Rhode Island, or the Jersies?

A. Certainly not without they should be assisted by the Royal army.[5]

Although an admission by one man is not decisive, an admission by one with the beliefs and prejudices of Galloway is not far short of it. If he could concede that the Loyalists could not have maintained themselves without support from the regular troops for an indefinite period, it seems unlikely that any contemporary whose judgment was worth anything would have claimed more. Galloway's self-esteem had been deeply wounded by the refusal of the Howes to place as high a value upon the support which he proffered them as he did himself, and we may be sure that any confession he made of the limited efficacy of that support was wrung from him only because it was an inescapable truth.

Thus it is fairly clear that the utmost help Howe could have secured from the Loyalists would have made possible but little alteration in his plan of campaign. In none of the districts which he occupied in 1776 or 1777 could he have organized a provincial force strong enough to hold the ground won after the regular army had moved on to other areas. Wherever provincial troops were used for garrison purposes, they needed stiffening by a considerable force of regulars. The exact amount of leaven needed is unimportant. Use of Loyalist troops would have decisively increased the power of the British field army only if they could have

5 Ibid.

been trusted to hold the conquered districts practically without assistance.

Although the raising of Loyalist troops did not provide a sure avenue to success, the Howes were diligent in recruiting them. Even hostile witnesses testified to the pains that they took.[6] Various inducements were offered, such as bounties and gifts of land after a certain period of service.[7] But the friends of government protested vigorously against the manner in which these troops were raised and organized. The Howes insisted that none of the Loyalists should receive arms unless enlisted in regularly organized provincial corps.[8] The provincial supporters of the Crown, on the other hand, wished to distribute arms to Loyalists without bothering about formal military organization.[9] They apparently believed that those thus armed would go forth, either individually or in impromptu groups, to terrify sympathizers with the Revolution and to make themselves masters of their districts. The real burden of the complaints against the Howes was not that they failed to raise provincial troops, but that they refused to sanction this indiscriminate issue of arms.

This reluctance on the part of the Howes was not surprising. Acquiescence in the demands of the Loyalist leader would have led either to nothing at all, with a consequent loss of military material, or to a sanguinary partisan strife that could not have failed to embitter the struggle beyond hope of ending it by reconciliation. An anecdote of Lord Howe puts the matter concisely.

The Admiral was some months ago applied to for letters of marque and commissions for privateers, to ferret out a

---

[6] Dom. State Papers, Geo. III, 18. The Howe Inquiry.
[7] *H.M.C. American Mss. in the Royal Institution*, vol. 5, no. 114.
[8] Dom. State Papers, George III, 18. The Howe Inquiry.
[9] Ibid.

numerous nest of small craft, which go between the Carolinas and the French West India islands and supply the
whole rebel continent.   With great heat and emotion, he
exclaimed, 'Good God! will you never have done with
teazing me? will you leave no room for reconciliation?'[10]

Obviously any hope of ending the conflict by conciliation would have disappeared promptly had a horde
of vengeful Loyalists been equipped with arms and
allowed to use them at will against anyone they thought
to be an enemy of the Crown.   The Howes rejected
the plan, not because they wished to ignore the help
which the Loyalists might give, but because this particular form of help would have ensured the defeat of
their own plans.

But the critics of the Howes denounced them not
only for refusing to distribute arms broadcast, but for
neglecting to recruit as many provincial troops as could,
by diligent effort, have been secured.   In these criticisms, however, an interesting discrepancy appears.
The critics were anxious to do two things, to prove that
the Howes had not made adequate use of the Loyalists,
and to demonstrate the depth of Loyalist enthusiasm
and devotion.   Hence they fell into the logical ab-
surdity of lamenting at one moment the inadequate
numbers of the provincial troops that were raised and
of citing figures the next instant to prove that they
were exceedingly numerous.   An address of the Loyalists in London in 1779 declared that their troops, then
in the army, 'exceeded in number the troops enlisted
(by Congress) to oppose them.'[11]   Another address in
1782 went even farther and asserted that 'there are
many more men in His Majesty's provincial regiments

[10] Historical Anecdotes, pp. 64-71.   Letter from New York, 7 February
1778.
[11] Sabine, *American Loyalists*, vol. 1, p. 72.

than there are in the continental service.'[12]   Sabine
said that many of the descendants of Loyalist officers,
with whom he had interviews, shared the belief that
the Loyalist troops were fully as numerous as the
American forces, although he himself felt somewhat
sceptical.

Still I doubt whether either the written or verbal statements are to be relied on implicitly, and for the reason
that, in the former, I am sure there are exaggerations on
other subjects, and the latter rest on the assertions of men
who were equally ready to attribute the success of the
Whigs and their own ruin to the inefficiency and bad management of Sir William Howe and other royal generals.[13]

If the figures claimed by the Loyalists were correct, the
Howes certainly achieved far more than had ever been
expected in the enlistment of provincials.   If those
figures were incorrect, the proof of Loyalist enthusiasm
becomes much less convincing.

The only figures of the Loyalist troops of any significance are those that show the total number of men
under arms at any one time.   Fortunately we have
these figures in the records of the Colonial Office.[14]
In 1777 the number was 3257 and in 1778, 7348.   In
1779, with Clinton in command, the figure was substantially the same as that for 1778.   The difference
between the figures for 1777 and 1778 was due of
course to the enlargement of the recruiting area occasioned by the Pennsylvania campaign.   Another
check on the number of Loyalist troops is Sabine's list
of the names of the Loyalist regiments, of which he
noticed twenty-six.   The average size of such regiments, under conditions of the time, was probably not

---

12 Sabine, *American Loyalists*, vol. 1, p. 72.
13 Ibid.
14 C.O.5/7, pp. 419-30.   Précis of orders for raising Provincials.

much over three hundred and certainly not over four hundred. That would bring the total to approximately the same figure indicated in the records of the Colonial Office.[15]

The testimony of General Robertson before the Inquiry, which was for the most part unfavourable to the Howes, brings further support to this conclusion. Upon examination by Burke he said:

> The loyal Provincials, in arms, amounted to between five and six thousand. . . He did not believe if the royal troops were withdrawn from his own government (New York), that the loyal Provincial military would be able to maintain their ground against the usurped power of the Congress.[16]

Yet it is difficult to think of any other place in America which it would have been as safe to entrust to the protection of Loyalist troops.

In seeking to judge whether the Howes made as much use of the Loyalists as was possible or wise, we must reject completely the idea that the Loyalist troops were so great in number as to have been almost sufficient by themselves to have ended the war. It cannot even be claimed for them that they could have held the ground won by British victories, except with the assistance of regular troops.

But were the seven or eight thousand provincials actually enrolled as many as could have been secured, subject to the conditions set by the Howes, namely, that they be organized as regular military units? As the precise number of Loyalist inhabitants can never be known, exact estimates of the potential military material among them can never be formed; but we

---

15 Sabine, *American Loyalists*, vol. 1, p. 73.
16 *A View of the Evidence*, p. 50.

can find a fairly satisfactory standard of comparison in the experience of the revolutionary party. At no time did Washington command an army appreciably more than double the numbers of the Loyalist troops. Yet the area from which he could recruit was many times larger than that held by the British, from which latter, for the most part, Loyalist soldiers must be secured. Furthermore, Washington's army, when at its largest, always contained a considerable percentage of militia under arms for a limited period. When he relied on regulars alone, his total force, especially in times of adversity, often sank below the totals of the Loyalist troops. Under the circumstances it seems that Sir William Howe secured as many Loyalist troops as could have reasonably been expected. He might, perhaps, have made a better showing on paper had he raised a Loyalist militia. But he never needed such uncertain support to win his battles, and the notorious unreliability of such troops would have made it utterly impossible to entrust to them the maintenance of the gains secured by the regulars.

Lord Howe was also denounced for refusing to make adequate use of the Loyalists in naval operations. Joseph Galloway, in particular, criticized him for refusing to allow certain Loyalists to take galleys to destroy American shipping in various inlets along the coast. Permission was first granted, then withdrawn. Galloway wrote :

Several of the inferior officers of the navy, it seems, murmured at seeing the captains of these galleys holding a commission above them. This was the ostensible reason, while many thought another was the true one. The navy officers did not wish to see others gaining the emoluments which must have been the result of these expeditions.[17]

17 *A Letter to the Rt. Hon. Lord Viscount H——e*, p. 40.

Probably Lord Howe's decision was in considerable part dictated by a desire to prevent Loyalists cruising about in semi-piratical fashion, vexing all and sundry, to the great embitterment of the struggle. But perhaps Galloway was partly right in attributing to him a professional dislike of turning over naval tasks to civilians and very possibly this feeling, plus pressure from his officers, prompted him to refuse the Loyalist mariners the opportunity they sought. Before we call the action short-sighted, however, we must remember the military and naval system of the day. Prize money in time of war was one of the few compensations for the hard work and meagre pay of a naval officer, and to turn opportunities for securing it over to civilians might have damaged naval morale. On land a problem of similar delicacy was to be faced. Regular army officers held their commissions by purchase, which made progress through the various grades a slow and costly process. Now, in wartime, civilians who had no other claim to preferment than an ability to produce a few motley individuals they chose to call a company, wished to receive commissions which, if granted, would make them outrank officers of long standing. A careful handling of this problem was necessary for the maintenance of the morale of the army; and if, both in the army and navy, the Howes may at times have been a little too considerate of the claims of regular officers, they would have been far more at fault had they ignored them.

Galloway also criticized Lord Howe's handling of the fleet. He argued that, had the ships of the fleet been sufficiently scattered, a ship could have been stationed at every important inlet and by such an arrangement the economic life of the colonies, and particularly that portion of it which facilitated the

supply of the American army, could have been stran-
gled.[18] The argument is plausible, but Galloway forgot that the fleet, thus scattered, would have required
weeks to concentrate sufficiently to defend itself against
a powerful adversary. Lord Howe clearly had this
possibility in mind when he explained his refusal to
authorize Loyalist privateers.

> The reason, and the only reason assigned, was an ap-
> prehension in your Lordship, that the privateers would
> take from the fleet under your command the seamen nec-
> essary to fight and navigate it.[19]

Of course the American naval force could never have
threatened the safety of the British fleet; but the possibility of war with France could never be neglected,
and, owing to the slowness of communications, it was
not at all improbable that a French fleet might arrive
ready for battle almost as soon as the news of the
declaration of war. Had such an event taken place
after Lord Howe had dispersed his fleet, he would
have been blamed without measure for the ensuing
disaster. Possibly Lord Howe did not quite appreciate the possibilities of close blockade, as developed later
during the wars of the French Revolution, but the
sort of blockade urged by Galloway would have been
safe only when there was no danger of war with a
great naval power.

Another important criticism of the British command
in America relates to the personal character of Sir
William Howe. Although he came to America with
as fine a reputation as any officer in the British army,
his lack of success was followed by insinuations that
he was either naturally incompetent or so given to
debauchery that his natural abilities had no opportu-

[18] *A Letter to the Rt. Hon. Lord Viscount H——e*, p. 28.
[19] Ibid., p. 37.

nity to make themselves felt. A number of writers have attributed to Howe's personal shortcomings a very decisive influence upon the outcome of the war.

These critics have some basis of fact for their charge. That Howe lived with a mistress, both at New York and Philadelphia, seems certain. She was a Mrs. Loring, a Boston lady whose husband was propitiated with certain employments in the army. Howe was also given to gambling, as was the lady, and helped to while away the long winter months in this fashion. Mrs. Loring was supposed to be the avenue whereby the General's favour could be secured.[20] All of these facts could certainly do the army no good, as has been frequently pointed out.

The most vivid description of the supposed personal incompetence of Sir William Howe is the letter of Charles Lee who, while a prisoner of the British, saw a good deal of Sir William.

He is, besides, the most indolent of mortals : never took farther pains to examine the merits or demerits of the cause in which he was engaged, than merely to recollect, that Great Britain was said to be the mother country, George the Third King of Great Britain, that the King and Parliament formed the supreme power, that a supreme power is absolute and uncontrollable, that all resistance must, consequently, be rebellion ; but, above all, that he was a soldier, and bound to obey in all cases whatever.

McKensey, Balfour, Galloway, were his counsellors : they urged him to all his acts of harshfulness ; they were his scribes ; all the damned stuff which was issued to the astonished world was theirs. I believe he scarcely ever read the letters he signed. . . You will say I am drawing my friend Howe in more ridiculous colours than he has yet been represented in : but that is his real character. He is naturally good humoured, complaisant, but illiterate and indolent to the last degree, unless as an executive sol-

20 *Historical Anecdotes*, pp. 38-48.

dier, in which capacity he is all fire and activity, brave and cool as Julius Caesar. His understanding is, as I observed before, rather good than otherwise, but was totally confounded and stupefied by the immensity of the task imposed upon him. He shut his eyes, fought his battles, drank his bottle, had his little whore, advised with his counsellors, received his orders from North and Germain (one more absurd than the other), took Galloway's opinion, shut his eyes, fought again, and is now, I suppose, to be called to account for acting according to instructions.[21]

This is a damning indictment which, at first sight, would seem to require either complete refutation or acceptance of the idea that Howe was an utterly inadequate commander. But on second thought, one may concede a certain element of truth in all that Lee wrote, yet create from it a very different picture of the British commander. That Howe was a great lunkhead, unaware of what he was doing, is too silly to be worthy of consideration. That he accepted the American command out of a desire for professional employment and a sense of military duty has already been indicated and may be accepted as having dulled, to some extent, the edge of his keenness. No doubt the individuals mentioned did influence him and did probably write some of his proclamations : but there is nothing unusual in that. The letters written in his own hand are of as high an intellectual standard as those which may possibly have been composed for him by his subordinates. That he was rather overwhelmed by the immensity and perplexity of his task seems in some degree probable. One gathers as much from his correspondence. But there is a difference between one who feels embarrassed and pessimistic

---

[21] *Memoirs of Charles Lee* (Langworthy, editor). Letter from Lee to Rush from Valley Forge, 4 June 1778, pp. 422-5.

because faced with an immensely difficult task and the utterly overwhelmed simpleton which Lee pictured. There was a kernel of truth in everything Lee alleged, but his description was so highly coloured as to be a rank caricature, which is only what one would have expected from Charles Lee, eager as ever to puff himself by condemning others.

We must also remember, as has been mentioned in a previous chapter, that in matters of general strategical importance Lord Howe shared equally with his brother the responsibility for the decisions taken. A certain class of decisions, of course, he could not influence, such as tactical decisions upon the field of battle. But, for the most part, these decisions were not those that have been attributed to the vices or other personal failings of Sir William Howe. His failure to form adequate plans, his excessive delay in beginning campaigns, his decision not to go up the Hudson, these and others of this type are those for which his private faults are usually made accountable. But these decisions were taken deliberately, in moments of comparative leisure, and it is certain that Lord Howe was party to them all. There is no evidence that Lord Howe suffered from similar temptation to neglect his duty nor any reason to believe he would have tolerated such a dereliction on the part of his brother. From the very nature of the dual command and the certain knowledge we have that the brothers collaborated in all important decisions, it seems out of the question to attribute to the personal habits of Sir William Howe the baleful influence upon large questions of strategy that some historians have professed to discover.

Had such inadequacy been so disastrously influential as is sometimes claimed, we ought to be able to sense the fact in the course of the Parliamentary investigation that followed the return of the Howes. The story of the investigation has been fully written by Worthington C. Ford, but a summary here may be worth something for the sake of the light it may shed on some of the points at issue.[22]

After the news of the Burgoyne disaster a rapidly growing volume of criticism of the Howes appeared in England, together with some directed against the ministry. Rumours began to circulate, prophesying the recall of Sir William Howe and the official letters to the commanders in America were thought to presage that action. Germain became increasingly hostile to the Howes.[23] In January 1778 Fox moved in Parliament for the instructions to Howe and Burgoyne. North, in reply, brought in a new commission of conciliation which was passed but pleased nobody. The recall of the Howes had been decided upon, but their names were included in the new commission.

At this point Israel Mauduit, inspired, so Mr. Ford concludes, by Germain, inaugurated the pamphlet war against the Howes. Burgoyne reached London in May and trouble began to brew in the House of Commons. Sir William Howe arrived in July, was received at court, and protested he had no intention of joining the Opposition, but said he must be allowed to justify himself, since he had been attacked by Germain and his friends. With the arrival of Lord Howe in October the air grew tense with rumours. Sir William moved that his correspondence with Germain be laid before the house, although at this time the King and ministry were considering what might be done for the

---

[22] *Parliament and the Howes,* in the *Massachusetts Historical Society Proceedings,* vol. 44, pp. 120-43.
[23] Donne, vol. 2, p. 116.

Howes, not what might be done to them. Lord Howe was even considered for the Admiralty, but made too difficult conditions. The government showed no anxiety to air the case or to make scapegoats of the Howes and the first motion for an inquiry was defeated without a division. Even Germain showed no great desire to defend himself. But the Opposition took the offensive and attacked the government for refusing an inquiry while stimulating hack writers to abuse the Howes. Germain, in answering an attack by Burgoyne, assailed the Howes and thus made it impossible to deny an inquiry.

The inquiry began in May 1779 and dragged on into June, rather overshadowed by the outbreak of war with Spain. The adjournment of Parliament on June 29 brought it to an inconclusive close. The pamphlet war continued several months longer and was as inconclusive as the inquiry, except that it has left a suspicion that has survived ever since that there was something sinister in the Howes' lack of success. In the Parliamentary Inquiry itself victory belonged to neither side. Most of the testimony that seems reliable or pertinent has been incorporated into the earlier chapters of this study.

The significant thing to remember about the Inquiry is that it was not the result of an angry demand of an outraged ministry for the trial of faithless or incompetent servants. The ministry sought as long as possible to avoid it. If any single minister provoked it, it was Germain through his inspiration of Mauduit. But there is no reason to think that Germain intended the matter to come before Parliament. It was only because of the fact that he was outmanoeuvred on the floor of the House of Commons and, in answering Burgoyne, tempted into an attack on the

Howes, that the government found it impossible to refuse the inquiry they demanded. In so far as the manner in which the inquiry came about indicates contemporary and informed opinion, we may say that the government feared it and the Howes welcomed it. But it would perhaps be unsafe to conclude much one way or another from that fact.

CHAPTER XVIII

CONCLUSION

WE HAVE reached a point where a general verdict upon the record of the Howes may be attempted, but the attempt ought to be preceded by a word of warning. General verdicts in history result inevitably in over-simplification owing to exigencies of space and language. The final result of the American command of the Howes was the product of a very complicated interplay of many factors. It is impossible in a single chapter to retrace all the intricate lines of the pattern. What is written here must be a summary of the principal influences at work. The reader must supply for himself, from his recollection of the previous pages, the background of uncertainty and misunderstanding that accompanies any military campaign and is part of any accurate picture of events.

The outbreak of the American Revolution presented the British government with a problem of extraordinary difficulty. Only a very superficial analysis of the situation in 1775 can lead to a conclusion that the revolution in America could have been crushed easily. It is true that the British did not find great difficulty in defeating the American army in the field, but the problem far transcended that. It was not an ordinary war that Great Britain had to fight, a contest against a government with a multitude of interests, where prompt acceptance of defeat in one field might be wise in order to avoid disaster in another. The very existence of the American government was at stake and peace on any terms but victory meant destruction. Individuals might make peace with the British government without great cost to themselves, but the government must win or collapse.

The British government was not in the grip of any such desperate necessity. British pride would have suffered from the loss of the American colonies, but the existence of the British nation was not imperilled. Greater dangers than the loss of the American colonies might well threaten, and consequently the British government could not afford to risk everything in that conflict. Strength had to be kept in reserve for a possible European crisis and, should that danger materialize, the support of the American war might have to be suddenly and drastically curtailed. Hence no British commander in America could be sure, from month to month, of the amount of support he could expect from home. Plans formed upon an expectation of consistent support might suddenly require radical revision through no fault of the government. Every possible plan for the defeat of the revolution had to face that hazard.

Quite apart from the possible intrusion of other factors, the perplexities facing the British command in America were sufficiently numerous. The defeat of the American army would not alone bring success. A revolt had to be subdued, a rebellious population brought to a willingness to accept once more the authority of the British government. This had to be done without excessive cost and in a fashion to ensure the future usefulness of the colonies. A mere harrying of all rebellious persons would not do. Ideally, the futility of resistance to the Crown ought to be proved by the use of the least possible severity, in order that the colonies would not be impoverished nor the colonists permanently embittered. To calculate the exact measures needed to achieve this result was far from easy; yet any plan of action that professed real statesmanship must attempt it.

The task of the British government was further complicated by political conditions at home and in America. In England George III and his friends were striving to carry out a political program disliked by a large section of the nation. If that irritation was to be kept within bounds, the nation must be spared as many burdens as possible. The government was not in a position to appeal to the country for unprecedented sacrifices. Until 1778 at least, a large section of public opinion regarded the conflict as a ministerial war, and so long as that was the case the government had to be wary about asking too much.

In the early stages of the war it was difficult to estimate the strength of the American resistance. The reports from the colonies were contradictory and Gage seldom seemed of the same mind twice in succession. Men in England who claimed to know the colonies well differed radically in their estimates of the military capacity of the colonials. Under the circumstances it was impossible for the government to discover with any degree of accuracy how serious an effort would be required for the defeat of the revolution.

These conditions made it impossible for the Howes to know how much of an effort the government was willing to make for the recovery of the colonies. They could not know whether their own view of what was necessary would be accepted at home. Even had there been momentary agreement at the outset, the rapid shifting of conditions in England and in America, and the slowness of communication between the two, made almost inevitable an ultimate divergence of view between the Howes and the ministry. The former, engrossed with their task, were certain to devote greater attention to deciding what they needed for success than they were to the ability of the government to meet their requests. The ministry, on the other hand, was equally certain to be more aware of its own embarrassments than of the perplexities of the Howes. It was only natural, therefore, that within a few months the Howes were looking to the government for more support than it was willing to give, and the government was looking to the Howes for a more rapid victory than they were in a position to provide.

The choice of the Howes for the American command did not, in the long run, prove fortunate, but some of their qualities which were later thought objectionable seemed at the time to recommend them. The Howes were neither members of the Opposition nor of the King's party. They were professional military men in search of employment. Owing possibly to their left-handed relationship to the royal family, their search had been rewarded by some promise of favour. The outbreak of the war in the colonies made it almost inevitable that this promise would materialize in the shape of an American command. They seemed well suited to the task, especially as the government hoped to make use of conciliatory methods. They had both served in America and had been well liked there. Their elder brother, slain at Ticonderoga, had enjoyed a real popularity. No commander of the British forces in America could have been expected to make the colonists predisposed to listen to reason so well as one by the name of Howe.

The Howes approached their task with mixed feelings. For war against the Americans they felt no enthusiasm; yet they objected to the toleration of rebellion. They felt a natural desire for professional employment, and they also hoped that their popularity with the colonists would help end the revolution with a minimum of armed conflict. The conciliatory policy which they were authorized to carry out did not, it is true, command the united support of the ministry. Some of its members consented only because they feared the Howes would drift into opposition unless given the American command on their own terms. But others, notably North, entertained a genuine hope that the revolution might be ended by some method short of relentless war. Even Germain felt that much might be accomplished by an appeal to Loyalist sentiment, although he thought only severity would prove effective against the originators of the revolt.

There was thus nothing illogical, nothing obviously mistaken, in the choice of the Howes for the American command or in their acceptance of it. Their professional competence was unquestioned and they seemed fortunately placed, by experience and conviction, to combine the arts of soldier and peacemaker. The fact that conciliation was the cornerstone of their policy, whereas some of the cabinet accepted it either with little faith or ill-concealed dislike, had not yet become the disastrous source of friction that it later was to be.

Military difficulties alone made the task of the Howes very formidable. The British army was one of the best in Europe, but its maintenance presented a difficult problem. Recruits were scarce and required long training. Throughout Europe governments and commanders sought to husband their military resources and often showed a greater anxiety to avoid losses than they did to win battles. Frederick the Great, who had to answer to no higher authority and who had to take desperate chances, could make tremendous demands of his troops and accept the resulting loss. But Frederick could not have done it had he been only a general, and he probably would not have done it had a less critical situation faced him.

Sir William Howe in America had, in this particular, less freedom of action than a commander in Europe would have enjoyed. Three thousand miles from home, in a position where even a request for reinforcements might take months in transit, and where a year must elapse before the troops could arrive at the scene of operations, the evil consequences of any serious loss were doubly injurious. His campaigns had to be fought in a region where the valour and discipline of the British regulars on the battlefield were of less importance than skill in marching and foraging, arts in which the British never enjoyed a great reputation. The American colonies, in comparison with Europe, were rough and inhospitable, characterized by a scarcity of good billets and ready supplies. The severe winters, doubly hard on unseasoned Europeans, took a heavy toll whenever extensive operations were attempted during that period of the year. Nature, the state of American civilization, and the conditions of the war, conspired to impose upon the British commander an unusual measure of caution.

In addition to all this, the eighteenth century was an age of military formalism. In this formalism Sir William Howe had been thoroughly steeped, although his work in developing light infantry during the years before the Revolution indicates that he was no mere slave of tradition. But the unusual situation that faced him, if to one type of mind it might have suggested a departure from rule, to another would have suggested strict adherence to convention as probably the safest path through a maze of difficulty too complex for precise survey. A reading of Sir William Howe's despatches leaves the impression that his mind took the latter path. The tremendous responsibility with which he was entrusted seemed to accentuate this trend. He seems to have felt that, if he followed the conventional rules and then failed, he could say in his own defence that he had observed the best accepted practice. His desire to succeed appeared gradually to transform itself into a wish to avoid mistakes. To this tendency can probably be attributed his failure to push advantages to the limit and his fear of taking chances that seemed to bolder minds to offer reasonable promise of success. It is, of course, impossible to prove that this frame of mind was decisive at any given moment, but a careful study of Sir William Howe's correspondence leaves me convinced, when looking upon his command as a whole, that it was an influence of major importance.

Various possibilities were open to the Howes when they devised their plan of operations. Only one policy, that of subjecting the colonies to the utmost severity and vexation, was ruled out. The simplest among those which the Howes might have chosen was that of concentrating upon the destruction of the American field army in the hope that the dispersal of that force would so discourage the Americans that the more minute work of pacification, the 'mopping up,' as it would be called today, could be left to take care of itself. Or certain key districts might have been occupied in order to cut the enemy's communications and cramp his movements and make impossible the support of his armed forces. In some measure both of these schemes were embodied in the plans of the Howes and of the government. Sir William always hoped to be able to bring Washington's army to decisive action. The Burgoyne expedition was designed to cut off New England from the other colonies; and Howe, when planning his expedition to Pennsylvania, had at one time an intention of cutting Washington off from contact with the southern colonies by interposing between him and the Susquehanna.

But these ideas only played a subordinate part in the plans of the Howes; they had in mind a more subtle and complicated scheme. First and foremost, they wished to convince the colonists that successful resistance to Great Britain was impossible and to effect that persuasion in a manner that would make return to British allegiance easy and permanent. The plan they devised bore close resemblance to the operations of a skilfully handled police force in times of public disturbance. The incorrigible and organized rioters, represented in this case by Washington's army, were to be attacked and broken up whenever safe and convenient to do so. The rest of the disorderly element, represented by the unorganized revolutionaries, was to be taught, by a steady and methodical enlargement of the area of British occupation, that continued resistance to law and order was impossible. One revolted district after another was to be reconquered in this fashion and held in subjection by a humane but masterful occupation. It was hoped that, in time, this steady progress of British arms would appear so irresistible that even remote centers of rebellion would recognize the futility of resistance and abandon the contest without waiting for the arrival of British troops.

Thus the actual fighting would be kept at a minimum and bitter memories be avoided.

This plan had much to recommend it. If carried through vigorously it was relatively safe. It called for no immediate risk. Where the enemy could not be safely attacked he could be manœuvred into retirement. So long as the British army could put into the field a force able to meet the enemy army on even terms, there was little danger of any major disaster. The plan would engender the minimum of bitterness in the defeated colonists; it might even be carried through in such fashion that the Americans would be brought to an attitude approaching cordiality. To help make this possible there was the commission which, although it offered little to the Americans unless they were prepared to submit, might have made their submission easier after they had concluded that no other course remained open to them.

Certain difficulties, however, stood in the way of success. First of all, the plan was costly. The nearer the work approached completion, the more expensive it would become, for more and more territory would have to be occupied at the same time that a sufficient field army for enlarging the area of occupation was kept available. To adopt such a scheme was unwise unless the British government could reasonably be expected to support it. It is a fair criticism of the Howes that they lacked sufficient reason for believing that the British government would be either able or willing to support such a plan. Had they been promised help to that extent, their complaints when it was later denied them would have been justified. But the government made no such pledge and it is doubtful whether it could have been fulfilled had it been made. The Howes failed to come to any understanding with the government about the amount of support they were to have in case the war lasted beyond the year 1776. After they had reached America and discovered that at least a second campaign would be necessary, they went ahead on the assumption that they could count on the forces needed for their plan. The ministry, on the other hand, proceeded on the assumption that the troops provided at first, plus just enough to maintain the original figure, ought to suffice.

The responsibility for this misunderstanding probably lies as much with one party as with the other. Yet neither ought to be blamed too severely. In a difficult task of co-operation such as this, even if all concerned acted both with skill and a desire to be as co-operative as possible, the risk of imperfect co-ordination was great. Few revolutions would have succeeded if the government in power had always been able to estimate accurately the seriousness of the danger and to mobilize effectively its potential power. But government is so complicated a business that miscalculations will occur. When sufficiently serious, an apparently unpromising revolt may succeed, and those involved in the failure of the government will be labelled incompetent.

In every human event present action is influenced greatly by the recollection of past experience. So it was with the Howes, particularly with Sir William.[1]

---

[1] It is not my intention to suggest that the horror of Bunker Hill so plagued his memory that he ever afterward had little nerve for vigorous action, as Henry Lee argued in his *Memoirs of the War in the Southern Department of the United States*, p. 55, vol. 1. That battle did teach him a respect for colonials behind breastworks, but his reluctance to attempt frontal assaults were due less to a morbid recollection of Bunker Hill than to a calculated desire to maintain his army in accordance with the routine military thought of the day. He could not afford the heavy losses that such assaults involved and retain sufficient strength for the plan of campaign he had adopted.

From the time of the siege of Boston it was his almost constant misfortune to suffer from a variety of annoyances and mortifications. These seldom came from big reverses, but rather from an inability to operate freely or from a failure to secure as favourable a permanent result as immediate success had seemed to warrant. The embarrassments of the British position at Boston made Howe fear that the revolt would prove more difficult to subdue than he had at first supposed. The refusal of the Americans to abandon the contest after the New York campaign served further to damage his optimism and to convince him that only a long and extensive effort could re-establish British authority. This series of disappointments gradually led him to overestimate the capacity of his opponent. He reconciled himself to the idea of a long war and therefore showed less eagerness to snatch at fleeting opportunities than he would have shown had he believed one or two resounding successes might end the contest. Brilliant assaults demanded risks which, in the light of Sir William Howe's estimate of the advantage to be secured, seemed unjustifiably great.

This steadily growing pessimism from which the Howes suffered throughout the period of their command certainly influenced their operations. Success seemed always to escape them and they sensed the disappointment that the indecisiveness of their operations occasioned at home. Instead of spurring them on to taking greater chances, it accentuated their belief in the need for extreme caution. They tended to exaggerate the powers of their opponents and to be excessively impressed by the hazards of any attempt to force an immediate decision.

Here the lack of touch between the Howes and the ministry showed its baleful influence. Had the Howes understood fully the difficulty the government was having in supporting the war, they might have felt justified in taking greater risks. Instead, they assumed that the government ought, and therefore probably would, support them so generously that serious risk would be unnecessary. In so doing they rejected a familiar principle of war, that the enemy should be attacked with full vigour wherever found. Commanders who have followed it have often found victory awaiting them where an objective estimate of their prospects would have made its achievement appear impossible. Perhaps Sir William Howe ought to have followed this rule. But his responsibilities were great, and the penalty for rashness apparently tremendous, so that we need not call him treasonous or incompetent if he chose to pursue a more cautious policy.

The Howes also were not always perfectly consistent in their devotion to their main plan of operations. At times Sir William's letters pointed in the direction of other plans, of pushing the enemy without relaxation and at all hazard, or of initiating a comprehensive scheme of interference with the communications and daily life of the colonies that would distress and embarrass them into submission. As the Howes never formulated in any one document the theory which, on the whole, seems to have guided them, they themselves were possibly not fully aware how much they were in its grip, and consequently these occasional stabs in the direction of a different policy probably did not seem to them inconsistent. As their pessimism grew from insufficient success, so also grew their tendency to oscillate between one scheme and another in the hope that opportunism would unlock the door of success which the key of consistent theory had failed to open.

Even at the very start the Howes approached their task without much confidence. All through their correspondence can be read the fear that the Revolution would resist the best calculated measures that could be devised against it, and this fear served to give a tentative quality to all their efforts. Their lack of confidence made them too sensitive to indications that a particular operation had collided with insuperable obstacles. Each too-readily-abandoned scheme increased their pessimism and lessened the likelihood that the next advance would be pushed with all the vigour possible.

It was pointed out in the previous chapter that the personal vices of Sir William Howe, often advanced as an explanation of the inertia ascribed to him, could not have been decisive in the major decisions of strategy. It is possible, however, that they may have had a slight influence in matters in which Lord Howe did not collaborate. It seems more probable, however, that his vices were the consequence of his ill success and discouragement rather than the cause. That is the proper interpretation of Lee's account. Of course, a surrender to debauch as a solace for discouragement would only add to a commander's difficulties, and perhaps that was the case with Sir William. It would be an exaggeration, however, to ascribe to this more than a subordinate influence in the course of events.

The most serious charge made against the Howes is that they did not wish to win and made no serious effort to do so. They are charged with having carried on this flirtation with treason because of their tenderness toward the Americans and their dislike of the ministerial party. There is absolutely no foundation for the assumption. No evidence exists to sup-

port it except the venomous complaints of certain
contemporaries who were disappointed at the failure
to defeat the Revolution, but who had no means of
knowing that the Howes were losing deliberately, even
had that been the case. The only argument for this
view is the belief that nothing less serious could have
explained the failure of the Howes to win. This argument ignores the fact, which it has been one of
the purposes of this book to point out, that the obstacles to British success were very great. Whatever the
circumstances, it is almost inconceivable that men of
the position and reputation of the Howes could have
betrayed their trust in the manner charged. Only
conclusive evidence that they did so would justify
giving credence to the accusation. Not a shred of
such evidence has ever been found.

In dismissing as absurd the charge of deliberate be-
trayal, we need not deny that the sympathy of the
Howes for the Americans had some importance.
They knew that elements in the ministry believed that
the colonists ought to be treated with severity and had
no sympathy with the careful mixture of force and
leniency which they themselves were endeavouring to
employ. With people who were more anxious to take
vengeance upon the Americans than to make them willing subjects once more the Howes had not a moment of
sympathy, whether such persons were located in
Whitehall or among Loyalist circles in America.
Their dislike of the advocates of vengeance appeared
frequently throughout their correspondence with the
government and apparently added to their feeling that
they and the government were working at cross purposes. This increased their own pessimism and possibly led to a less vigorous policy than might have

been adopted by commanders who felt themselves more in harmony with their superiors.

The criticism of the Howes for inadequate utilization of Loyalist support was fully considered in the previous chapter. At this point it will be sufficient to recall that the Loyalist enthusiasts had in mind a general arming of their friends as a prelude to a grandiose guerilla war upon all rebel sympathizers. Such a scheme, however, would have ruined any prospect of achieving peace by reconciliation. The Howes were only safeguarding their own plan of operations in refusing to accept it. Within the more limited plan of enrolling Loyalists as regular troops the Howes showed creditable vigour and probably secured about as many troops as circumstances permitted. Even a slightly greater return of recruits would not have altered the fact, admitted by Galloway, that the Loyalists could not hold the colonies in subjection without the continued presence of the British army.

In discussing the Howes we must also guard against assuming that the opposition of Washington and his army was of small importance. Much has been written in recent years belittling Washington's military reputation. Very possibly he is not entitled to rank with the great commanders of history, but at certain moments critical for the American cause, he showed a combination of fortitude and bold initiative that made him, for the moment at least, a leader of the highest order. Trenton and Germantown were riposts of great daring and decisive influence. Sir William Howe faced an opponent in the field who made serious mistakes but who possessed unusual tenacity and showed a capacity approaching genius for denying the British the full fruits of victory.

Before passing a final judgment on the Howes we must ask how near they came to success. Although their story is one of eventual failure, there is reason to believe they were not as far short of victory as usually supposed. The American situation before Trenton was certainly desperate and, had Washington been compelled to go through the winter without the restorative effect of that victory, we cannot feel certain that his army would have survived. Perhaps only a chance of war, a risk deliberately but reluctantly taken by Howe in an endeavour to make the power of British arms felt as widely as possible, saved the day for his adversary. From a very similar, although less acute, crisis the Americans were saved by the moral effect of Germantown. Had the British remained in Philadelphia, instead of abandoning it precipitately as soon as Clinton assumed command, would they not have produced a drain upon the resources and morale of the revolt that would have been very critical? The strain of supporting the war over a long period nearly brought about an American collapse before Yorktown. How much more serious would have been that strain had Philadelphia, as well as New York, remained constantly in British possession? It is perhaps risky to speculate about what might have happened, but it seems quite possible that the Howes were nearer victory than their recall and the subsequent abandonment of Philadelphia have led the world to believe.

Since, however, the government was unwilling and perhaps unable to support them as liberally as they desired, their plan of operations had reached its limit. We may say that the Howes were near victory only by imagining that the government could have reinforced them enough to make possible a further extension of

British occupation. The unwillingness or inability of the government to do so required the adoption of some less expensive plan. It was impossible to operate as the Howes proposed to operate and do so inexpensively.

Thus the ill success of the Howes is traceable primarily to their failure to adjust their methods to the support that the government was willing to provide. They had a plan that might have succeeded, that would have produced a superior type of reconciliation ; but it was costly in time, money, and troops. The government would not, probably could not, foot the bill. For this failure to adjust plans to resources both the Howes and the government were responsible. This lack of co-ordination was aggravated by the fact that neither party knew, nor could know, exactly in advance the vitality of the Revolution or the strength of Loyalist sentiment. By the time the Howes were in a position to make an accurate estimate of these decisive factors, they were out of touch with the ministry at home. Under the conditions, only extraordinary luck could have prevented confusion and misunderstanding.

But this confusion of ideas, although a natural product of the conditions of the struggle, cannot entirely exculpate Sir William Howe. We may acquit him of treachery or of the grosser forms of incompetence, but we must recognize that he continually fell a little short of the most vigorous and effective use of his opportunities. All commanders have missed opportunities, but Sir William Howe continually failed to rise to the full possibilities of the occasion. In the face of difficulty his mind took refuge in routine ideas. He developed the habit of underestimating his prospects of success. He failed to push his advantages as vigorously as possible, partly because of pessimism, partly because of fear that reverses would destroy the powerful and majestic impression he wished British arms to make upon the Americans. He played safe too often and did so when only a more daring policy would have brought success. His anxiety to subdue the revolt in a way to make possible harmonious relations in the future between the colonies and the mother country, although sound in substance, led him to the use of half measures.

Men of excellent records, with well deserved reputations for ability and energy, frequently prove disappointing when at length they arrive at positions of high and independent responsibility, especially when their previous training and experience have not provided ready answers for the new problems with which they find themselves confronted. Sir William Howe was a case in point. In the face of a truly appalling measure of personal responsibility, Howe's personality and capacity seemed to strike a hitherto undiscovered limitation. The situation demanded a great man: Sir William Howe was just a competent man. In the face of a need for greatness his mere competence looked weak in comparison. He himself seemed dimly aware of the fact and, as a result, he did not manifest his ordinary competence and vigour.

Recognition of this personal element in the story must not blind us, however, to the fact that the confusion and misunderstanding attendant upon such a peculiar war as that of the American Revolution must bear the major responsibility for the failure of the Howes. To put it in its simplest terms, the Howes built a plan too expensive for the British government to use for more than a single year, a mistake for which the blame must be attributed to the Howes, to the government, and to the inevitable confusion of events. This, qualified by the personal equation that has been described, rather than some easy explanation of treason, vice, or sheer incompetence, is the key to the mystery of the Howe brothers' American command.

BIBLIOGRAPHY

ANY attempt to provide an exhaustive bibliography for even the purely military side of the American Revolution would require a volume in itself and is unnecessary for this work. This bibliography will contain only such material as is of service in forming an estimate of the work of the Howe brothers, with the addition, for the several phases of their career in America, of a few of the more important works from which can be secured the best account of the general course of operations.

It is always a problem to know how best to organize the materials of a bibliography. It has seemed wisest here to divide them into five classes: (1), printed works covering the war and its problems in a broad way; (2), manuscript materials and printed guides to the same; (3), source material that may be obtained in printed form; (4), the controversial literature that centred round the Parliamentary Inquiry into the work of the Howes; and (5), printed works dealing with particular phases of the war.

I

Although nearly fifty years have elapsed since the publication in 1886 of volume VI of Winsor's *Narrative and Critical History* (Houghton Mifflin, Boston & N. Y.), that still remains the greatest single mine of information about the detailed military events of the American Revolution and particularly about the source material from which any history of the period must be written. This work contains all the material that was to be found in the original edition of Winsor's *Handbook of the American Revolution,* published in 1879 (Houghton Osgood, Boston). Each chapter is written by an expert on his subject and the text is small in comparison with the bibliographical footnotes.

No attempt need be made to list modern histories of the American Revolution, for their number is legion. Among the works of large scope and real distinction, that of Sir George Otto Trevelyan, *The American Revolution* (4 vols., Longmans, Green, N. Y., 1899–1912) stands out, although it may be objected to on grounds of its Whig bias. Another modern history of the Revolution that is peculiarly suggestive for students of the career of the Howes is Sydney G. Fisher's *The Struggle for American Independence* (2 vols., Lippincott, Phila. & London, 1908). This work has the distinction of coming nearer than any other general history to a correct appreciation of the command of the Howes. The most recent general history of the period, *The War of Independence* by C. H. Van Tyne (Houghton Mifflin, Boston & N. Y., 1929), falls into a number of errors in interpreting the activities of the Howes.

While the Revolutionary War was still fresh in the memories of contemporaries, Stedman produced his *History of the American War* (2 vols., London, 1794). Stedman served with the British army in America, and that experience gave a very intimate quality to what he wrote. The most valuable copy of Stedman is in the John Carter Brown Library at Providence, Rhode Island. It belonged to Sir Henry Clinton, who made marginal comments that often shed a great deal of light upon the proper interpretation of events recorded in the text. Clinton also embodied his observations on Stedman's History in a pamphlet entitled, *Observations on Mr. Stedman's History of the American War*, which was published in London in 1794. Another contemporary work of real value is an anonymous production known as *The Boston History*, so-called from its place of publication, where it was printed in 1781–82. It is particularly useful for a long account of political conditions in England at the outbreak of the war and for a very full narrative of the meeting of Lord Howe and the American commissioners in 1776.

Of modern works devoted strictly to the military history of the war, the best known is Sir John Fortescue's *History of the British Army* (Macmillan, London & N. Y., 1899 et seq.), of which volume three is devoted largely to the American Revolution. This work, although extremely useful because of its detailed account of military events, suffers on the interpretative side from too great a propensity to attribute all failures of operations to the incompetence of the civil authorities. Among military histories of the war written in America, *The Revolutionary War and the Military Policy of the United States* (Scribners, N. Y., 1911) by General Francis V. Greene is a good brief account. *Washington, Commander-in-Chief* by Thomas G. Frothingham (Houghton Mifflin, Boston & N. Y., 1930), is also valuable. On the naval side A. T. Mahan's *Major Operations of the Royal Navy, 1762–1783* (Little, Brown, Boston, 1898) is probably the best account. A recent book by W. M. James, *The British Navy in Adversity* (Longmans, Green, London & N. Y., 1926), also gives a good summary but adds nothing new. For the character of the British army and the difficulties that beset its enlistment and organization one may consult E. E. Curtis, *Organization of the British Army in the American Revolution* (Yale Univ. Press, New Haven ; Humphrey Milford, Oxford U. Press, London, 1926). J. F. C. Fuller's *British Light Infantry in the Eighteenth Century* (Hutchinson, London, 1925) describes the effort, to which Sir William Howe contributed, to give greater flexibility to operations by the use of light troops.

Foremost among the writers who have addressed themselves to the problem of the Howes was Charles Francis Adams, in whose *Studies Military and Diplomatic* (Macmillan, N. Y., 1911) is contained the criticism of the British campaign of 1777 which he first contributed to the *Proceedings of the Massachusetts Historical Society* in 1883. He condemns the Howes almost without stint. On the other side is Charlemagne Tower in his *Essays Political and Historical* (Lippincott, Philadelphia & London, 1914), of which one is devoted to the campaigns of the Howes. It is, in my judgment, the most accurate analysis that has been made of the motives of the Howes.

Three other works are of great value to the student of the detailed military events of the Revolution because of the many factual items that they provide : H. B. Carrington, *Battles of the American Revolution, 1775–1781. Historical and Military Criticism with topographical illustration* (A. S. Barnes & Co., N. Y., 1876) ; Henry B. Dawson, *Battles of the United States* (Johnson, Fry, N. Y., 1858) ; and B. J. Lossing, *Pictorial Field Book of the Revolution* (Harper, N. Y., 1855).

II

Any student preparing to study the records of the British campaigns in America will turn for guidance to C. M. Andrews, *Guide to the Materials for American History to 1783 in the Public Record Office of Great Britain* (Carnegie Institution, Washington, 1912–14). Also of great assistance is the companion volume by the same author, *Guide to the Manuscript Materials for the History of the United States to 1783 in the British Museum and in Minor London Archives and in the Libraries of Oxford and Cambridge* (Carnegie Institution, Washington, 1908).

The great source for the British side of military operations during the Revolution, and especially for the motives that actuated the British commanders, is found in the records of the Colonial Office deposited in the Public Record Office. The correspondence between the Colonial Office and the commanders-in-chief in America is found in class five, cited in this work as C.O.5. Both incoming and outgoing letters are arranged in the order of receipt and despatch. Each volume contains a year's business and makes no attempt to segregate letters sent from letters received. Hence, for example, the volume for 1776 will not contain all the despatches written by Sir William Howe in that year, but only such as reached Whitehall before 1 January 1776. On the other hand, all of Germain's despatches for the year will be there. Those of Howe which arrived after the beginning of the year are in the 1777 volume.

The important volumes begin with class 5, vol. 92, cited as C.O.5/92, which contains the correspondence for 1775, including all of Gage's letters from late in 1774 until his recall, and a number from Howe written in the weeks just before and after his assumption of command. In general, one could count on letters written in America being received at Whitehall about a month after writing, but letters travelling westward across the Atlantic usually required at least double the time. Volumes 93, 94 and 95 contain the remainder of the correspondence between Germain and Sir William Howe, the several volumes representing 1776, 1777, and 1778 respectively.

The contents were not confined to official letters, but contain a great quantity of other material. Howe forwarded many letters he had received from various people in the colonies and also sent returns of troops, provisions, and the like. A large part of this material was incorporated in these volumes of records. Germain, on his part, not infrequently forwarded to Howe information which had come to him, so that probably half of each volume is made up of this illustrative material. Its inclusion makes consecutive reading of the volumes particularly valuable, for these various pieces form a commentary on the ideas contained in the official letters and indicate the sort of information that was considered significant by both Howe and Germain.

There are other volumes in class 5 of the Colonial Office Records that are valuable for a study of the Howes. Volume 139 is filled largely with returns of the German mercenaries and contains the treaties whereby their services were secured. Volume 155 has a few odds and ends that are of use. Volume 242 contains a list of the papers on the American campaigns laid before the House of Commons. Volume 7 has a précis of the orders for raising provincial troops and is valuable for estimating their importance in the British plans.

Of particular importance is volume 177, which contains the correspondence of both the Howes with Germain in regard to the use of their commission to negotiate peace, together with a copy of the commission itself. This volume also contains copies of the proclamations which the Howes issued in furtherance of their plans for conciliation.

Volume 229 has the correspondence between Germain and Col. Guy Johnson, the son of Sir William, who was carrying on his father's work with the Indians. It throws some light on the situation in America. Volume 253 contains various précis, of which the most important concern the reasons for the Canadian expedition and the measures for reinforcing the British army under Howe in 1776. In addition to the facts contained, these précis are useful in showing the attitude which Germain's office took toward these measures and the light in which it wished its actions regarded.

For an understanding of the Burgoyne expedition and the real intention behind it, the primary source lies in C.O.5, class 42, volumes 36 and 37. The former in particular is important. It contains the correspondence between Germain and Carleton for 1777 and also a number of letters from Burgoyne. In it can be traced the genesis of the Canadian campaign and Burgoyne's reinterpretation of it as difficulties began to gather round him. There is also some Burgoyne material in volume 37, that for 1778.

The despatches from Lord Howe to the Admiralty for the years 1776 and 1777 are contained in the Admiralty Records, class 1, volume 487. Except for a very occasional ray of light upon the motives of Lord Howe, these despatches yield comparatively little that is of significance for the present study.

In the Domestic Papers, George III, three volumes yield

various items of some value. Volumes 11 and 12 contain odds and ends, chiefly minutes of cabinet meetings. Volume 18 is more important, as it contains the full minutes of the Parliamentary Inquiry. It is only in a very nominal sense, however, that these State Papers may be called volumes, for they are merely stray papers tied together, without any binding or permanent arrangement. The Colonial Office and Admiralty documents are bound and in many cases have the pages numbered.

This enumeration covers only a fraction of the records in the Public Record Office that deal with the American Revolution. Many of the others, such as the War Office Records and other Colonial Office volumes not mentioned here, would be necessary for the writing of a complete history of the Revolutionary War but are of very secondary value for a study confined to the British command.

The British Museum has some manuscripts of value. Most important is Additional Manuscripts, 21,680, the correspondence between Major Hutcheson, who served in America, and General Haldimand, who had been much in America but was in England during the period of the Howe brothers' command. Additional Manuscripts, 34,413, the Auckland Papers, have various letters from America, some of which are useful, as have also No. 35,912, the Hardwick Papers. No. 21,661 has the correspondence between Haldimand and Amherst. The Egerton Manuscripts contain a journal of the operations of the British army under Howe, but it is of little value, the sort of thing that could be thrown together from any good textbook. There are a few other pertinent documents to be found among the British Museum manuscripts, but nothing of importance for this study that is not obtainable elsewhere.

Within the past few years some very important documentary material has been brought to this country by Mr. William L. Clements and has been kept in his private library at Bay City, Michigan.[1] This material has been described by Mr. Randolph G. Adams, the Librarian of the William L. Clements Library at Ann Arbor, in two short volumes, *The Headquarters Papers of the British Army in North America during the War of the American Revolution; a brief description of Sir Henry Clinton's papers in the William L. Clements Library* (Wm. L. Clements Library, Ann Arbor, 1926) and *The Papers of Lord George Germain; a brief description of the*

[1] As a consequence of Mr. Clements's death, this material will presumably be transferred to the William L. Clements Library at Ann Arbor.

Stopford-Sackville papers now in the William L. Clements Library (Wm. L. Clements Library, Ann Arbor, 1928). The Germain Papers contain a number of items not previously known but are of far less importance to this study than are the Clinton Papers. These latter contain the great mass of Clinton's correspondence. Naturally, the major portion of it covers the later years of the war, when Clinton held the chief command, but there is a great deal on the period when Clinton was subordinate to Sir William Howe. In addition to the correspondence, there is a work in manuscript entitled *An Historical Detail of Seven Years Campaigns in North America from 1775 to 1782*, in which Clinton makes many interesting observations upon the work of the Howes.

The Clinton Papers contain a great deal of information important for a correct understanding of the British actions during the period we have under consideration. If, on the whole, Clinton's testimony tends to support the conclusions drawn from the more familiar sources, much that is definitely new appears in connexion with various details. The papers also present an extraordinary picture of Clinton, who reveals himself as a person with so overdeveloped a sensitivity to slights, real and imagined, that one almost questions his sanity. This morbid state of mind has to be kept in view in reading his criticisms of the Howes.

In their present arrangement it is impossible to give volume or folio citations for the Clinton Papers. The real guide to the papers is Miss Jane Clark, who has been doing the work of sorting them and preparing typewritten transcripts to accompany each letter. This last service is really a vital one, for Clinton's handwriting is so difficult that only a person as experienced and skilful as Miss Clark could hope to decipher it in any reasonable length of time.

Mr. Clements also made possible the bringing to this country of the Knox and Shelburne Papers, which contain a few things of value for the history of the Howes. These collections, however, are not in Mr. Clements's residence, but are in the William L. Clements Library at Ann Arbor.

III

The student of the American Revolution is fortunate in finding a good deal of source material already in print. *The Parliamentary History,* especially volume 18, is of great value in showing the ideas of the time as reflected in the debates in Parliament. It also contains the papers on the American situation submitted to Parliament at the beginning of the war. The most convenient source for Gage's opinions on that subject is now Clarence C. Carter's *The Correspondence of General Thomas Gage* (2 vols., Yale Univ. Press, New Haven ; Humphrey Milford, Oxford Univ. Press, London, 1931–33). *The Annual Register* and the *Gentleman's Magazine* are also valuable for contemporary politics. For many years W. B. Donne's *The Correspondence of King George the Third with Lord North from* 1768 *to* 1783 (J. Murray, London, 1867) was indispensable for studying the position and influence of the King. It still is essential for the story of the relations between the King and his Prime Minister, but as a compilation of the King's correspondence it has been superseded by Sir John Fortescue's *Correspondence of King George the Third from* 1760 *to December* 1783 (Macmillan, London, 1927–28) which contains all the King's correspondence for that period. Horace Walpole's *Last Journals* (J. Lane, London, N. Y., 1910) although full of the bias of the diarist, nevertheless afford a valuable commentary on events of the period.

But the greatest collection of printed sources is found in the reports of the Historical Manuscripts Commission. Most important of all are the two volumes of the *Manuscripts of Mrs. Stopford-Sackville,* which contain the papers of Lord George Germain. Volume one contains correspondence between Germain and various officials in the administration, Pownall, Knox, and Eden especially. Volume two contains correspondence between him and the Howes. Some of it only duplicates what may be found in the Colonial Office Records, but it also contains some very valuable letters not found in the official records.

Material of use in this study is also found in the reports on the *Manuscripts of Miss M. Eyre Matcham* in *Various Collections,* vol. 5, and in the *Report on the American Manuscripts in the Royal Institution.* The reports on the *Manuscripts of the Earl of Dartmouth,* the *Manuscripts of the Earl of Carlisle,* and the *Manuscripts of the Marquess of Lothian* also contain Revolutionary material.

The volumes of *Almon's Remembrancer* contain many letters that were known to contemporaries and are important for showing the information upon which contemporary opinion was based.

In the *Collections of the New York Historical Society* for 1883 is published the *Journal of Stephen Kemble.* Kemble was Adjutant-General to the British army in America. The two volumes of the *Collections* for that year, known generally as the *Kemble Papers,* also contain Sir William Howe's Orderly Book. The latter, in so far as it concerns the siege of Boston, can be found in B. F. Stevens, *General Sir William Howe's Orderly Book at Charlestown, Boston, and Halifax, June 17, 1775 to 26 May 1776; to which is added the official abridgment of General Howe's correspondence with the English government during the siege of Boston* (London, 1890). In the Howe Orderly Books reproduced in the *Kemble Papers* there are certain large gaps. These have, for the most part, been filled through the discovery of several of the missing books by Major M. V. Hay, of Seaton, Aberdeen, Scotland. The information about this discovery may be found in *Americana* for April, 1924. In general, however, for the purposes of this study, the Orderly Books do not yield as much as might be hoped.

Two compilations of source material are of great value to the student: Peter Force, *American Archives,* series 4 (Washington, 1837–46) and B. F. Stevens, *Facsimiles of Manuscripts in European Archives relating to America, 1773-83* (London 1889–95). Force's work, which was intended to gather together all the pertinent material on the Revolution was, however, never completed, and so is useful only for the first eighteen months of the war.

The records of the American Loyalists may be studied in *Papers relating to the American Loyalists,* published by order of the House of Commons, 1821, and in *The Royal Commission on the Losses and Services of the American Loyalists, 1783–1785, being the notes of Mr. Daniel Parker Coke, M.P., one of the commissioners,* edited by Hugh E. Egerton (Oxford University Press, 1915). In this connexion may be cited *The Diary and Letters of His Excellency Thomas Hutchinson* (2 vols., London, S. Low Marston, Searle & Rivington, 1883–86). Hutchinson had been governor of Massachusetts, and in his diary in England can be read the fears and hopes of the Loyalists, together with various pieces of information that throw light upon the problems of the British government.

A number of diaries or collections of letters of British officers and civilians in America at the time of the Revolution have come down to us. C. K. Bolton has edited the *Letters of Hugh Earl Percy* (C. E. Goodspeed, Boston, 1902) which provide some information about British difficulties, although Percy was very young at the time and his estimates varied exceedingly with his mood. *André's Journal,* edited by H. C. Lodge (Bibliophile Society, Boston, 1903) has a record of British movements from June 1777 to November 1778, and has a tragic interest because of the fate of its author. *The Journal of Nicholas Cresswell, 1774–1777* (L. MacVeagh, The Dial Press, N. Y., 1924) is an account of the experiences of a young Englishman who, during the first months of the Revolution, was in those parts of America held by the Revolutionaries, from whence he made interesting observations about the effect of military events upon the American morale. *Montressor's Journal,* published by the New York Historical Society in 1882, is the journal of a captain of engineers whose testimony figured prominently in the Parliamentary Inquiry. *Simcoe's Military Journal* (Bartlett & Welford, N. Y., 1884) is the journal of John G. Simcoe, a prominent officer in the Loyalist troops. It is mostly concerned with the second half of the war, but has some information about events round Philadelphia in the winter of 1777–78. There is a certain amount of illustrative material in a volume printed in 1779 entitled *Historical Anecdotes, civil and military : in a series of letters written from America in the years* 1777–78. Of much the same sort is W. H. Wilkin, *Some British Soldiers in America* (H. Rees, London, 1914), most of the material being letters from British soldiers serving in America.

A certain amount of primary material has been gathered from letters and journals written by the Germans who served in America. Best known is that written by Baroness Riedesel, the wife of the general who served under Burgoyne, *Letters and Journals relating to the War of the American Revolution and the capture of the German troops at Saratoga,* translated by W. L. Stone (J. Munsell, Albany, 1867). W. L. Stone also published in 1891 *Letters of Brunswick and Hessian Officers during the American Revolution* (J. Munsell, Albany). Additional material of this nature is found in R. W. Pettengill, *Letters from America, 1776-1779 ; being the letters of Brunswick, Hessian, and Waldeck officers with the British armies during the Revolution* (Houghton Mifflin, Boston, 1914). Some information about the procuring of German troops for the American service may be found in Charles Rainsford, *Transactions as commissary for embarking foreign troops in the English service from Germany,* printed in the *New York Historical Society Collection* of 1879.

On the American side the two best known intimate records of the war are the *Memoirs of Major-General William Heath, by himself,* edited by William Abbatt in 1901, New York, and James Thacher, *A Military Journal during the American Revolutionary War* (Richardson & Lord, Boston,

1823). The printed material on the American side of the war is copious, but a mention of some of the most important will suffice. The edition of the writings of Washington cited in this book is that of Worthington C. Ford (Putnams, N. Y. & London, 1889–93), which replaced the older edition of Jared Sparks. Sparks edited in 1853 *Correspondence of the American Revolution, being the letters of eminent men to George Washington* (Little, Brown, Boston). The letters of General Greene are described in the *Calendar of Correspondence of Major-General Nathanael Greene, Quarter-Master General, United States Army, in the library of the American Philosophical Society. Proceedings of the Society,* vol. 39, pp. 154-344, Philadelphia, 1900.

IV

A great mass of controversial literature arose over the campaigns of the Howes. The best general guide to the controversy is *Parliament and the Howes,* by Worthington C. Ford, in vol. 44 of the *Proceedings of the Massachusetts Historical Society.* Charles Francis Adams also published an article in 1910 in the same Proceedings on *Contemporary Opinion on the Howes.*

The pamphlet campaign against the Howes began in 1778, and it is Mr. Ford's belief that it was directly inspired by Germain. The chief writer at first was Israel Mauduit, although the pamphlets were published anonymously. This pamphleteer put forth in 1778 *Remarks upon General Howe's account of his proceedings on Long Island in the Extraordinary Gazette of October 10, 1776.* It was very critical of Howe's conduct on Long Island and condemned him for having missed a chance for decisive victory. The next year the same writer wrote *Observations upon the Conduct of S—r W—m H—e at the White Plains, as related in the Gazette of December 30, 1776,* in which was contained a scathing attack on the failure of Howe to push his operations on that occasion. Mauduit also published in the same year *Strictures on the Philadelphia Mischianza.*

There is a large collection of Howe pamphlets in the Massachusetts Historical Society Library, with annotations by Mauduit. The Bancroft Collection in the New York Public Library also has a number of Mauduit's pamphlets.

In 1779 Joseph Galloway joined in the pamphlet war with his *The Examination of Joseph Galloway, late Speaker of the House of Assembly of Pennsylvania before the House of Commons in a Committee on the American Papers.* The

Letters to a Nobleman on the Conduct of the War in the Middle Colonies by the same author was an attack on the conduct of the British campaign in 1777. An unidentified person published *Two Letters from Agricola to Sir William Howe.* Robert Dallas published anonymously *Considerations upon the American Inquiry.* There was also published *A View of the Evidence relative to the Conduct of the American War under Sir William Howe, Lord Viscount Howe, and General Burgoyne as given before a Committee of the House of Commons last Session of Parliament. To which is added A Collection of the Celebrated Fugitive Pieces that are said to have given rise to that Important Enquiry.* This gives the evidence before the Enquiry in considerable detail. In 1780 Joseph Galloway published *Plain Truth, or a Letter to the Author of Dispassionate Thoughts on the American War.* Josiah Tucker was the author of the *Dispassionate Thoughts.* Sir William Howe entered the lists in his own defence by printing *The Narrative of Lieutenant-General Sir William Howe in a committee of the House of Commons on the 29th of April 1779 relative to his conduct during his late command of the King's troops in North America, to which are added, Some Observations upon a Pamphlet entitled, Letters to a Nobleman.* This *Narrative* contains a very full explanation of the motives which Howe stated to have actuated him during the disputed points of his campaign. Galloway met it with *A Reply to the Observations of Lieutenant-General Sir William Howe on a pamphlet entitled Letters to a Nobleman, in which his Misrepresentations are detected, and those letters are supported by a Variety of New Matter and Argument.* A pamphlet entitled *The Detail and Conduct of the American War, etc.,* gave, with some additions, the same information contained in *A View of the Evidence* and attested to the public interest in the dispute.

In 1781 Galloway attacked Lord Howe especially in *A Letter to the Rt. Hon. Lord Viscount H—e on his Naval Conduct in the American War.* He charged Lord Howe with general failure to use the fleet in a vigorous manner so as to bring pressure to bear on the revolting colonies. Mauduit returned to the lists with *Three Letters to Lieutenant-General Sir William Howe,* in which he charged Howe with having accepted the command with deliberate intent of losing the war. Galloway published a *Letter from Cicero to the Rt. Hon. Lord Viscount H—e; occasioned by his late Speech in the H—e of C—ns,* and also *Letters from Cicero to Catiline the Second.*

Burgoyne's expedition also occasioned pamphlet controversy which bore more or less directly on the conduct and record of the Howes. In 1779 appeared *A Brief Examination of the plan and conduct of the northern expedition in America in 1777*, which attacked Burgoyne for endeavouring to do what was not justified in his orders. In 1780 the *Essay on Modern Martyrs ; with a lettter to General Burgoyne* also charged Burgoyne with recklessly sacrificing his army. Burgoyne replied in *A State of the expedition from Canada as laid before the House of Commons by Lieutenant-General Burgoyne*. This defence contained a collection of documents appertaining to the expedition, as well as Burgoyne's own version of the affair.

This pamphlet material is of very uneven value in the assistance it brings to a study of the conduct of the Howes. Much of it is scarcely worth the reading, if one has already read the earlier pamphlets ; for the later pamphlets, for the most part, merely reiterate the earlier attacks. Most useful have been *A View of the Evidence, Howe's Narrative, The State of the Expedition from Canada,* Galloway's *Examination* and *Letter to a Nobleman,* and *Reply to the Observations, etc.* A general reading of the pamphlets is of value in indicating the points most severely attacked in the record of the Howes. Although the Howes' answers give valuable information about their motives and intentions, that evidence has to be handled carefully, for it was put together in such fashion as to meet specific objections and often avoids an answer that would satisfy the historian but not a contemporary political opponent. The Howes tried to prove that they did what their opponents argued they ought to have done, and in some cases neglected the better historical justification for their course.

v

No attempt can be made to draw up a bibliography of English politics at the time of the American Revolution but, in addition to works already mentioned that touch upon the subject, one may notice Fitzmaurice, *Life of William Earl of Shelburne* (Macmillan, London, 1875–76) and F. A. Mumby, *George III and the American Revolution* (Houghton Mifflin, Boston & N. Y., 1923).

No biography of Sir William Howe had been written before the recent publication of Bellamy Partridge's *Sir Billy Howe* (Longmans, Green, London & N. Y., 1932). This, however, is a piece of historical journalism and makes no contribution toward a solution of the difficult problems connected with

Howe's career. The standard life of Lord Howe is Sir John Barrow's *Life of Howe* (J. Murray, London, 1838). It is, however, very uninformative for the period of the American Revolution except in so far as purely naval events are concerned. Paul Leicester Ford published an article in the *Atlantic Monthly* in June 1896, 'Lord Howe's Commission to Pacify the Colonies,' which contains a contemporary account written by the Howes' secretary. James Parton's *Life and Times of Benjamin Franklin* (Mason Bros., N. Y. & Mason & Hamlin, Boston, 1864) gives a very full account of the Staten Island interview and also has some material on the earlier relations between Franklin and Lord Howe.

The Loyalists have received the attention of a number of writers. Most venerable among them is Lorenzo Sabine, whose *The American Loyalists* (C. C. Little & J. Brown, Boston) was published in 1847. In 1864 he brought out *Biographical Sketches of Loyalists of the American Revolution* (2 vols., Little, Boston). Sabine's judgments are still in many cases the most balanced that have been made on this subject. A. C. Flick published in 1901 *Loyalism in New York during the American Revolution*. (Columbia Univ. Press, N. Y.; P. S. King & Son, London). The latest general work on the Loyalists is by C. H. Van Tyne, *The Loyalists in the American Revolution* (Macmillan, N. Y., London, 1902). Although this book is well thought of by many authorities on the period, it suffers from too strenuous an endeavour to point out the importance and numbers of the Loyalists. An acceptance of its conclusions would lead one to believe that the Loyalists could have rendered much greater aid to the British cause than was actually within their power.

There is a vast amount of literature on the battle of Bunker Hill, but most of it concerns points of detail rather than the view that is of importance to this study. Charles Francis Adams has a very good short account in the *American Historical Review,* vol. I, pp. 401-13. The centennial of the battle led to the appearance of several studies. Justin Winsor prepared a volume. *Celebration of the centennial for the anniversary of the battle of Bunker Hill. With an appendix containing a survey of the literature of the battle, its antecedents and results* (Published by Boston City Council, 1875). The same year Richard Frothingham published *The Centennial: battle of Bunker Hill* (Little, Brown, Boston). The next year the same author brought out *The battlefield of Bunker Hill: with a relation of the action by William Prescott, and illustrative documents* (Printed for author, Boston). The most recent study is by Harold Murdock, *Bunker Hill : notes and queries on a famous battle* (Houghton Mifflin, Boston, 1927).   Another work worth noting is John Clarke, *An impartial and authentic narrative of the battle fought on the 17th of June, 1775* (London, 1775).   Clarke was a British lieutenant of marines.   Samuel A. Drake printed in 1875 *Bunker Hill : the story told in letters from the battlefield by British officers engaged* (Nichols & Hall, Boston).   One of the earliest histories of the battle was by Samuel Swett, *History of Bunker Hill* (Munroe & Francis, Boston, 1826).   Several years later Swett entered into controversy with Frothingham on the topic.   But the amount of literature is greater than the real importance of the battle warrants and is to be explained by the sentimental interest attaching to the first regularly contested engagement of the new American army.

   The great authority for the siege of Boston has long been Richard Frothingham's *History of the Siege of Boston, and also of the battles of Lexington, Concord, and Bunker Hill* (C. C. Little & J. Brown, Boston, 1849), with later editions. Mr. Allen French, author of *The Day of Lexington and Concord* (Little, Brown, Boston, 1925), edited in 1926 *A British fusilier in revolutionary Boston : being the diary of Lieutenant Frederick MacKenzie, adjutant to the Royal Welsh Fusiliers, Jan. 5–April 30, 1775* (Harvard Press, Cambridge).   Mr. French's latest work, *The First Year of the American Revolution* (Houghton Mifflin, Boston, 1934) is of great importance both for Bunker Hill and for the whole story of the siege and may replace Frothingham as the leading authority on the subject.   Information on the siege may also be secured from William Carter, *A Genuine detail of the several engagements, positions, and movements of the royal and American armies during the years 1775 and 1776* (London, 1784).

   The German mercenaries who served in America have elicited some interest.   In 1863 Max von Eelking produced a study which was translated by J. G. Rosengarten in 1893 under the title of *The German allied troops in the North American War of Independence, 1776-1783* (J. Munsell's Sons, Albany).   Von Eelking also prepared *Memoirs and journals of Major-General Riedesel during his residence in America*, translated by W. L. Stone in 1868 (J. Munsell, Albany).   Edward J. Lowell's *The Hessians and the other German auxiliaries of Great Britain in the revolutionary war* (Harpers, N. Y., 1884) is a standard work on the subject. J. G. Rosegarten, the translator of von Eelking, brought out in 1899 *A defence of the Hessians* (Reprint from Pa. Mag.

of History & Biography, Philadelphia), and in 1904 *American History from German Archives* (New Era Press, Lancaster, Pa.)

The campaign round New York in 1776 has attracted the attention of several writers. Thomas W. Field brought out an elaborate study, *The Battle of Long Island in 1869* (Long Island Historical Society Memoirs, vol. 2, Brooklyn). The great authority for the period is Henry P. Johnston, *The Campaign of 1776 around New York and Brooklyn* (1878). It is volume III of the Memoirs of the *Long Island Historical Society*. John C. Schwab's *The Revolutionary history of Fort Number Eight on Morris Heights, New York City* (Privately printed, New Haven, 1897), contains some material on the operations around New York. For the White Plains campaign there is *Westchester County, New York in the American Revolution*, (Morrisania, N. Y., 1886) by Henry B. Dawson. William Abbatt's *The Battle of Pell's Point, Pelham* (New York, 1901) argues for the importance of that action in delaying the British advance. Edward F. de Lancey in *The Capture of Mount Washington the Result of Treason* (New York, 1877) gives an explanation of Howe's failure to push his attack at White Plains and of the surprisingly easy capture of Fort Washington.

The events in New Jersey have called forth two valuable books, Charles C. Haven's *A new historic manual concerning the three battles at Trenton and Princeton, New Jersey* (W. T. Nicholson, Trenton, 1871) and William Stryker's *The battles of Trenton and Princeton* (Houghton Mifflin, Boston & N. Y., 1898), which is the standard work on that topic. An interest in local history has led to a study of New York City during the Revolution. In 1861 the Mercantile Library Association printed privately *New York City during the American Revolution*, which is a collection of original paperes. The principal work on the subject has long been that by Thomas Jones, *History of New York during the Revolutionary War*, (N. Y. Historical Society, 1879). The value of this book is discussed by Henry P. Johnston in *Observations on Judge Jones' Loyalist history of the American revolution. How far is it an authority?* (D. Appleton, N. Y., 1880). An account by Wilbur C. Abbott, *New York in the American Revolution* (Scribners, N. Y. & London, 1929) adds little of any value. The most recent study is by Oscar T. Barck, *New York City during the war for independence* (Columbia Univ. Press, New York, 1931).

The part that Charles Lee may have played in the formation of the plans of the Howes for 1777 is discussed in George

H. Moore's *Treason of Charles Lee* (C. Scribner, N. Y., 1860). The New York Historical Society printed *The Lee Papers* in 1872–75, which contain Lee's memoirs and also a reprint of Moore's *Treason of Charles Lee*. The memoirs had been separately printed in London in 1792 shortly after Lee's death.

Until very recently the great work on Burgoyne's expedition was that of E. B. de Fonblanque, *Political and Military Episodes in the latter half of the 18th century. Derived from the life and correspondence of the Rt. Hon. John Burgoyne, general, statesman, dramatist* (Macmillan, London, 1876). In 1877 W. L. Stone brought out *The Campaign of Lieutenant-General John Burgoyne* (J. Munsell, Albany). The one hundred and fiftieth anniversary of Saratoga has provoked a renewed interest in Burgoyne, which has resulted in the appearance of two new books on the subject, *Gentleman Johnny Burgoyne* (J. Cape, London, 1927) by F. J. Hudleston, and *The Turning Point of the Revolution, or Burgoyne in America* (Houghton Mifflin, Boston & N. Y., 1928) by Hoffmann Nickerson. The former of the two makes a point of treating Burgoyne as an interesting and often amusing personality, but beneath it is found some good history. The latter is more serious in intent, and excellent for the general setting of the expedition and its international repercussions, but puts forward an interpretation of the campaign itself that seems to me inaccurate.

There is no history of the Pennsylvania campaign of 1777 that does for that event what Johnston does for the campaign of 1776. *The Defences of Philadelphia in 1777*, collected and edited by Worthington C. Ford in 1897 (Historical Printing Club, Brooklyn), contains a full presentation of contemporary documents. The battle of Brandywine has elicited more interest than the campaign in general. There appeared in 1846 *Some account of the British army — and of the battle of Brandywine — which came to the knowledge and observation of Joseph Townsend* (T. Ward, Philadelphia). The same year the Pennsylvania Historical Society published, as a supplement to Townsend, *Papers of the Historical Society of Pennsylvania relative to the battle of Brandywine*. There is a pamphlet by W. D. Stone, *Battle of Brandywine* (1895) and in Charlemagne Tower's *The Marquis de Lafayette in the American Revolution* (2 vols., J. B. Lippincott, Philadelphia, 1895) there is an account of the battle.

Some material on the occupation of Philadelphia may be secured from Winthrop Sargent's *The Life and Career of Major John André* (Ticknor & Fields, Boston, 1861). Among other biographies of military men associated with the war ought also to be mentioned G. W. Greene's three volume *Life of Nathanael Greene* (Putnams, N. Y., 1867–71). But it might be remarked in concluding, that a definitive history of the military side of the American Revolution is yet to be written and that a wealth of material, of which the present bibliography is a mere suggestion, awaits the use of someone who will undertake for the War of the American Revolution what, for instance, Sir Charles Oman has done for the Peninsular War.

INDEX

A

Aborn, Muster Master General, describes plundering of Hessians, 197.

Adams, John, meets Lord Howe, 158.

American army, revival of offensive spirit after Trenton, 235.

American Revolution, peculiar character of, 10 *et seq.*

Amherst, Sir Jeffrey, considered for American command, 43 ; refuses it, 45.

B

Barrington, Viscount, explains appointment of Sir William Howe, 45.

Boston, siege of, 85 *et seq. ;* British difficulties in, 89 *et seq. ;* unruliness of soldiers in, 91 ; British shortage of supplies, 92-7 ; British decide to evacuate, 100 ; British evacuation, 102-04 ; plight of Loyalists in city, 103.

Brandywine, battle of, 287.

British army, its qualities, 18 *et seq. ;* its tactical limitations, 20-21.

British fleet, sails from New York, 277 ; sails into Delaware Bay, 277 ; enters Chesapeake Bay, 282.

Bronx River, operations upon, 189.

Brooklyn lines, Howe's failure to attack, 134 ; controversy over it, 135-141 ; Americans evacuate, 142.

Bull, Lieutenant-Governor, reports on conditions in America, 33.

Bunker Hill, battle of, British plans for battle, 74-78 ; British failure to pursue after battle, 80-81.

Burgoyne, General John, considered for post in America, 44 ; ap-pointed to command in America, 45 ; seeks post at New York, 46 ; complains about his post, 47 ; describes conditions at Boston, 82 ; arrives in England, 87 ; complains of lack of information at Boston, 92 ; genesis of his expedition from Canada, 245 ; submits plan to Germain, 246 ; instructions from Germain, 249 ; complains of restrictions upon his actions, 253 ; Lord North's attitude toward his expedition, 257 *et seq. ;* changes view of purpose of his expedition, 260 *et seq. ;* seeks assistance from Clinton, 260.

C

Canada, genesis of expedition from, 245.

Carleton, Sir Guy, named to independent command, 84 ; his military plans, 246 ; Germain's instructions to him, 249.

Charlestown, British failure to occupy, 72.

Chesapeake Bay, preferred as landing place by Sir William Howe, 278 ; British fleet enters, 282.

Clinton, Sir Henry, considered for post in America, 44 ; appointed, 45 ; urges Gage to move army to New York, 109 ; remarks about Brooklyn lines, 139 ; commands British landing at Kipp's Bay, 176 ; explains failure to cut off Americans in New York, 177 ; explains British actions at White Plains, 191-2 ; describes Burgoyne's confidence, 254 ; conversations with Sir William Howe about Burgoyne, 258, 265-6 ; feels unable to assist Burgoyne, 260 ; opinion of expedition to Pennsylvania, 263 ; urges importance of Hud-